MURTY CLASSICAL
LIBRARY OF INDIA

Sheldon Pollock, General Editor

TULSIDAS

THE EPIC OF RAM

VOLUME 2

MCLI 8

TULSIDAS

तुलसीदास

THE EPIC OF RAM

VOLUME 2

Translated by
PHILIP LUTGENDORF

MURTY CLASSICAL LIBRARY OF INDIA

HARVARD UNIVERSITY PRESS

Cambridge, Massachusetts

London, England

2016

SERIES DESIGN BY M9DESIGN

Library of Congress Cataloging-in-Publication Data

Tulasidasa, 1532–1623.
The epic of Ram / Tulsidas ; translated by Philip Lutgendorf.
volume cm. — (Murty Classical Library of India ; 8)
In English and Awadhi on facing pages.
Includes bibliographical references and index.
ISBN 978-0-674-42501-9 (cloth : alk. paper) (vol. 1)
ISBN 978-0-674-08861-0 (cloth: alk. paper) (vol. 2)
I. Lutgendorf, Philip, translator.
II. Tulasidasa, 1532–1623. Ramacaritamanasa. English.
III. Tulasidasa, 1532–1623. Ramacaritamanasa. IV. Title.
PK1947.9.T83R313 2016
891.4'312—dc23   2015016322

CONTENTS

INTRODUCTION

This volume presents the text and translation of the second half of Tulsidas's monumental "First Stair"—conventionally called *Bālkāṇḍ* or "The Book of Youth"—the first and longest sub-book in his retelling of the Ramayana story, *Rāmcarit-mānas* (frequently translated in English as "Divine lake of Ram's deeds").[1] Following a lengthy prologue, presented in volume 1, in which the poet pays homage to his sources of inspiration, divine and worldly, and presents tales of gods, divine sages, and earthly kings and queens (who all have a role to play in setting the stage for the advent of Ram as world-saving avatar), the life story of Ram, as generally understood, begins in the present volume, at *Bālkāṇḍ*'s one hundred and seventy-sixth stanza. Just concluded was the tragic tale, narrated by the sage Yajnavalkya to his friend Bharadvaj, of King Pratapbhanu ("sun of glory"), an illustrious monarch who was destroyed through the machinations of a wily enemy and by the power of a curse uttered by Brahmans (1.153–175). Condemned to die, together with his entire clan, by these "gods on earth" (as Tulsi regularly calls them), the king is soon slain in battle.

As this volume commences, Yajnavalkya continues his narration: King Pratapbhanu and his brother and chief minister are reborn as "night-stalkers" (*nisācara*), another name for the class of demonic antagonists in Hindu lore who are more commonly known as *rākṣasas*. These powerful, protean beings—earthly avatars of the dark *asuras* or senior cousins of the luminous celestial gods or *devas*—possess superhuman abilities yet lack immortality, for the gods cheated the *asuras* of the nectar that gives deathlessness, when both sets of cosmic cousins obtained it by churning the infinite milk-ocean. Ever bent on revenge, *asuras* and *rākṣasas*—the mostly unavoidable English rendering, "demons," tends to obscure their more ambivalent nature—attempt to claim their lost immortality through performing awesome austerities that force the gods, and especially Brahma, creator-god and "grandfather" to both sets of cousins, to grant them desired boons—although these invariably contain a loophole that will allow the gods, once again, to defeat and suppress them. As Yajnavalkya's story continues, King Pratapbhanu is reborn as Ravan (usually understood etymologically as "he who causes lamentation"), the ten-headed and twenty-armed *rākṣasa* grandson of a divine sage named Pulastya. The king's powerful brother becomes his brother once more, now in the form of a voracious giant named Kumbhakaran ("pot-ears"), and his sagacious chief minister takes birth as their third brother, the wise and uncharacteristically virtuous Vibhishan, who, despite his name (which means "terrifying"), is in Tulsi's telling a lifelong devotee of Vishnu/Ram.

The first section of this volume, "The Tyranny of Ravan," tells of the *rākṣasa* warlord's rise to power, both on earth and throughout the cosmos. Once he has obtained his desired boon of near-immortality, he acquires an impregnable stronghold on the magical island of Lanka and commences a reign of terror, directed especially against Brahmans, cows, gods, and pious devotees. In this he is much assisted by his formidable eldest son, known both as Meghnad ("thunder") and, following his triumph in a war with the celestial gods, as Indrajit ("victor over Indra"). The atrocities of father, son, and their demonic hordes become so horrendous that the earth goddess herself feels unbearably burdened. Assuming the form of a cow, embodiment of maternal nurture and beneficence, she begs the gods for relief; with her, and with Brahma's help, they petition the supreme and transcendent deity, Vishnu, to descend as an earthly avatar. The opening section concludes with Vishnu's promise to be born as Ram and his brothers in the city of Avadh (1.187).

Tulsidas's spirited retelling, in the two sections that follow and that comprise the bulk of this volume, of Ram's birth, childhood, and adolescent adventures, culminating in his marriage to Princess Sita of Videha, continues to depart in some notable ways from the classical archetype of the Sanskrit *Vālmīki Rāmāyaṇa*. Ram's divine nature, always foregrounded in Tulsi's version, is twice dramatically displayed to his mother, Kausalya, when he is still a baby (1.192, 1.201–202), and these theophanies, together with his playful toddler activities that are then so lovingly portrayed, seem to echo the accounts of young Krishna in the *Bhāgavatapurāṇa*. The poet shows relatively little interest in Ram's first martial exploits and other learning experiences under the tutelage of Sage Vishvamitra; the demon Taraka and her two sons are killed or driven away in a mere three lines (1.209.3, 1.210.2–3), and the famous tale of the descent of the River Ganga from heaven, which occupies ten chapters in Valmiki's *Bālakāṇḍa* (1.34–1.43), is alluded to in a single half-line (1.212.1). Yet, in keeping with Tulsi's focus on fervent devotion to Ram as the embodiment of love and mercy, the story of his liberation of Ahalya, a penitent ascetic woman, from an ancient curse is expanded to include four lyrical *chand* quatrains in which she adores Ram as her compassionate savior (1.211.1–4).

Once Ram, accompanied by his brother Lakshman and sage Vishvamitra, reaches the court of King Janak of Videha, where a great tournament is to be held to find a suitable bridegroom for the king's daughter, Sita, Tulsi crafts a long interlude that has become especially beloved. Popularly known as the *phūlvārī* or "flower garden" episode, this ten-stanza passage (1.227–236) depicts a seemingly chance encounter between Ram and Sita, when he and Lakshman go to the royal garden to gather materials for their guru's morning rituals, and she and a group of young women companions pass their way to worship in a temple dedicated to goddess Parvati, Shiva's wife and the granter of marital happiness. This intensely romantic episode of mutual "love at first sight," resonant with both theological and mystical overtones, has long been savored by commentators and is also a special favorite of many audiences at the autumnal Ramlila pageants, which enact the Ramayana story as a series of outdoor dramas, often drawing extensively on Tulsi's text.

In another striking departure from the Valmiki narrative, Tulsi repositions the tense encounter between Ram and Parashuram—an earlier avatar of Vishnu—in a scene that the poet likewise expands, playing on the tension sometimes present in the relationship between Brahman priest-sages and their kingly Kshatriya patrons (1.268–284). He moves the encounter from just after Ram and Sita's wedding to just before it. This repositioning is dramatically effective, as the wrathful sage's arrival puts an end to the angry kings' protests over Sita's choice of Ram as her husband, while also introducing uncertainty (at least, for the characters in the narrative) as to whether their union will actually come to pass. But a further motive for the move might well have been that Tulsi did not want to allow anything to distract from, or form an anticlimax to, the spectacular and ecstatic wedding festivities with which he brings this imposing book to its auspicious conclusion. Though the painful episodes of palace intrigue, separation from loved ones, and forest exile in the "Second Stair"—commonly known as *Ayodhyākāṇḍ* or "The Book of Ayodhya"—lie just ahead, *Bālkāṇḍ* itself ends with a blissful vision of marital love and familial harmony, as well as with a promise of blessing to all its readers and listeners.

NOTES

1 An extended general introduction to the epic, with information concerning the poet's life and other works and an explanation of the allegory of Manas Lake and its stairways, is found in volume 1 of this translation.

NOTE ON THE TEXT
AND TRANSLATION

Despite its prestige and popularity, the *Rāmcaritmānas* has not been accorded a truly critical edition, which might yet be assembled from careful comparative study of (reportedly) surviving manuscripts dating to the first hundred years after its composition. Copies of some of these were in the possession of celebrated *Mānas* expounders of the nineteenth century and became the basis for published versions, edited by them and issued by the new vernacular presses of the period. Differences among these editions were (by the standards of premodern Hindi literature) comparatively minor but of course much debated, and in the twentieth century three more authoritative and scholarly editions attempted to resolve them—though none could claim to have adhered to the standards followed, for example, in the long-term projects to reconstruct the early texts of the Sanskrit *Rāmāyaṇa* and *Mahābhārata*.[1] The first of these, issued by the industrious Gita Press of Gorakhpur and accompanied by a readable gloss in Hindi (GP), has become, by default, the standard edition of the epic, and has been used by every translator since Growse, including me. However, I also constantly consult the most elaborate and celebrated of published commentaries, *Mānaspīyūṣ* (Nectar of the Mānas; MP), which incorporates the insights of many traditional scholars of the nineteenth and twentieth centuries. It, too, uses the GP edition as basic text, but it periodically offers variant readings from manuscripts and older published editions. When such variations seem significant, I explain this in an endnote, as I do in the (very rare) instances in which I adopt a variant reading in preference to that found in the Gita Press version.

Readers may note occasional discrepancies between the Avadhi of Tulsidas's Devanagari text and the transliteration scheme adopted for characters' names in the translation, notes, and glossary. Thus, "Shankar," one of the common names of the god Shiva, appears as *saṅkara* (in its Devanagari equivalent) in the original text and in any notes that quote it directly, but as "Shankar" (the common, modern Hindi pronunciation) in the translation. Standard Sanskritic transliteration (e.g., *śaṅkara*), used in much scholarly writing, is additionally offered in the glossary.

The *Rāmcaritmānas* has already seen nine complete English translations.[2] Although this is not surprising for such an influential scripture—the *Bhagavadgītā* can boast of more than two hundred—it is more than have been accorded any other long premodern vernacular work in the Indian tradition. Why, then, a tenth? The obvious reason, of course, is to try to improve on them. Seven of the translations are into prose, and although two of them have considerable merit (Growse's is spirited and Hill's is admirably accurate), they all produce an effect that is on the whole turgid and "prosaic"—a sad fate for a poem that regularly urges the "singing" of its lines, and whose rhythmic recitation has been moving audiences for more than four centuries. On the other hand, two complete rhyming-verse renditions (by Atkins and Satya Dev), though certainly labors of love and tours de force in their way, take unfortunate liberties with the meaning of the verses in order to produce a metrical effect that often sounds jangling and trite, like a Victorian greeting card.

The challenges inherent in rendering the *Mānas* in English have been noted before.[3] As a devotional work intended for episodic oral performance, the text seems repetitious when set in a linguistic medium that is normally experienced through individual, silent communion with the printed page, and its frequent use of formulaic phrases (though common in epic poetry worldwide) may appear redundant and saccharine—e.g., "eyes filling with tears" and "limbs thrilling with love" (the latter, one choice for the nearly untranslatable *pulak*—in plain English, "goosebumps" or the dismally medical "horripilation"; besides "thrilling," I sometimes use "trembling," "quivering," "flushed," or "shivering"), or the poet's often-repeated assertion that some person, place, event, or emotion "cannot be described"— which he usually follows with its very apt description. Some of Tulsi's apparent "repetitiveness," however, actually reflects the great asymmetry in lexicons between the two languages. English has more than one verb for "seeing"— the most important and recurrent act in which *Mānas* characters engage, especially "seeing" the unworldly beauty of Ram and Sita—but it does not have (as I have counted in *Bālkāṇḍ* alone) fourteen. Similarly, one can think of several synonyms for the adjective "beautiful"—but not the twenty -two, each slightly different, that Tulsi deploys to convey the overwhelming visual attraction of his divine characters and their world. And, like "camel" in the Arabic lexicon, "lotus" in the *Mānas* is not a single word—rather, it is, by my count, twenty-nine, each nuanced and suited to different contexts of meaning, meter, rhyme, and alliteration. Tulsi's vocabulary is indeed immense, and he is often credited with having expanded the lexicon of what would become modern Hindi through his revival and adaptation of Sanskrit loan-words; no Sanskrit chauvinist, he also used, according to a recent count, more than ninety Arabic and Persian ones.[4] In English, much of this verbal richness (to echo the poet) simply "cannot be expressed."

What, then, is my impetus and aim in this new translation? My own engagement with the epic began more than three decades ago, after several periods of travel in north India made me realize the extent to which the *Mānas* was ingrained in its living culture. In my initial study of the text as a graduate student, I was fortunate to have a teacher who insisted that I learn to chant its verses aloud to simple melodies—a skill that I have since shared with many students, since I know that it enhances both enjoyment and understanding of the work.[5] My first book grew out of that in-class "performance" and examined the many ways in which the *Mānas* "lives" in its cultural context. My first effort at translation of a section of the epic—its beloved "Fifth Stair," *Sundarkāṇḍ*—came much later.[6] Although I was not altogether happy with it, I loved the opportunity it gave me to engage deeply with the poem and (imaginatively) with its author. It was also my first sustained attempt at what, following the commission and editorial guidelines of the Murty Classical Library of India, I am now attempting to do for the complete epic: produce a straightforward, readable, free-verse rendering in contemporary language. I readily concede that most of the enchanting music of Tulsidas—his rhyme, alliteration, and almost hypnotic rhythm—is lost in my version. What I seek to preserve, as much as possible, is clarity, compactness of expression, and a certain momentum. I am especially happy to be contributing to a dual-language version, and I hope that serious readers, even if they do not know Hindi, might at least acquire facility with its easy, phonetic script so that they can begin to sound out the lines of the original—for truly, there is verbal magic in every stanza of the *Mānas*.

NOTES

1   The three scholarly editions are Poddar 1938, Mishra 1962, and Shukla et al. 1973.
2   A list appears in the Bibliography.
3   Growse 1891 (1978): lvii–lviii; Hill 1952: xx; Lutgendorf 1991: 29–33.
4   McGregor 2003: 938; Stasik 2009.
5   I would like to pay tribute to my University of Chicago mentors, Kali Charan Bahl (who taught me to chant the *Mānas*) and Colin P. Masica (who helped me understand its cultural impact). A. K. Ramanujan and Wendy Doniger were also inspirations, both as scholars and translators.
6   Lutgendorf 1994, 1995, 2001.

The Epic of Ram

The Tyranny of Ravan

१ काल पाइ मुनि सुनु सोइ राजा ।
  भयउ निसाचर सहित समाजा ॥
  दस सिर ताहि बीस भुजदंडा ।
  रावन नाम बीर बरिबंडा ॥

२ भूप अनुज अरिमर्दन नामा ।
  भयउ सो कुंभकरन बलधामा ॥
  सचिव जो रहा धरमरुचि जासू ।
  भयउ बिमात्र बंधु लघु तासू ॥

३ नाम बिभीषन जेहि जग जाना ।
  बिष्नुभगत बिग्यान निधाना ॥
  रहे जे सुत सेवक नृप केरे ।
  भए निसाचर घोर घनेरे ॥

४ कामरूप खल जिनस अनेका ।
  कुटिल भयंकर बिगत बिबेका ॥
  कृपा रहित हिंसक सब पापी ।
  बरनि न जाहिं बिस्व परितापी ॥

१७६ उपजे जदपि पुलस्त्यकुल पावन अमल अनूप ।
   तदपि महीसुर श्राप बस भए सकल अघरूप ॥

१ कीन्ह बिबिध तप तीनिहुँ भाई ।
  परम उग्र नहिं बरनि सो जाई ॥
  गयउ निकट तप देखि बिधाता ।
  मागहु बर प्रसन्न मैं ताता ॥

And so, sage, in due course that very king*   1
became a night-stalker, along with his kin.
With ten heads and twenty stout arms
that mighty hero was named Ravan.
The king's younger brother, Arimardan,   2
became Kumbhakaran, citadel of strength,
and his chief minister, Dharmaruchi,
became their junior stepbrother,
named Vibhishan, as everyone knows,   3
a treasury of wisdom and Vishnu's votary.
And all the sons and servants of the king
became great and terrifying demons,
shape-shifting villains of countless kinds,   4
perverse, frightening, and irrational.
All were pitiless and evil, prone to violence
and indescribably cruel to all of creation.

Though born in the matchlessly pure   176
and holy lineage of sage Pulastya,
by the power of the earth-gods' curse
they all became sin incarnate.

The three brothers performed many ascetic acts   1
of a rigor surpassing description.
Brahma observed their ardor and approached,
saying, "Ask a wish, sons, for I am pleased."

---

* Pratapbhanu; see 1.153–175.

२ करि बिनती पद गहि दससीसा ।
बोलेउ बचन सुनहु जगदीसा ॥
हम काहू के मरहिं न मारें ।
बानर मनुज जाति दुइ बारें ॥

३ एवमस्तु तुम्ह बड़ तप कीन्हा ।
मैं ब्रह्माँ मिलि तेहि बर दीन्हा ॥
पुनि प्रभु कुंभकरन पहिं गयऊ ।
तेहि बिलोकि मन बिसमय भयऊ ॥

४ जौं एहिं खल नित करब अहारू ।
होइहि सब उजारि संसारू ॥
सारद प्रेरि तासु मति फेरी ।
मागेसि नीद मास षट केरी ॥

१७७ गए बिभीषन पास पुनि कहेउ पुत्र बर मागु ।
तेहिं मागेउ भगवंत पद कमल अमल अनुरागु ॥

१ तिन्हहि देइ बर ब्रह्म सिधाए ।
हरषित ते अपने गृह आए ॥
मय तनुजा मंदोदरि नामा ।
परम सुंदरी नारि ललामा ॥

२ सोइ मयँ दीन्हि रावनहि आनी ।
होइहि जातुधानपति जानी ॥
हरषित भयउ नारि भलि पाई ।
पुनि दोउ बंधु बिआहेसि जाई ॥

4

The ten-headed one* bowed humbly, clasping his feet, 2
and petitioned him: "Lord of creation,
let none be able to slay me,
save the two species of monkeys and men."[1]
"So be it," Brahma said, "for your asceticism is great." 3
Shiva said, "I, along with Brahma, gave this boon."
Then the creator went to Kumbhakaran
and when he saw him, was taken aback
and thought, "Were this villain to eat every day, 4
my whole creation would be consumed."
So he induced Sharada to addle his wits
and he asked to sleep for six straight months!

Then he went to Vibhishan and said, 177
"Choose a boon, my son,"
and he requested pure, ardent love
for the lotus-like feet of the supreme Lord.

Granting these boons, Brahma departed, 1
and the three went happily homeward.
The demon Maya[2] had a daughter named Mandodari,
supremely lovely, a jewel among women.
He brought her and presented her to Ravan, 2
knowing he would be ruler of all their kind.
Delighted to get a good wife, Ravan
arranged marriages for his two brothers.

* Ravan.

३ गिरि त्रिकूट एक सिंधु मझारी ।
बिधि निर्मित दुर्गम अति भारी ॥
सोइ मय दानवँ बहुरि सँवारा ।
कनक रचित मनिभवन अपारा ॥

४ भोगावति जसि अहिकुल बासा ।
अमरावति जसि सक्रनिवासा ॥
तिन्ह तें अधिक रम्य अति बंका ।
जग बिख्यात नाम तेहि लंका ॥

१७८क खाईं सिंधु गभीर अति चारिहुँ दिसि फिरि आव ।
कनक कोट मनि खचित दृढ़ बरनि न जाइ बनाव ॥

१७८ख हरि प्रेरित जेहिं कलप जोइ जातुधानपति होइ ।
सूर प्रतापी अतुलबल दल समेत बस सोइ ॥

१ रहे तहाँ निसिचर भट भारे ।
ते सब सुरन्ह समर संघारे ॥
अब तहँ रहहिं सक्र के प्रेरे ।
रच्छक कोटि जच्छपति केरे ॥

२ दसमुख कतहुँ खबरि असि पाई ।
सेन साजि गढ़ घेरेसि जाई ॥
देखि बिकट भट बड़ि कटकाई ।
जच्छ जीव लै गए पराई ॥

In the sea's midst, a triple-peaked summit   3
had been made impregnable by Brahma.
It was further adorned by the titan Maya
with countless gem-studded buildings of gold.
Like Bhogavati, abode of the serpent clans,   4
and Amaravati, Indra's own capital,
yet more lavish and formidable than these,
it was famed throughout the world by the name Lanka.

Surrounded on four sides by a moat   178a
of fathomless ocean,
it was a mighty fortress of gold, inlaid with gems,
of indescribable craft.

In any aeon, whomever Hari inspires   178b
to become ruler of the demons
dwells there with his minions,
a powerful and incomparably fiery hero.

Great night-stalking warriors once lived there,   1
but they were all slain by the gods in battle
and now it was occupied, at Indra's command,
by ten million *yakṣa* demigods,[3] soldiers of Kuber.
As soon as the ten-headed one got word of this,   2
he raised an army and laid siege to it.
Seeing that awesome warrior and his legions,
the guards all fled for their lives.

३ फिरि सब नगर दसानन देखा ।
गयउ सोच सुख भयउ बिसेषा ॥
सुंदर सहज अगम अनुमानी ।
कीन्हि तहाँ रावन रजधानी ॥

४ जेहि जस जोग बाँटि गृह दीन्हे ।
सुखी सकल रजनीचर कीन्हे ॥
एक बार कुबेर पर धावा ।
पुष्पक जान जीति लै आवा ॥

१७९ कौतुकहीं कैलास पुनि लीन्हेसि जाइ उठाइ ।
मनहुँ तौलि निज बाहुबल चला बहुत सुख पाइ ॥

१ सुख संपति सुत सेन सहाई ।
जय प्रताप बल बुद्धि बड़ाई ॥
नित नूतन सब बाढ़त जाई ।
जिमि प्रतिलाभ लोभ अधिकाई ॥

२ अतिबल कुंभकरन अस भ्राता ।
जेहि कहुँ नहिं प्रतिभट जग जाता ॥
करइ पान सोवइ षट मासा ।
जागत होइ तिहूँ पुर त्रासा ॥

३ जौं दिन प्रति अहार कर सोई ।
बिस्व बेगि सब चौपट होई ॥
समर धीर नहिं जाइ बखाना ।
तेहि सम अमित बीर बलवाना ॥

8

The ten-faced one roamed about inspecting the city   3
and became free of cares and utterly content.
Reckoning it beautiful and naturally secure,
Ravan made his capital there.
He apportioned dwellings suitable to rank   4
and made all his night-stalkers happy.
Then one day he attacked Kuber,
seized the Pushpak vehicle,* and brought it back.

Then he went to Mount Kailash   179
and, just for fun, lifted it up,
as if to gauge the might of his arms,
and went away well pleased.

Pleasures, riches, sons, armies, allies,   1
victory, splendor, might, intellect, and fame—
all went on constantly increasing,
since with every gain, greed only grows.
For a brother, he had mighty Kumbhakaran,   2
whose equal in battle was never born.
He drank much and slept for six months,
but his waking terrified the three worlds,
for if he were to eat his fill daily   3
the cosmos would soon be laid waste.
In war, his resoluteness was indescribable,
and there were countless mighty heroes like him.

---

* A flying palace.

४ बारिदनाद जेठ सुत तासू।
भट महुँ प्रथम लीक जग जासू॥
जेहि न होइ रन सनमुख कोई।
सुरपुर नितहिं परावन होई॥

१८० कुमुख अकंपन कुलिसरद धूमकेतु अतिकाय।
एक एक जग जीति सक ऐसे सुभट निकाय॥

१ कामरूप जानहिं सब माया।
सपनेहुँ जिन्ह कें धरम न दाया॥
दसमुख बैठ सभाँ एक बारा।
देखि अमित आपन परिवारा॥

२ सुत समूह जन परिजन नाती।
गनै को पार निसाचर जाती॥
सेन बिलोकि सहज अभिमानी।
बोला बचन क्रोध मद सानी॥

३ सुनहु सकल रजनीचर जूथा।
हमरे बैरी बिबुध बरूथा॥
ते सनमुख नहिं करहिं लराई।
देखि सबल रिपु जाहिं पराई॥

४ तेन्ह कर मरन एक बिधि होई।
कहउँ बुझाइ सुनहु अब सोई॥
द्विजभोजन मख होम सराधा।
सब कै जाइ करहु तुम्ह बाधा॥

10

The king's eldest son was Meghnad,[4]   4
first among the world's warriors,
whom no one could face in battle
and who caused constant panic in heaven.

Besides these, there were Durmukh, Akampan,   180
Vajradant, Dhumketu, Atikay,[5]
and an army of stalwarts, each of whom
could single-handedly conquer the world.

All were adept at sorcery and shape-shifting   1
and paid no heed to compassion and dharma.
Once, the ten-headed one sat in his assembly
gazing at his numberless clansmen,
swarms of sons, servants, subjects, and kin—   2
for who can count the race of demons?
With inborn arrogance he looked at his army
and spoke with animosity and heady pride.
"Hear me, night-stalker legions: 3
the gods are our enemies,
yet they will not face us in battle,
for seeing a powerful foe, they flee.
But there is one way to kill them—   4
listen as I explain it to you.
The feeding of Brahmans, fire rites,
and ancestral oblations[6]—go and stop it all!

१८१ छुधा छीन बलहीन सुर सहजेहिं मिलिहहिं आइ ।
तब मारिहउँ कि छाड़िहउँ भली भाँति अपनाइ ॥

१ मेघनाद कहुँ पुनि हँकरावा ।
दीन्हीं सिख बलु बयरु बढ़ावा ॥
जे सुर समर धीर बलवाना ।
जिन्ह कें लरिबे कर अभिमाना ॥

२ तिन्हहि जीति रन आनेसु बाँधी ।
उठि सुत पितु अनुसासन काँधी ॥
एहि बिधि सबही अग्या दीन्ही ।
आपुनु चलेउ गदा कर लीन्ही ॥

३ चलत दसानन डोलति अवनी ।
गर्जत गर्भ स्रवहिं सुर रवनी ॥
रावन आवत सुनेउ सकोहा ।
देवन्ह तके मेरु गिरि खोहा ॥

४ दिगपालन्ह के लोक सुहाए ।
सूने सकल दसानन पाए ॥
पुनि पुनि सिंघनाद करि भारी ।
देइ देवतन्ह गारि पचारी ॥

५ रन मद मत्त फिरइ जग धावा ।
प्रतिभट खोजत कतहुँ न पावा ॥
रबि ससि पवन बरुन धनधारी ।
अगिनि काल जम सब अधिकारी ॥

Powerless and faint with hunger, the gods   181
will naturally come together,
and then I can annihilate them, or just
send them off, nicely enslaved."

Later, he summoned Meghnad   1
and instructed him, fanning his ardor and enmity.
"If there are gods who are brave and strong,
with enough self-respect to make a stand,
defeat them in war and bring them in chains."   2
The son rose, shouldering his sire's edict.
Thus issuing commands to everyone,
he too went forth, mace in hand.
When the ten-faced one walked, earth shook,   3
and at his roar, heavenly women miscarried.
Hearing that Ravan was coming in rage,
the gods took shelter in Mount Meru's caverns.
The lovely realms of the guardians of space[7]   4
the ten-headed one found wholly deserted.
Sending up mighty, lion-like roars,
he challenged the gods with abuse.
Drunk with war lust, he scoured the world   5
seeking his match, but nowhere found one.
The gods of sun, moon, wind, waters, wealth,
fire, death, and dharma—all the authorities,

६ किंनर सिद्ध मनुज सुर नागा ।
हठि सबही के पंथहिं लागा ॥
ब्रह्मसृष्टि जहँ लगि तनुधारी ।
दसमुख बसबर्ती नर नारी ॥

७ आयसु करहिं सकल भयभीता ।
नवहिं आइ नित चरन बिनीता ॥

१८२क भुज बल बिस्व बस्य करि राखेसि कोउ न सुतंत्र ।
मंडलीक मनि रावन राज करइ निज मंत्र ॥

१८२ख देव जच्छ गंधर्ब नर किंनर नाग कुमारि ।
जीति बरीं निज बाहु बल बहु सुंदर बर नारि ॥

१ इंद्रजीत सन जो कछु कहेऊ ।
सो सब जनु पहिलेहिं करि रहेऊ ॥
प्रथमहिं जिन्ह कहुँ आयसु दीन्हा ।
तिन्ह कर चरित सुनहु जो कीन्हा ॥

२ देखत भीमरूप सब पापी ।
निसिचर निकर देव परितापी ॥
करहिं उपद्रव असुर निकाया ।
नाना रूप धरहिं करि माया ॥

३ जेहि बिधि होइ धर्म निर्मूला ।
सो सब करहिं बेद प्रतिकूला ॥

kinnaras, perfected ones, men, deities, snakes— 6
he relentlessly pursued them all.
Every embodied being in Brahma's creation,
male and female, came under ten-faced's fist.
Terrified, they followed his commands 7
and constantly fell in submission at his feet.

He conquered the cosmos by his arms' might, 182a
leaving no one independent.
Ravan kept his own counsel and ruled,
the supreme emperor of all spheres.

The daughters of gods, demigods, heavenly musicians, 182b
men, *kinnaras,* and serpent kings—
countless beautiful women, won by his brute strength—
he took in marriage.

Any command he gave to Indrajit* 1
was already as good as done.
The first orders to be issued
and the deeds that ensued—hear them now.
Terrifying to behold, steeped in evil, 2
the demonic armies tormented the gods.
Legions of demons committed atrocities,
assuming countless forms by sorcery.
Whatever would serve to uproot dharma— 3
they did it all, in defiance of the Veda.

---

* Meghnad.

जेहिं जेहिं देस धेनु द्विज पावहिं ।
नगर गाउँ पुर आगि लगावहिं ॥

४   सुभ आचरन कतहुँ नहिं होई ।
देव बिप्र गुरु मान न कोई ॥
नहिं हरिभगति जग्य तप ग्याना ।
सपनेहुँ सुनिअ न बेद पुराना ॥

५   जप जोग बिरागा तप मख भागा
श्रवन सुनइ दससीसा ।
आपुनु उठि धावइ रहै न पावइ
धरि सब घालइ खीसा ॥
अस भ्रष्ट अचारा भा संसारा
धर्म सुनिअ नहिं काना ।
तेहि बहुबिधि त्रासइ देस निकासइ
जो कह बेद पुराना ॥

१८३   बरनि न जाइ अनीति घोर निसाचर जो करहिं ।
हिंसा पर अति प्रीति तिन्ह के पापहि कवनि मिति ॥

१   बाढ़े खल बहु चोर जुआरा ।
जे लंपट परधन परदारा ॥
मानहिं मातु पिता नहिं देवा ।
साधुन्ह सन करवावहिं सेवा ॥

Wherever they found cows and the twice-born,[8]
that village, town, or city they put to the torch.
Acts of merit ceased to be done,   4
and no one heeded god, Brahman, or guru,
or practiced devotion, sacrifice, asceticism, or wisdom.
No whisper of Veda or *purāṇa* could be heard.

Repetition of mantras, yoga, asceticism, offerings to 5
  gods—
if the ten-headed one heard of it,
he personally rose and rushed to pounce
and exterminate, sparing none.
Such tyranny pervaded the universe
that the ears never heard of dharma
and anyone who spoke of Veda and *purāṇa*
was terrorized and banished.

The atrocities committed by the night-stalkers   183
were beyond counting,
for is there any limit to the sins
of those enamored of violence?

Scoundrels, thieves, and gamblers multiplied   1
who lusted after others' wealth and wives.
Heedless of mother, father, and god,
they forced holy ones to serve them.

17

२ जिन्ह के यह आचरन भवानी ।
ते जानेहु निसिचर सब प्रानी ॥
अतिसय देखि धर्म कै ग्लानी ।
परम सभीत धरा अकुलानी ॥

३ गिरि सरि सिंधु भार नहिं मोही ।
जस मोहि गरुअ एक परद्रोही ॥
सकल धर्म देखइ बिपरीता ।
कहि न सकइ रावन भय भीता ॥

४ धेनु रूप धरि हृदयँ बिचारी ।
गई तहाँ जहँ सुर मुनि झारी ॥
निज संताप सुनाएसि रोई ।
काहू तें कछु काज न होई ॥

५ सुर मुनि गंधर्बा मिलि करि सर्बा
गे बिरंचि के लोका ।
सँग गोतनुधारी भूमि बिचारी
परम बिकल भय सोका ॥
ब्रह्माँ सब जाना मन अनुमाना
मोर कछू न बसाई ।
जा करि तैं दासी सो अबिनासी
हमरेउ तोर सहाई ॥

१८४ धरनि धरहि मन धीर कह बिरंचि हरि पद सुमिरु ।
जानत जन की पीर प्रभु भंजिहि दारुन बिपति ॥

Those who behave like this, Bhavani,[9]   2
whatever creatures they be, know to be demons!
Seeing dharma gravely weakened,
goddess Earth became frightened and fretful:
"Mountains, rivers, and seas do not burden me   3
so much as one who is hostile to others."
She saw all righteous practices overturned
but in terror of Ravan, could say nothing.
Pondering this, she took the form of a cow   4
and went where gods and sages had gathered.
Weeping, she recounted her afflictions,
yet none of them could do anything.

All the gods, sages, and celestial singers   5
went together to the world of Brahma
along with wretched Earth in her cow form,
distracted by fear and sorrow.
Brahma understood it all and mused,
"I can exercise no power in this,
but that eternal One, whose maidservant you are,
can aid both me and you."

Then the creator spoke: "Be firm in heart,   184
all-bearing Earth, recalling Hari's feet,
for the Lord knows his servants' suffering
and will destroy your afflictions."

१ बैठे सुर सब करहिं बिचारा ।
कहँ पाइअ प्रभु करिअ पुकारा ॥
पुर बैकुंठ जान कह कोई ।
कोउ कह पयनिधि बस प्रभु सोई ॥

२ जाके हृदयँ भगति जसि प्रीती ।
प्रभु तहँ प्रगट सदा तेहिं रीती ॥
तेहिं समाज गिरिजा मैं रहेऊँ ।
अवसर पाइ बचन एक कहेऊँ ॥

३ हरि ब्यापक सर्बत्र समाना ।
प्रेम तें प्रगट होहिं मैं जाना ॥
देस काल दिसि बिदिसिहु माहीं ।
कहहु सो कहाँ जहाँ प्रभु नाहीं ॥

४ अग जगमय सब रहित बिरागी ।
प्रेम तें प्रभु प्रगटइ जिमि आगी ॥
मोर बचन सब के मन माना ।
साधु साधु करि ब्रह्म बखाना ॥

१८५ सुनि बिरंचि मन हरष तन पुलकि नयन बह नीर ।
अस्तुति करत जोरि कर सावधान मतिधीर ॥

१ जय जय सुरनायक जन सुखदायक
प्रनतपाल भगवंता ।
गो द्विज हितकारी जय असुरारी
सिंधुसुता प्रिय कंता ॥

Then the gods all sat and pondered   1
where to find the Lord and entreat him.
One proposed going to Vaikunth city,
another said he resides on the ocean of milk.
In a devoted heart, according to its love,   2
the Lord is ever revealed—that is his way.
I, too, was in that assembly, Parvati,
and at an opportune moment, I spoke.
"Hari is all-pervading and omnipresent,   3
but this I know: he manifests through love.
Tell me, is there any place, or time,
or quadrant of space from which the Lord is absent?
Filling all beings, yet aloof and detached,   4
he appears through love, like hidden fire."
My speech was approved by all
and Brahma proclaimed, "Well said!"

Hearing me, the creator rejoiced, his body thrilling,   185
and his eyes shed tears.
That profound one joined his palms
and solemnly began a hymn of praise.[10]

"Glory to the Lord of gods, who gladdens his servants;   1
to God, the guardian of suppliants!
Hail, friend of cows and Brahmans, foe of demons,
dear spouse of ocean's daughter!

पालन सुर धरनी अद्भुत करनी
मरम न जानइ कोई ।
जो सहज कृपाला दीनदयाला
करउ अनुग्रह सोई ॥

२ जय जय अबिनासी सब घट बासी
ब्यापक परमानंदा ।
अबिगत गोतीतं चरित पुनीतं
मायारहित मुकुंदा ॥
जेहि लागि बिरागी अति अनुरागी
बिगत मोह मुनिबृंदा ।
निसि बासर ध्यावहिं गुन गन गावहिं
जयति सच्चिदानंदा ॥

३ जेहिं सृष्टि उपाई त्रिबिध बनाई
संग सहाय न दूजा ।
सो करउ अघारी चिंत हमारी
जानिअ भगति न पूजा ॥
जो भव भय भंजन मुनि मन रंजन
गंजन बिपति बरूथा ।
मन बच क्रम बानी छाड़ि सयानी
सरन सकल सुरजूथा ॥

४ सारद श्रुति सेषा रिषय असेषा
जा कहुँ कोउ नहिं जाना ।
जेहि दीन पिआरे बेद पुकारे
द्रवउ सो श्रीभगवाना ॥

Protector of gods and earth, worker of wonders,
whose mystery none comprehends,
who is innately merciful and compassionate to the lowly—
may he be gracious to us!
Glory to you, indestructible pervader,   2
imminent in all beings, ultimate bliss,
imperishable and imperceptible doer of holy deeds,
beyond illusion, Mukunda!*
You, on whom dispassionate sages
who have transcended delusion, with fervent love
meditate night and day, singing your glories—
hail to you, being-consciousness-bliss!
You who, assuming triple attributes,   3
birthed creation all alone, without aid,
adversary of evil—give a thought to us,
who know neither devotion nor worship.
Destroyer of rebirth's dread, delight of sages' hearts,
remover of myriad afflictions—
giving up on our ingenuity[11] in thought, word, and deed
we gods in unison humbly seek your shelter.
You whom Sharada, Veda, Shesh,   4
and all divine seers fail to comprehend,
whom the Veda proclaims to love the lowly,
Supreme Lord, have mercy!

---

* "Giver of liberation," an epithet of Vishnu.

भव बारिधि मंदर सब बिधि सुंदर
गुनमंदिर सुखपुंजा ।
मुनि सिद्ध सकल सुर परम भयातुर
नमत नाथ पद कंजा ॥

१८६ जानि सभय सुर भूमि सुनि बचन समेत सनेह ।
गगनगिरा गंभीर भइ हरनि सोक संदेह ॥

१ जनि डरपहु मुनि सिद्ध सुरेसा ।
तुम्हहि लागि धरिहउँ नर बेसा ॥
अंसन्ह सहित मनुज अवतारा ।
लेहउँ दिनकर बंस उदारा ॥

२ कस्यप अदिति महातप कीन्हा ।
तिन्ह कहुँ मैं पूरब बर दीन्हा ॥
ते दसरथ कौसल्या रूपा ।
कोसलपुरीं प्रगट नर भूपा ॥

३ तिन्ह कें गृह अवतरिहउँ जाई ।
रघुकुल तिलक सो चारिउ भाई ॥
नारद बचन सत्य सब करिहउँ ।
परम सक्ति समेत अवतरिहउँ ॥

४ हरिहउँ सकल भूमि गरुआई ।
निर्भय होहु देव समुदाई ॥
गगन ब्रह्मबानी सुनि काना ।
तुरत फिरे सुर हृदय जुड़ाना ॥

Mandara mountain[12] in the sea of existence,
lovely abode of virtue, treasury of delight!
All sages, perfected ones, and gods, dreadfully frightened,
bow at your holy feet."

Knowing the terror of gods and Earth, 186
hearing their loving address,
a deep voice came from the sky,
dispelling doubt and distress.

"Do not fear, sages and celestials. 1
For your sake, I will take human guise
along with my aspects, descending as man
in the glorious solar lineage.
Kashyap and Aditi performed great austerity 2
and I have given them a boon.
In the form of Dasarath and Kausalya,
they have appeared as rulers of Kosala.
I will come down to their home 3
as four eminent brothers of the Raghu line.
Fulfilling all of Narad's prophecy,
I will incarnate, together with my supreme energy,[13]
and will lift the earth's entire burden. 4
So do not be afraid, hosts of gods."
Having heard that divine voice in the sky,
the gods went back at once, hearts calmed.

५   तब ब्रह्माँ धरनिहि समुझावा ।
अभय भई भरोस जियँ आवा ॥

१८७   निज लोकहि बिरंचि गे देवन्ह इहइ सिखाइ ।
बानर तनु धरि धरि महि हरि पद सेवहु जाइ ॥

Then Brahma comforted Earth   5
and she lost her fear and found faith.

As he returned to his own realm,   187
the creator instructed the celestials,
"Take on various monkey forms and go to earth
to serve at Hari's feet."

Ram's Birth and Youth

१ गए देव सब निज निज धामा ।
भूमि सहित मन कहुँ बिश्रामा ॥
जो कछु आयसु ब्रह्माँ दीन्हा ।
हरषे देव बिलंब न कीन्हा ॥

२ बनचर देह धरी छिति माहीं ।
अतुलित बल प्रताप तिन्ह पाहीं ॥
गिरि तरु नख आयुध सब बीरा ।
हरि मारग चितवहिं मतिधीरा ॥

३ गिरि कानन जहँ तहँ भरि पूरी ।
रहे निज निज अनीक रचि रूरी ॥
यह सब रुचिर चरित मैं भाषा ।
अब सो सुनहु जो बीचहिं राखा ॥

४ अवधपुरीं रघुकुलमनि राऊ ।
बेद बिदित तेहि दसरथ नाऊँ ॥
धरम धुरंधर गुननिधि ग्यानी ।
हृदयँ भगति मति सारँगपानी ॥

१८८ कौसल्यादि नारि प्रिय सब आचरन पुनीत ।
पति अनुकूल प्रेम दृढ़ हरि पद कमल बिनीत ॥

१ एक बार भूपति मन माहीं ।
भै गलानि मोरें सुत नाहीं ॥
गुर गृह गयउ तुरत महिपाला ।
चरन लागि करि बिनय बिसाला ॥

The gods went to their respective abodes,   1
at peace, along with Mother Earth.
Whatever orders Brahma had given
they gladly fulfilled without delay,
taking earthly form as woodland beings,   2
heroes of matchless might and splendor,
with rocks, trees, and nails for weapons,
to patiently await Hari's coming.
They thronged every hill and forest,   3
living in diverse and splendid troops.
I have recounted these wondrous events,
but now hear what occurred meanwhile.
In Avadh city reigned a jewel of the Raghus,   4
famed in the Veda, by the name of Dasarath,
an upholder of dharma, virtuous, wise,
devoted in heart and mind to bow-bearing Vishnu.[1]

Kausalya and his other dear consorts   188
were all of purest behavior,
humbly heeding their husband
and firm in love for Hari's feet.

Yet once in that sovereign's heart   1
this grief arose: "Alas, I have no son."
The king went straight to his guru's abode
and fell at his feet in profound entreaty,

२ निज दुख सुख सब गुरहि सुनायउ ।
कहि बसिष्ठ बहुबिधि समुझायउ ॥
धरहु धीर होइहहिं सुत चारी ।
त्रिभुवन बिदित भगत भय हारी ॥

३ सृंगी रिषिहि बसिष्ठ बोलावा ।
पुत्रकाम सुभ जग्य करावा ॥
भगति सहित मुनि आहुति दीन्हें ।
प्रगटे अगिनि चरू कर लीन्हें ॥

४ जो बसिष्ठ कछु हृदयँ बिचारा ।
सकल काजु भा सिद्ध तुम्हारा ॥
यह हबि बाँटि देहु नृप जाई ।
जथा जोग जेहि भाग बनाई ॥

१८९ तब अदृस्य भए पावक सकल सभहि समुझाइ ।
परमानंद मगन नृप हरष न हृदयँ समाइ ॥

१ तबहिं रायँ प्रिय नारि बोलाई ।
कौसल्यादि तहाँ चलि आई ॥
अर्ध भाग कौसल्यहि दीन्हा ।
उभय भाग आधे कर कीन्हा ॥

२ कैकेई कहँ नृप सो दयऊ ।
रह्यो सो उभय भाग पुनि भयऊ ॥
कौसल्या कैकेई हाथ धरि ।
दीन्ह सुमित्रहि मन प्रसन्न करि ॥

32

telling him all his sorrows and hopes.   2
Vasishtha spoke many words of solace,
"Take heart, for you will have four sons
of universal fame, who will remove devotees' fears.
Then Vasishtha summoned sage Shringi   3
to perform a blessed son-granting rite.
As the sage devoutly made oblations,
fire-god Agni appeared, vessel in hand,
and said, "Vasishtha's heart's desire,   4
and your entire aim, is achieved!
Go, king, and divide this holy food
as is fitting, apportioning shares."

Then Agni the purifier vanished,   189
having instructed the whole assembly.
The king was lost in bliss,
his heart overflowing with joy.

He quickly summoned his beloved wives,   1
Kausalya and the rest, who came there.
To Kausalya the king gave half of it
and divided the remainder in equal parts.
The lord of men presented one to Kaikeyi   2
and what remained was again halved,
offered to Kausalya and Kaikeyi,
and given to Sumitra, gladdening her heart.

३ एहि बिधि गर्भसहित सब नारी ।
भईं हृदयँ हरषित सुख भारी ॥
जा दिन तें हरि गर्भहिं आए ।
सकल लोक सुख संपति छाए ॥

४ मंदिर महँ सब राजहिं रानीं ।
सोभा सील तेज की खानीं ॥
सुख जुत कछुक काल चलि गयऊ ।
जेहिं प्रभु प्रगट सो अवसर भयऊ ॥

११० जोग लगन ग्रह बार तिथि सकल भए अनुकूल ।
चर अरु अचर हर्षजुत राम जनम सुखमूल ॥

१ नौमी तिथि मधु मास पुनीता ।
सुकल पच्छ अभिजित हरिप्रीता ॥
मध्यदिवस अति सीत न घामा ।
पावन काल लोक बिश्रामा ॥

२ सीतल मंद सुरभि बह बाऊ ।
हरषित सुर संतन मन चाऊ ॥
बन कुसुमित गिरिगन मनिआरा ।
स्रवहिं सकल सरिताऽमृतधारा ॥

३ सो अवसर बिरंचि जब जाना ।
चले सकल सुर साजि बिमाना ॥
गगन बिमल संकुल सुर जूथा ।
गावहिं गुन गंधर्ब बरूथा ॥

Thus all the king's wives conceived 3
and their hearts were filled with delight.
From the day Hari entered the womb,
joy and plenty pervaded all the worlds.
Within the palace, all the queens 4
were radiant with beauty and goodness.
And so the days passed happily
till it was time for the Lord's advent.

All asterisms, signs, and planetary alignments 190
became auspicious
and all created beings blissful, for Ram's birth
is the root of happiness.

On the ninth of spring's sacred month, 1
in its bright half, under Hari's victory sign,[2]
at midday, when it was neither too cold nor hot,
a pure time, giving ease to all,
a cool, fragrant breeze began to blow, 2
pleasing the hearts of gods and sages.
Woods bloomed, hills sparkled with gems,
and rivers poured forth nectar-streams.
When Brahma divined that the time had come, 3
the gods set out in decorated chariots.
The clear sky thronged with deities
and troops of heavenly praise-singers

४ बरषहिं सुमन सुअंजुलि साजी ।
गहगहि गगन दुंदुभी बाजी ॥
अस्तुति करहिं नाग मुनि देवा ।
बहुबिधि लावहिं निज निज सेवा ॥

१११ सुर समूह बिनती करि पहुँचे निज निज धाम ।
जगनिवास प्रभु प्रगटे अखिल लोक बिश्राम ॥

१ भए प्रगट कृपाला दीनदयाला
कौसल्या हितकारी ।
हरषित महतारी मुनि मन हारी
अद्भुत रूप बिचारी ॥
लोचन अभिरामा तनु घनस्यामा
निज आयुध भुज चारी ।
भूषन बनमाला नयन बिसाला
सोभासिंधु खरारी ॥

२ कह दुइ कर जोरी अस्तुति तोरी
केहि बिधि करौं अनंता ।
माया गुन ग्यानातीत अमाना
बेद पुरान भनंता ॥
करुना सुख सागर सब गुन आगर
जेहि गावहिं श्रुति संता ।
सो मम हित लागी जन अनुरागी
भयउ प्रगट श्रीकंता ॥

showering handfuls of flowers   4
while celestial drums resounded.
Serpents, sages, and gods chanted
and offered their diverse adoration.

The divine hosts offered praise and returned   191
to their respective realms,
and the Lord—abode of the world and comforter of all—
became manifest.[3]

He manifested, that merciful one,   1
compassionate to the lowly, Kausalya's benefactor.
His mothers rejoiced and sages were stunned,
contemplating his extraordinary form,
cloud-dark to soothe the eyes and holding
his divine weapons in four arms,
bejeweled, with wildflower garland and great eyes—
beauty's sea and Khara's slayer!
Hands joined in prayer, his mother said,   2
"Infinite one, how shall I praise you?
Beyond illusion, attributes, and knowledge,
        immeasurable—
so Veda and *purāṇa* proclaim.
Sea of joy and mercy, abode of all merit,
of whom scriptures and the saintly sing—
Shri's husband, who loves his faithful ones,
for my sake has appeared.

३ ब्रह्मांड निकाया निर्मित माया
रोम रोम प्रति बेद कहै ।
मम उर सो बासी यह उपहासी
सुनत धीर मति थिर न रहै ॥
उपजा जब ग्याना प्रभु मुसुकाना
चरित बहुत बिधि कीन्ह चहै ।
कहि कथा सुहाई मातु बुझाई
जेहि प्रकार सुत प्रेम लहै ॥

४ माता पुनि बोली सो मति डोली
तजहु तात यह रूपा ।
कीजै सिसुलीला अति प्रियसीला
यह सुख परम अनूपा ॥
सुनि बचन सुजाना रोदन ठाना
होइ बालक सुरभूपा ।
यह चरित जे गावहिं हरिपद पावहिं
ते न परहिं भवकूपा ॥

१९२ बिप्र धेनु सुर संत हित लीन्ह मनुज अवतार ।
निज इच्छा निर्मित तनु माया गुन गो पार ॥

१ सुनि सिसु रुदन परम प्रिय बानी ।
संभ्रम चलि आईं सब रानी ॥

Countless universes crafted of illusion   3
crowd his pores—so the Veda declares.
That he should be in my womb is a jest
to unsteady even steadfast intellects!"
At this nascent knowledge the Lord smiled,
for he wished to perform many deeds,
and reassured his mother with sweet tales,[4]
that she might love him as her son.
Her insight wavering, his mother spoke again,   4
"My child, abandon this form!
Play as an infant, and so beguilingly
that I may know matchless joy."
Hearing her, that wisest of ones began to wail.
The Lord of gods became a babe!
One who sings this story finds Hari's feet
and will not fall into rebirth's abyss.

For the sake of seers, saintly ones, cows, and gods,   192
he came down as man,
shaping a body by his own will,
far beyond illusion's sensory attributes.

Hearing the dear sound of an infant's cries,   1
the queens distractedly hurried there.

हरषित जहँ तहँ धाईं दासी ।
आनँद मगन सकल पुरबासी ॥

२ दसरथ पुत्रजन्म सुनि काना ।
मानहुँ ब्रह्मानंद समाना ॥
परम प्रेम मन पुलक सरीरा ।
चाहत उठन करत मति धीरा ॥

३ जाकर नाम सुनत सुभ होई ।
मोरें गृह आवा प्रभु सोई ॥
परमानंद पूरि मन राजा ।
कहा बोलाइ बजावहु बाजा ॥

४ गुर बसिष्ठ कहँ गयउ हँकारा ।
आए द्विजन सहित नृपद्वारा ॥
अनुपम बालक देखेन्हि जाई ।
रूप रासि गुन कहि न सिराई ॥

१९३ नंदीमुख सराध करि जातकरम सब कीन्ह ।
हाटक धेनु बसन मनि नृप बिप्रन्ह कहँ दीन्ह ॥

१ ध्वज पताक तोरन पुर छावा ।
कहि न जाइ जेहि भाँति बनावा ॥
सुमनबृष्टि अकास तें होई ।
ब्रह्मानंद मगन सब लोई ॥

२ बृंद बृंद मिलि चलीं लोगाईं ।
सहज सिंगार किएँ उठि धाईं ॥

40

Joyous maidservants bustled about
and all the townspeople were overjoyed.
Dasarath, hearing of his son's birth,   2
was as if filled with ultimate bliss.
Supreme love in his heart, his body thrilling,
he sought to rise, steadying his mind.
"He whose name, once heard, brings blessing—   3
that Lord has come into my home!"
His heart filled with rapture, the king
commanded musicians to perform
and had guru Vasishtha summoned.   4
He came with Brahmans to the king's door
to see that incomparable infant,
utterly beautiful and beyond description.

When all ancestral offerings and auspicious birth rites[5]   193
had been performed,
the king distributed gold, cattle, clothes,
and jewels to the priestly seers.

Bedecked with banners and arches,   1
the city was indescribably adorned.
Flowers rained from the firmament
and everyone was lost in divine bliss.
Crowds of townswomen assembled,   2
hastily adorning themselves to hurry forth

कनक कलस मंगल भरि थारा ।
गावत पैठहिं भूप दुआरा ॥

३ करि आरति नेवछावरि करहीं ।
बार बार सिसु चरनन्हि परहीं ॥
मागध सूत बंदिगन गायक ।
पावन गुन गावहिं रघुनायक ॥

४ सर्बस दान दीन्ह सब काहू ।
जेहिं पावा राखा नहिं ताहू ॥
मृगमद चंदन कुंकुम कीचा ।
मची सकल बीथिन्ह बिच बीचा ॥

१९४ गृह गृह बाज बधाव सुभ प्रगटे सुषमा कंद ।
हरषवंत सब जहँ तहँ नगर नारि नर बृंद ॥

१ कैकयसुता सुमित्रा दोऊ ।
सुंदर सुत जनमत भैं ओऊ ॥
वह सुख संपति समय समाजा ।
कहि न सकइ सारद अहिराजा ॥

२ अवधपुरी सोहइ एहि भाँती ।
प्रभुहि मिलन आई जनु राती ॥
देखि भानु जनु मन सकुचानी ।
तदपि बनी संध्या अनुमानी ॥

३ अगर धूप बहु जनु अँधिआरी ।
उड़इ अबीर मनहुँ अरुनारी ॥

with gold water vessels and heaped offering trays.
Singing, they entered the king's gate.
Worshiping with lamps, making gestures of blessing,[6]   3
they fell time and again at the baby's feet.
Bards, minstrels, and singers of every sort
intoned the virtues of the Raghu king.
Immense wealth was given away to all[7]   4
and the receivers just passed it along!
Costly musk, sandal, and vermilion
collected like mud in every lane.

Every home rang with rejoicing, for the source   194
of splendor was made manifest,
and everywhere, townsmen and women
celebrated in delirious throngs.

When both Kaikeya's daughter* and Sumitra   1
likewise gave birth to beautiful sons,
the joy and splendor of that celebration
could not be told by Sharada and the serpent king!
The city of Avadh looked as glorious   2
as Lady Night come to meet her lord,
but, as if abashed at seeing the sun still there,
she decided to turn into twilight;
clouds of rich incense were its dusk,   3
tinted by tossed vermilion powder;

---

* Kaikeyi.

मंदिर मनि समूह जनु तारा ।
नृप गृह कलस सो इंदु उदारा ॥

४ भवन बेद धुनि अति मृदु बानी ।
जनु खग मुखर समयँ जनु सानी ॥
कौतुक देखि पतंग भुलाना ।
एक मास तेइँ जात न जाना ॥

१९५ मास दिवस कर दिवस भा मरम न जानइ कोइ ।
रथ समेत रबि थाकेउ निसा कवन बिधि होइ ॥

१ यह रहस्य काहूँ नहिं जाना ।
दिनमनि चले करत गुनगाना ॥
देखि महोत्सव सुर मुनि नागा ।
चले भवन बरनत निज भागा ॥

२ औरउ एक कहउँ निज चोरी ।
सुनु गिरिजा अति दृढ़ मति तोरी ॥
काकभुसुंडि संग हम दोऊ ।
मनुजरूप जानइ नहिं कोऊ ॥

३ परमानंद प्रेम सुख फूले ।
बीथिन्ह फिरहिं मगन मन भूले ॥
यह सुभ चरित जान पै सोई ।
कृपा राम कै जापर होई ॥

४ तेहि अवसर जो जेहि बिधि आवा ।
दीन्ह भूप जो जेहि मन भावा ॥

the massed gems of mansions were stars,
and the palace finial the full moon;
inside, the sweet sound of Vedic chant   4
was like the evening chorus of birds.
Seeing this spectacle, the sun forgot himself
and, unawares, let a month go by.

A month became a mere day,   195
yet no one fathomed this mystery.
The sun and his chariot stood still,
so how could night come on?

No one grasped this secret,   1
and the sun moved on, praising Ram.
Gods, sages, and serpents witnessed the celebrations
and went home, reckoning their good fortune.
Let me disclose a little secret of my own,[8]   2
Girija, for your mind is now firm:
with Bhushundi the crow, I went there, too,
in human form, unknown to all.
Exulting in the supreme bliss of love   3
we roamed the lanes, lost in delight.
But this blessed adventure can only be known
by one who receives Ram's grace.
To whomever came at that time, in whichever way,   4
the king gave whatever would please his heart.

गज रथ तुरग हेम गो हीरा ।
दीन्हे नृप नानाबिधि चीरा ॥

१९६ मन संतोषे सबन्हि के जहँ तहँ देहिं असीस ।
सकल तनय चिर जीवहुँ तुलसिदास के ईस ॥

१ कछुक दिवस बीते एहि भाँती ।
जात न जानिअ दिन अरु राती ॥
नामकरन कर अवसरु जानी ।
भूप बोलि पठए मुनि ग्यानी ॥

२ करि पूजा भूपति अस भाषा ।
धरिअ नाम जो मुनि गुनि राखा ॥
इन्ह के नाम अनेक अनूपा ।
मैं नृप कहब स्वमति अनुरूपा ॥

३ जो आनंद सिंधु सुखरासी ।
सीकर तें त्रैलोक सुपासी ॥
सो सुखधाम राम अस नामा ।
अखिल लोक दायक बिश्रामा ॥

४ बिस्व भरन पोषन कर जोई ।
ताकर नाम भरत अस होई ॥
जाके सुमिरन तें रिपु नासा ।
नाम सत्रुहन बेद प्रकासा ॥

Elephants, chariots, horses, gold, cows, and gems,
the lord of men gave out, and all sorts of clothes.

When all hearts were sated, benedictions   196
were heard on every hand:
"Let all the boys be blessed with long lives!"—
those lords of Tulsidas.

In this way, many days passed,   1
though no one reckoned day or night.
Knowing it was time for the naming ceremony,
the king summoned his wise family priest,
venerated him, and declared,   2
"Bestow the names you have chosen, sage."
Vasishtha said, "Their names are many and matchless,
Your Majesty, yet I will speak from my own
    understanding:
he who is the ocean of bliss and delight,   3
one drop of which sates the triple spheres—
that abode of joy shall be named Ram,
for he gives comfort to the whole universe.
He who supports and succors the world   4
will be named Bharat, 'the bearer,'
and he whose mere recollection destroys foes
will be Shatrughna,* glorified in the Veda."

* "Enemy-killer."

१९७ लच्छन धाम राम प्रिय सकल जगत आधार ।
गुरु बसिष्ट तेहि राखा लछिमन नाम उदार ॥

१ धरे नाम गुर हृदयँ बिचारी ।
बेद तत्व नृप तव सुत चारी ॥
मुनि धन जन सरबस सिव प्राना ।
बाल केलि रस तेहिं सुख माना ॥

२ बारेहि ते निज हित पति जानी ।
लछिमन राम चरन रति मानी ॥
भरत सत्रुहन दूनउ भाई ।
प्रभु सेवक जसि प्रीति बड़ाई ॥

३ स्याम गौर सुंदर दोउ जोरी ।
निरखहिं छबि जननीं तृन तोरी ॥
चारिउ सील रूप गुन धामा ।
तदपि अधिक सुखसागर रामा ॥

४ हृदयँ अनुग्रह इंदु प्रकासा ।
सूचत किरन मनोहर हासा ॥
कबहुँ उछंग कबहुँ बर पलना ।
मातु दुलारइ कहि प्रिय ललना ॥

१९८ ब्यापक ब्रह्म निरंजन निर्गुन बिगत बिनोद ।
सो अज प्रेम भगति बस कौसल्या कें गोद ॥

The abode of all merit, beloved of Ram,   197
and very basis of the vast world—
on him Guru Vasishtha bestowed
the lofty name Lakshman—"auspicious."

The guru gave names, searching his heart.   1
"Sire, your four sons are the Vedas' essence,
the prize of sages, the people's all, Shiva's soul,
and yet they delight in infant play!"
Knowing from boyhood his benevolent master,   2
Lakshman ever adored Ram's feet.
And between brothers Bharat and Shatrughna
was the praiseworthy love of lord and servant.
Seeing the two comely pairs, dark and fair,   3
their mothers prayed to avert the evil eye.[9]
All four were abodes of beauty and merit,
yet the surpassing sea of joy was Ram.
His heart held the moonlight of mercy   4
revealed by beams of his beguiling smile.
On him, at her breast or in a pretty cradle,
his mother doted, cooing, "Little darling!"

All-pervading God, stainless, unqualified,   198
and in need of no diversion—
that birthless one, bound by love and devotion,
lay in Kausalya's lap.

१ काम कोटि छबि स्याम सरीरा ।
नील कंज बारिद गंभीरा ॥
अरुन चरन पंकज नख जोती ।
कमल दलन्हि बैठे जनु मोती ॥

२ रेख कुलिस ध्वज अंकुस सोहे ।
नूपुर धुनि सुनि मुनि मन मोहे ॥
कटि किंकिनी उदर त्रय रेखा ।
नाभि गभीर जान जेहिं देखा ॥

३ भुज बिसाल भूषन जुत भूरी ।
हियँ हरि नख अति सोभा रूरी ॥
उर मनिहार पदिक की सोभा ।
बिप्र चरन देखत मन लोभा ॥

४ कंबु कंठ अति चिबुक सुहाई ।
आनन अमित मदन छबि छाई ॥
दुइ दुइ दसन अधर अरुनारे ।
नासा तिलक को बरनै पारे ॥

५ सुंदर श्रवन सुचारु कपोला ।
अति प्रिय मधुर तोतरे बोला ॥
चिक्कन कच कुंचित गभुआरे ।
बहु प्रकार रचि मातु सँवारे ॥

६ पीत झगुलिया तनु पहिराई ।
जानु पानि बिचरनि मोहि भाई ॥
रूप सकहिं नहिं कहि श्रुति सेषा ।
सो जानइ सपनेहुँ जेहिं देखा ॥

His dark form was lovely as a billion love gods,   1
blue lotuses, or massed monsoon clouds,
with red-lotus feet and bright little nails,
like pearls perched on lily-pads,
and soles marked by thunderbolt, flag, and goad.[10]   2
With tinkling anklets to stop sages' hearts,
belt of tiny bells, belly with three folds,
and deep navel one must see to believe.
His long arms were richly bejeweled   3
and his chest adorned with tiger claws,
a glorious diamond necklace,
and the mind-stealing mark of a sage's sole.[11]
He had a conch-like neck, pretty little chin,   4
and a face more beautiful than countless Kamas,
with two pairs of tiny teeth and ruddy lips.
Who can describe his nose and brow-mark?
His ears were lovely, cheeks charming,   5
and his speech endearingly lisping.
His glistening, curly infant locks[12]
were lovingly arranged by his mother.
His little body bedecked in yellow,   6
he crawls on hands and knees, to my delight.[13]
This form, indescribable by Veda and Shesh,
is known only to one who sees within.[14]

१९९ सुख संदोह मोहपर ग्यान गिरा गोतीत ।
दंपति परम प्रेम बस कर सिसुचरित पुनीत ॥

१ एहि बिधि राम जगत पितु माता ।
कोसलपुर बासिन्ह सुखदाता ॥
जिन्ह रघुनाथ चरन रति मानी ।
तिन्ह की यह गति प्रगट भवानी ॥

२ रघुपति बिमुख जतन कर कोरी ।
कवन सकइ भव बंधन छोरी ॥
जीव चराचर बस कै राखे ।
सो माया प्रभु सों भय भाखे ॥

३ भृकुटि बिलास नचावइ ताही ।
अस प्रभु छाड़ि भजिअ कहु काही ॥
मन क्रम बचन छाड़ि चतुराई ।
भजत कृपा करिहहिं रघुराई ॥

४ एहि बिधि सिसुबिनोद प्रभु कीन्हा ।
सकल नगरबासिन्ह सुख दीन्हा ॥
लै उछंग कबहुँक हलरावै ।
कबहुँ पालने घालि झुलावै ॥

२०० प्रेम मगन कौसल्या निसि दिन जात न जान ।
सुत सनेह बस माता बालचरित कर गान ॥

Utter bliss, beyond delusion, knowledge,   199
speech, and sense perception,
mastered by a royal couple's love,
performs the pure play of a babe.

So, Ram, creation's father and mother,   1
delights the dwellers in Kosala.
Those who adore the Raghu master's feet
may aspire to this state, Bhavani.
But even with a billion efforts, how can those   2
averse to Ram slip from the fetters of rebirth?
Though in control of all created souls,
Maya, too, is in terror of that master
whose merest glance makes her dance.   3
Turning away from such a Lord, whom will you praise?
Give up guile in mind, word, and deed
and worship Ram—he will be gracious.
In this way, the Lord frolicked as an infant   4
giving delight to all the townspeople.
Sometimes his mother rocked him in her lap
or swung him in a cradle.

Lost in love, Kausalya never knew   200
the passing of days and nights.
Overcome by affection, she constantly sang
of her little son's sports.

१   एक बार जननीं अन्हवाए ।
करि सिंगार पलनाँ पौढ़ाए ॥
निज कुल इष्टदेव भगवाना ।
पूजा हेतु कीन्ह अस्नाना ॥

२   करि पूजा नैबेद्य चढ़ावा ।
आपु गइ जहँ पाक बनावा ॥
बहुरि मातु तहवाँ चलि आई ।
भोजन करत देख सुत जाई ॥

३   गै जननी सिसु पहिं भयभीता ।
देखा बाल तहाँ पुनि सूता ॥
बहुरि आइ देखा सुत सोई ।
हृदयँ कंप मन धीर न होई ॥

४   इहाँ उहाँ दुइ बालक देखा ।
मतिभ्रम मोर कि आन बिसेषा ॥
देखि राम जननी अकुलानी ।
प्रभु हँसि दीन्ह मधुर मुसुकानी ॥

२०१   देखरावा मातहि निज अद्भुत रूप अखंड ।
रोम रोम प्रति लागे कोटि कोटि ब्रह्मंड ॥

१   अगनित रबि ससि सिव चतुरानन ।
बहु गिरि सरित सिंधु महि कानन ॥
काल कर्म गुन ग्यान सुभाऊ ।
सोउ देखा जो सुना न काऊ ॥

Once, his mother bathed him,   1
groomed him, and laid him in his bed.
Preparing to worship the family god,
she performed her own ablutions.
She did the rites and made offerings   2
and then went to the kitchen.
When she returned to that place
she saw her son eating the holy food.
She went in alarm to the nursery   3
and saw the babe still sleeping there.
Coming back, she saw him at the shrine.
Her heart and mind were shaken.
"Here, there—I see two babies!   4
Is it my delusion or something more?"
Seeing his mother's distress, Lord Ram
laughed and gave a charming smile.

He made his mother behold   201
his own wondrous, indivisible form,
each pore imbued with millions
upon millions of universes.

Countless suns, moons, Shivas, four-faced Brahmas,   1
multiple mountains, rivers, seas, fields, forests,
time, karma, all traits, wisdom, and innate nature,
and even unheard-of things—she saw it all.

२　देखी माया सब बिधि गाढ़ी ।
　अति सभीत जोरें कर ठाढ़ी ॥
　देखा जीव नचावइ जाही ।
　देखी भगति जो छोरइ ताही ॥

३　तन पुलकित मुख बचन न आवा ।
　नयन मूदि चरननि सिरु नावा ॥
　बिसमयवंत देखि महतारी ।
　भए बहुरि सिसुरूप खरारी ॥

४　अस्तुति करि न जाइ भय माना ।
　जगत पिता मैं सुत करि जाना ॥
　हरि जननी बहुबिधि समुझाई ।
　यह जनि कतहुँ कहसि सुनु माई ॥

२०२　बार बार कौसल्या बिनय करइ कर जोरि ।
　अब जनि कबहुँ ब्यापै प्रभु मोहि माया तोरि ॥

१　बालचरित हरि बहुबिधि कीन्हा ।
　अति अनंद दासन्ह कहँ दीन्हा ॥
　कछुक काल बीतें सब भाई ।
　बड़े भए परिजन सुखदाई ॥

२　चूड़ाकरन कीन्ह गुरु जाई ।
　बिप्रन्ह पुनि दछिना बहु पाई ॥
　परम मनोहर चरित अपारा ।
　करत फिरत चारिउ सुकुमारा ॥

She saw wholly impenetrable Illusion 2
standing worshipfully, in utter terror,
and the soul, whom Maya makes dance,
and Bhakti, who brings it release.
Her body trembling, unable to speak, 3
she shut her eyes and lay her head at his feet.
Seeing his mother awestruck,
Khara's foe[15] again took infant form.
She was too frightened even to praise him. 4
"I've taken the world's Father as my son!"
But Hari thoroughly instructed her:
"Listen, mother, never speak of this!"

Palms joined in reverence, 202
Kausalya repeatedly entreated him,
"May I never again be overcome, Lord,
by your illusory power."

Hari performed many childlike acts 1
giving great joy to his servants.
With the passage of time, the brothers
grew bigger, delighting the household.
The guru came to do the tonsure rite 2
and Brahmans again received many gifts.
Supremely and endlessly beguiling
are the doings of the four little princes.[16]

३   मन क्रम बचन अगोचर जोई ।
दसरथ अजिर बिचर प्रभु सोई ॥
भोजन करत बोल जब राजा ।
नहिं आवत तजि बाल समाजा ॥

४   कौसल्या जब बोलन जाई ।
ठुमुकु ठुमुकु प्रभु चलहिं पराई ॥
निगम नेति सिव अंत न पावा ।
ताहि धरै जननी हठि धावा ॥

५   धूसर धूरि भरें तनु आए ।
भूपति बिहसि गोद बैठाए ॥

२०३   भोजन करत चपल चित इत उत अवसरु पाइ ।
भाजि चले किलकत मुख दधि ओदन लपटाइ ॥

१   बालचरित अति सरल सुहाए ।
सारद सेष संभु श्रुति गाए ॥
जिन्ह कर मन इन्ह सन नहिं राता ।
ते जन बंचित किए बिधाता ॥

२   भए कुमार जबहिं सब भ्राता ।
दीन्ह जनेऊ गुरु पितु माता ॥
गुरगृहँ गए पढ़न रघुराई ।
अलप काल बिद्या सब आई ॥

३   जाकी सहज स्वास श्रुति चारी ।
सो हरि पढ़ यह कौतुक भारी ॥

The Lord who eludes perception by mind, act,   3
and speech, frolics in Dasarath's courtyard.
When the king summons him to eat
he refuses to leave his playmates and come.
And when Kausalya goes to call him,   4
the Lord runs away with toddling gait.
He of whom Veda says, "Not this!"—whose infinitude
  eludes Shiva—
is chased and grabbed by his mother.
He comes, his body covered with dust,   5
and the chuckling king takes him on his lap.

He eats distractedly, and when he gets   203
the chance, tears off
this way and that, shrieking,
his face smeared with curd and rice.

Guileless and beguiling, these child-sports   1
are sung by Sharada, Shesh, Shiva, and Veda.
Those whose hearts are not attached
to them have been cheated by providence.
When all the brothers had become youths,   2
their guru and parents gave them sacred threads.
Ram went to his teacher's house to study
and quickly acquired all knowledge.
That Hari, whose very breath is the four Vedas,   3
should learn—what a great farce!

बिद्या बिनय निपुन गुन सीला ।
खेलहिं खेल सकल नृप लीला ॥
४ करतल बान धनुष अति सोहा ।
देखत रूप चराचर मोहा ॥
जिन्ह बीथिन्ह बिहरहिं सब भाई ।
थकित होहिं सब लोग लुगाई ॥

२०४ कोसलपुर बासी नर नारि बृद्ध अरु बाल ।
प्रानहु ते प्रिय लागत सब कहुँ राम कृपाल ॥

१ बंधु सखा सँग लेहिं बोलाई ।
बन मृगया नित खेलहिं जाई ॥
पावन मृग मारहिं जियँ जानी ।
दिन प्रति नृपहि देखावहिं आनी ॥
२ जे मृग राम बान के मारे ।
ते तनु तजि सुरलोक सिधारे ॥
अनुज सखा सँग भोजन करहीं ।
मातु पिता अग्या अनुसरहीं ॥
३ जेहि बिधि सुखी होहिं पुर लोगा ।
करहिं कृपानिधि सोइ संजोगा ॥
बेद पुरान सुनहिं मन लाई ।
आपु कहहिं अनुजन्ह समुझाई ॥
४ प्रातकाल उठि कै रघुनाथा ।
मातु पिता गुरु नावहिं माथा ॥

Perfect in wisdom, humility, judgment,
he played out every princely role.
To see his beauty, with bow and arrows   4
in hand, intoxicated all beings.
In whatever lanes the brothers ambled,
all the townsmen and women were stunned.

To all who dwelled in Kosala city,   204
men, women, elders, and children,
merciful Ram was dearer
than their own life's breath.

Gathering his brothers and friends   1
he would go hunting in the forests,
selecting and killing game of pure species[17]
and daily bringing them to show the king.
The creatures slain by Ram's arrows   2
shed their bodies and entered heaven.
Ram ate with his brothers and friends
and abided by his parents' commands.
Whatever would make the citizens happy,   3
he, the treasury of mercy, so arranged.
He listened attentively to Veda and *purāṇas*
and explained them to his young brothers.
Arising before dawn, the lord of Raghus   4
bowed his head to parents and guru,

आयसु मागि करहिं पुर काजा ।
देखि चरित हरषइ मन राजा ॥

२०५ ब्यापक अकल अनीह अज निर्गुन नाम न रूप ।
भगत हेतु नाना बिधि करत चरित्र अनूप ॥

१ यह सब चरित कहा मैं गाई ।
आगिलि कथा सुनहु मन लाई ॥
बिस्वामित्र महामुनि ग्यानी ।
बसहिं बिपिन सुभ आश्रम जानी ॥

२ जहँ जप जग्य जोग मुनि करहीं ।
अति मारीच सुबाहुहि डरहीं ॥
देखत जग्य निसाचर धावहिं ।
करहिं उपद्रव मुनि दुख पावहिं ॥

३ गाधितनय मन चिंता ब्यापी ।
हरि बिनु मरहिं न निसिचर पापी ॥
तब मुनिबर मन कीन्ह बिचारा ।
प्रभु अवतरेउ हरन महि भारा ॥

४ एहूँ मिस देखौं पद जाई ।
करि बिनती आनौं दोउ भाई ॥
ग्यान बिराग सकल गुन अयना ।
सो प्रभु मैं देखब भरि नयना ॥

and with their leave, attended to the city's affairs,
and his good deeds gladdened the king's heart.

All-pervasive, perfect, desireless, unborn,   205
unqualified by name and form—
for the sake of devotees he performed
diverse and matchless deeds.

I have sung you all these acts,   1
now listen to the next episode.
Vishvamitra, the great and wise sage,
lived in the forest in a holy ashram
where he practiced asceticism, sacrifice, and yoga,   2
though fearful of Marich and Subahu.*
Seeing a fire rite, those night-stalkers attacked
and caused mayhem, saddening the sage.
Vishvamitra, Gadhi's son, pondered in his heart,   3
"Hari alone can slay these sinful demons."
Then that best of sages reflected,
"The Lord has descended to remove earth's burden.
On this pretext I will go to his holy feet   4
and ask to bring back the two brothers.
The abode of all wisdom, detachment, and virtue—
on that Lord I will feast my eyes!"

---

* Forest-dwelling demons (*rākṣasas*).

२०६ बहुबिधि करत मनोरथ जात लागि नहिं बार ।
करि मज्जन सरऊ जल गए भूप दरबार ॥

१ मुनि आगमन सुना जब राजा ।
मिलन गयउ लै बिप्र समाजा ॥
करि दंडवत मुनिहि सनमानी ।
निज आसन बैठारेन्हि आनी ॥

२ चरन पखारि कीन्हि अति पूजा ।
मो सम आजु धन्य नहिं दूजा ॥
बिबिध भाँति भोजन करवावा ।
मुनिबर हृदयँ हरष अति पावा ॥

३ पुनि चरननि मेले सुत चारी ।
राम देखि मुनि देह बिसारी ॥
भए मगन देखत मुख सोभा ।
जनु चकोर पूरन ससि लोभा ॥

४ तब मन हरषि बचन कह राऊ ।
मुनि अस कृपा न कीन्हिहु काऊ ॥
केहि कारन आगमन तुम्हारा ।
कहहु सो करत न लावउँ बारा ॥

५ असुर समूह सतावहिं मोही ।
मैं जाचन आयउँ नृप तोही ॥
अनुज समेत देहु रघुनाथा ।
निसिचर बध मैं होब सनाथा ॥

64

His heart filled with yearning,   206
he lost no time in leaving,
bathed in the Sarayu's waters,
and went to the king's court.

When the king heard of the sage's approach   1
he went with all the Brahmans to meet him,
fell at the sage's feet in homage,
and then seated him on his own throne.
He washed his feet and worshiped him,   2
saying, "Today, none is more blessed than I."
He had him served varied fare
that greatly pleased the sage's heart,
then brought his four sons to the master's feet.   3
Seeing Ram, the sage lost bodily awareness
and gazed intoxicated at his lovely face,
like a *cakor* bird thirsty for the full moon.
Glad at heart, the king spoke,   4
"Your holiness has never graced us before.
Please reveal the motive for your visit
that I may act on it without delay."
The sage said, "A swarm of demons torments me,   5
so I come, king, to beg a favor of you.
Give me Ram and his young brother
to slay the night-stalkers and be my protectors.

२०७ देहु भूप मन हरषित तजहु मोह अग्यान ।
धर्म सुजस प्रभु तुम्ह कौं इन्ह कहँ अति कल्यान ॥

१ सुनि राजा अति अप्रिय बानी ।
हृदय कंप मुख दुति कुमुलानी ॥
चौथेंपन पायउँ सुत चारी ।
बिप्र बचन नहिं कहेहु बिचारी ॥

२ मागहु भूमि धेनु धन कोसा ।
सर्बस देउँ आजु सहरोसा ॥
देह प्रान तें प्रिय कछु नाहीं ।
सोउ मुनि देउँ निमिष एक माहीं ॥

३ सब सुत प्रिय मोहि प्रान कि नाईं ।
राम देत नहिं बनइ गोसाईं ॥
कहँ निसिचर अति घोर कठोरा ।
कहँ सुंदर सुत परम किसोरा ॥

४ सुनि नृप गिरा प्रेम रस सानी ।
हृदयँ हरष माना मुनि ग्यानी ॥
तब बसिष्ठ बहुबिधि समुझावा ।
नृप संदेह नास कहँ पावा ॥

५ अति आदर दोउ तनय बोलाए ।
हृदयँ लाइ बहु भाँति सिखाए ॥
मेरे प्रान नाथ सुत दोऊ ।
तुम्ह मुनि पिता आन नहिं कोऊ ॥

Give them, king, with glad heart, 207
surrendering attachment and ignorance.
To you, lord, will accrue merit and fame,
and to them, the greatest good."

When he heard these most unwelcome words, 1
the king's heart quavered and his face lost its glow.
"In my old age I acquired four sons,
and you spoke without due consideration, brahman.
Ask for land, cattle, wealth, or treasure, 2
and at once I will gladly give it all away.
Even body and breath, most dear to all,
I would give, sage, in the blink of an eye.
But all my sons are dear to me as life, 3
and Ram, master, I can never give up.
Just think of those dreadful, savage demons
and then of my beautiful, tender boy!"
Hearing the king's speech, imbued with love, 4
the wise recluse was inwardly pleased.
But then Vasishtha admonished the king
and the monarch's doubts were assuaged.
He reverently summoned his two sons, 5
hugged them, and gave them much instruction.
"Master, these two boys are my very breath,
but now, sage, you are their only father."

२०८क सौंपे भूप रिषिहि सुत बहुबिधि देइ असीस ।
जननी भवन गए प्रभु चले नाइ पद सीस ॥

२०८ख पुरुषसिंह दोउ बीर हरषि चले मुनि भय हरन ।
कृपासिंधु मतिधीर अखिल बिस्व कारन करन ॥

१ अरुन नयन उर बाहु बिसाला ।
नील जलज तनु स्याम तमाला ॥
कटि पट पीत कसें बर भाथा ।
रुचिर चाप सायक दुहुँ हाथा ॥

२ स्याम गौर सुंदर दोउ भाई ।
बिस्वामित्र महानिधि पाई ॥
प्रभु ब्रह्मन्यदेव मैं जाना ।
मोहि निति पिता तजेउ भगवाना ॥

३ चले जात मुनि दीन्हि देखाई ।
सुनि ताड़का क्रोध करि धाई ॥
एकहिं बान प्रान हरि लीन्हा ।
दीन जानि तेहि निज पद दीन्हा ॥

४ तब रिषि निज नाथहि जियँ चीन्ही ।
बिद्यानिधि कहुँ बिद्या दीन्ही ॥
जाते लाग न छुधा पिपासा ।
अतुलित बल तनु तेज प्रकासा ॥

The ruler of the earth, with many blessings,   208a
handed his sons over to the seer.
Then the Lord went to his mother's abode
and bowed his head at her feet.

The two heroes, lions among men, went off joyfully   208b
to relieve the sage's fear—
ocean of mercy, supremely resolute,
and all creation's ultimate cause.[18]

His eyes are reddish, chest broad, arms long,   1
and body dark as a blue lotus or evergreen tree,
waist bound with yellow cloth and fine quiver,
and his hands hold beautiful bow and arrows.
Dark and fair, both brothers were handsome.   2
Vishvamitra had gained a great treasure, and thought,
"Now I know that God favors Brahmans,
for the Lord left his own father for my sake."
As they went along, the sage guided them.[19]   3
Hearing them, demon Taraka rushed out in a rage.
With a single arrow, Ram took her life,
and knowing her misery, gave her his own state.[20]
Then the seer, fully convinced that Ram was his Lord, 4
taught secret knowledge to its very source,
so he would never feel hunger or thirst
and have matchless bodily strength and luster.

२०९ आयुध सर्ब समर्पि कै प्रभु निज आश्रम आनि ।
कंद मूल फल भोजन दीन्ह भगति हित जानि ॥

१ प्रात कहा मुनि सन रघुराई ।
निर्भय जग्य करहु तुम्ह जाई ॥
होम करन लागे मुनि झारी ।
आपु रहे मख कीं रखवारी ॥

२ सुनि मारीच निसाचर क्रोही ।
लै सहाय धावा मुनिद्रोही ॥
बिनु फर बान राम तेहि मारा ।
सत जोजन गा सागर पारा ॥

३ पावक सर सुबाहु पुनि मारा ।
अनुज निसाचर कटकु सँघारा ॥
मारि असुर द्विज निर्भयकारी ।
अस्तुति करहिं देव मुनि झारी ॥

४ तहँ पुनि कछुक दिवस रघुराया ।
रहे कीन्हि बिप्रन्ह पर दाया ॥
भगति हेतु बहु कथा पुराना ।
कहे बिप्र जद्यपि प्रभु जाना ॥

५ तब मुनि सादर कहा बुझाई ।
चरित एक प्रभु देखिअ जाई ॥
धनुषजग्य सुनि रघुकुल नाथा ।
हरषि चले मुनिबर के साथा ॥

Having presented him with all weapons,   209
he brought the Lord to his hermitage
and fed him roots and fruits,
knowing his beneficence to devotees.

At dawn, the Raghu lord said to the sage,   1
"Go and perform your sacrifice without fear."
The host of ascetics began their oblations
while he stood guard over the rite.
Hearing this, the enraged night-stalker Marich,   2
enemy of sages, rushed in with his forces.
Ram struck him with a blunt arrow
that hurled him a hundred leagues over the sea.
He then slew Subahu with a fiery arrow,   3
and his brother slaughtered the demon host.
Killing demons, he freed the twice-born of fear,
and throngs of gods and sages hymned his praise.
Then for some days the Raghu prince   4
stayed on, showing mercy to the Brahmans,
who devoutly recounted many holy tales,
though the Lord already knew them.
The sage then respectfully proposed   5
that the Lord might go and see a wonder.
Hearing of the bow rite,[21] the Raghu lord
happily set out with that best of sages.

६ आश्रम एक दीख मग माहीं ।
   खग मृग जीव जंतु तहँ नाहीं ॥
   पूछा मुनिहि सिला प्रभु देखी ।
   सकल कथा मुनि कहा बिसेषी ॥

२१० गौतम नारि श्राप बस उपल देह धरि धीर ।
     चरन कमल रज चाहति कृपा करहु रघुबीर ॥

१ परसत पद पावन सोक नसावन
   प्रगट भई तपपुंज सही ।
   देखत रघुनायक जन सुखदायक
   सनमुख होइ कर जोरि रही ॥
   अति प्रेम अधीरा पुलक सरीरा
   मुख नहिं आवइ बचन कही ।
   अतिसय बड़भागी चरननि्ह लागी
   जुगल नयन जलधार बही ॥
२ धीरजु मन कीन्हा प्रभु कहुँ चीन्हा
   रघुपति कृपाँ भगति पाई ।
   अति निर्मल बानी अस्तुति ठानी
   ग्यानगम्य जय रघुराई ॥
   मैं नारि अपावन प्रभु जग पावन
   रावन रिपु जन सुखदाई ।
   राजीव बिलोचन भव भय मोचन
   पाहि पाहि सरनहिं आई ॥

Along the way, an ashram came into view,   6
devoid of birds, beasts, and all other beings.
Seeing a great stone there, the Lord inquired
of the sage, who recounted the whole tale.[22]

"Gautam's wife, under a curse, patiently endures   210
embodiment in stone.
She craves the dust of your holy feet.
So be gracious, Raghu hero!"[23]

Touched by his holy feet, destroyers of sorrow,   1
that great ascetic woman appeared.
Seeing the Raghu lord, who gives joy to his people,
she stood prayerfully before him
distracted by intense love, her body thrilling,
and unable to utter a word.
Supremely fortunate, she fell at his feet,
tears streaming from her eyes.
Calming her mind, she recognized Lord Ram   2
and by his grace attained devotion.
In a clear voice she began praising him:
"Hail, Raghu Lord, attained by wisdom!
I am an impure woman, and you, Ravan's foe,[24] purify the
        worlds
and please your people.
Lotus-eyed liberator from rebirth's dread,
save me, save me! I take refuge at your feet.

३ मुनि श्राप जो दीन्हा अति भल कीन्हा
परम अनुग्रह मैं माना ।
देखेउँ भरि लोचन हरि भव मोचन
इहइ लाभ संकर जाना ॥
बिनती प्रभु मोरी मैं मति भोरी
नाथ न मागउँ बर आना ।
पद कमल परागा रस अनुरागा
मम मन मधुप करै पाना ॥

४ जेहिं पद सुरसरिता परम पुनीता
प्रगट भई सिव सीस धरी ।
सोइ पद पंकज जेहि पूजत अज
मम सिर धरेउ कृपाल हरी ॥
एहि भाँति सिधारी गौतम नारी
बार बार हरि चरन परी ।
जो अति मन भावा सो बरु पावा
गै पति लोक अनंद भरी ॥

२११ अस प्रभु दीनबंधु हरि कारन रहित दयाल ।
तुलसिदास सठ तेहि भजु छाड़ि कपट जंजाल ॥

१ चले राम लछिमन मुनि संगा ।
गए जहाँ जग पावनि गंगा ॥
गाधिसूनु सब कथा सुनाई ।
जेहि प्रकार सुरसरि महि आई ॥

74

In cursing me, the sage has done me great good,   3
for I regard it as supreme grace
to feast my eyes on Hari, liberator from illusion
and ultimate reward, as Shiva knows.
I have one request, divine master, simple-witted as I am,
and ask no other favor:
may the bee of my mind constantly sip love-nectar
from the pollen of your feet!
Those feet where the sacred river springs   4
that Shiva bears on his brow,
pure feet that birthless Brahma worships—
merciful Hari has placed on my head."
With this, Gautam's wife fell again and again
at the Lord's feet.
Gaining the boon most pleasing to her heart,
she went blissfully to her husband's world.

Such is Lord Hari, friend of the lowly,   211
who shows kindness without cause.
Tulsidas says, "Scoundrel, forsake your web of wiles
and adore him alone."[25]

Then Ram and Lakshman accompanied the sage   1
to where world-purifying Ganga flowed.
Gadhi's son recounted the whole tale
of how the gods' river had come to earth.

२   तब प्रभु रिषिन्ह समेत नहाए ।
बिबिध दान महिदेवन्हि पाए ॥
हरषि चले मुनि बृंद सहाया ।
बेगि बिदेह नगर निअराया ॥

३   पुर रम्यता राम जब देखी ।
हरषे अनुज समेत बिसेषी ॥
बापीं कूप सरित सर नाना ।
सलिल सुधासम मनि सोपाना ॥

४   गुंजत मंजु मत्त रस भृंगा ।
कूजत कल बहुबरन बिहंगा ॥
बरन बरन बिकसे बनजाता ।
त्रिबिध समीर सदा सुखदाता ॥

२१२   सुमन बाटिका बाग बन बिपुल बिहंग निवास ।
फूलत फलत सुपल्लवत सोहत पुर चहुँ पास ॥

१   बनइ न बरनत नगर निकाई ।
जहाँ जाइ मन तहँइँ लोभाई ॥
चारु बजारु बिचित्र अँबारी ।
मनिमय बिधि जनु स्वकर सँवारी ॥

२   धनिक बनिक बर धनद समाना ।
बैठे सकल बस्तु लै नाना ॥
चौहट सुंदर गलीं सुहाई ।
संतत रहहिं सुगंध सिंचाई ॥

The Lord bathed with the seers there   2
and the gods of earth received many gifts.
He departed joyously in the holy company
and soon approached the city of Videha.
Beholding the splendor of the city   3
Ram and his brother felt a special joy.
There were many wells, streams, and pools
of nectar-like water, with gemstone stairs.
Bees hummed in heady intoxication   4
and multicolored birds cooed sweetly.
Wild lotuses of every hue blossomed
and a cool, fragrant breeze gave constant delight.

Flower gardens, parks, and preserves,   212
the abode of countless birds,
verdant and full of flowers and fruit,
adorned the city on its four sides.[26]

The excellence of this city cannot be described,   1
and wherever the mind ranges in it, it becomes transfixed.
Its fine markets had colorful bejeweled awnings,
as if adorned by the creator's own hand.
Lordly merchants, each like the god of wealth,   2
sat behind abundant goods of every kind.
The beautiful squares and lovely lanes
were constantly sprinkled with perfumes.

३ मंगलमय मंदिर सब केरें ।
चित्रित जनु रतिनाथ चितेरें ॥
पुर नर नारि सुभग सुचि संता ।
धरमसील ग्यानी गुनवंता ॥

४ अति अनूप जहँ जनक निवासू ।
बिथकहिं बिबुध बिलोकि बिलासू ॥
होत चकित चित कोट बिलोकी ।
सकल भुवन सोभा जनु रोकी ॥

२१३ धवल धाम मनि पुरट पट सुघटित नाना भाँति ।
सिय निवास सुंदर सदन सोभा किमि कहि जाति ॥

१ सुभग द्वार सब कुलिस कपाटा ।
भूप भीर नट मागध भाटा ॥
बनी बिसाल बाजि गज साला ।
हय गय रथ संकुल सब काला ॥

२ सूर सचिव सेनप बहुतेरे ।
नृपगृह सरिस सदन सब केरे ॥
पुर बाहेर सर सरित समीपा ।
उतरे जहँ तहँ बिपुल महीपा ॥

३ देखि अनूप एक अँवराई ।
सब सुपास सब भाँति सुहाई ॥
कौसिक कहेउ मोर मनु माना ।
इहाँ रहिअ रघुबीर सुजाना ॥

Everyone's home was auspicious 3
and painted as if by Kama's own artistry.
The citizens were handsome, holy, and true,
virtuous, wise, and endowed with merit.
As for King Janak's incomparable abode— 4
even the gods were stunned by its luxury.
The sight of the citadel awed the mind
and seemed to seize the splendor of all the worlds.

A radiant house curtained with cloth of gold, 213
embroidered with gems—
it was the lovely abode of Sita,
so how can its glory be told?

At its grand gates and adamantine doors 1
thronged kings, actors, praise-singers, and bards.
Nearby stood vast stables, ever crowded
with horses, elephants, and chariots.
Innumerable warriors, ministers, and generals 2
all dwelt in homes like that of the king.
Outside the city, by its river and lakes
hosts of kings were everywhere encamped.
Seeing a splendid grove of mango trees, 3
pleasantly endowed with every comfort,
Sage Kaushik declared, "My heart is inclined
to stay here, wise Raghu hero."

४   भलेहिं नाथ कहि कृपानिकेता ।
उतरे तहँ मुनि बृंद समेता ॥
बिस्वामित्र महामुनि आए ।
समाचार मिथिलापति पाए ॥

२१४   संग सचिव सुचि भूरि भट भूसुर बर गुर ग्याति ।
चले मिलन मुनिनायकहि मुदित राउ एहि भाँति ॥

१   कीन्ह प्रनामु चरन धरि माथा ।
दीन्हि असीस मुदित मुनिनाथा ॥
बिप्रबृंद सब सादर बंदे ।
जानि भाग्य बड़ राउ अनंदे ॥

२   कुसल प्रस्न कहि बारहिं बारा ।
बिस्वामित्र नृपहि बैठारा ॥
तेहि अवसर आए दोउ भाई ।
गए रहे देखन फुलवाई ॥

३   स्याम गौर मृदु बयस किसोरा ।
लोचन सुखद बिस्व चित चोरा ॥
उठे सकल जब रघुपति आए ।
बिस्वामित्र निकट बैठाए ॥

४   भए सब सुखी देखि दोउ भ्राता ।
बारि बिलोचन पुलकित गाता ॥
मूरति मधुर मनोहर देखी ।
भयउ बिदेहु बिदेहु बिसेषी ॥

"Very good, master," said the merciful one, 4
and made camp there along with the sages.
"Great sage Vishvamitra has come!"—
this news soon reached Mithila's lord,*

and accompanied by counselors, champions, 214
learned Brahmans, guru, and kin,
that king went forth happily
to meet the king of sages.

He greeted him and prostrated at his feet 1
and the sage was pleased and gave his blessing.
The king then saluted the Brahman host,
joyfully realizing his great fortune.
Repeatedly asking after his well-being, 2
Vishvamitra bade the king be seated.
Just then the two brothers arrived,
after going to see the flower gardens.
Tender youths, dark and fair, 3
they delighted the eyes and stole all hearts.
The whole assembly rose when Ram approached
and Vishvamitra seated him close to himself.
Everyone felt joy on seeing the brothers— 4
their eyes grew moist, their limbs thrilled—
and beholding Ram's sweet and captivating form,
"bodiless" King Videha became truly so![27]

* King Janak.

२१५ प्रेम मगन मनु जानि नृपु करि बिबेकु धरि धीर ।
बोलेउ मुनि पद नाइ सिरु गदगद गिरा गभीर ॥

१ कहहु नाथ सुंदर दोउ बालक ।
मुनिकुल तिलक कि नृपकुल पालक ॥
ब्रह्म जो निगम नेति कहि गावा ।
उभय बेष धरि की सोइ आवा ॥

२ सहज बिरागरूप मनु मोरा ।
थकित होत जिमि चंद चकोरा ॥
ताते प्रभु पूछउँ सतिभाऊ ।
कहहु नाथ जनि करहु दुराऊ ॥

३ इन्हहि बिलोकत अति अनुरागा ।
बरबस ब्रह्मसुखहि मन त्यागा ॥
कह मुनि बिहसि कहेहु नृप नीका ।
बचन तुम्हार न होइ अलीका ॥

४ ए प्रिय सबहि जहाँ लगि प्रानी ।
मन मुसुकाहिं रामु सुनि बानी ॥
रघुकुल मनि दसरथ के जाए ।
मम हित लागि नरेस पठाए ॥

२१६ रामु लखनु दोउ बंधुबर रूप सील बल धाम ।
मख राखेउ सबु साखि जगु जिते असुर संग्राम ॥

Knowing his heart was intoxicated by love,   215
the king wisely controlled himself,
bowed at the sage's feet, and spoke
in a quavering yet deep voice.

"Master, do these two handsome youths   1
adorn a sage's line or defend a royal clan?
Or has *brahma,* whom the Veda hymns as 'not this'[28]
perhaps assumed dual guise and come here?
My mind, innately detached from worldly things,   2
is as stunned as a *cakor* bird on seeing the moon.
Hence I question you, master, most earnestly.
Tell me, lord, and do not conceal anything.
When I behold them, I feel an intense love   3
that tears my mind away from divine bliss!"
The sage replied with a smile, "You speak rightly,
lord of men, and your words are never false.
For these two are beloved of all living beings"—   4
(hearing this, Ram smiled to himself)—
"sons of Dasarath, jewel of the Raghu clan,
whom the king sent forth for my sake.

Ram and Lakshman, these noble brothers,   216
abodes of beauty, virtue, and strength,
guarded my rite, as the world bears witness,
by defeating demons in battle."

१ मुनि तव चरन देखि कह राऊ ।
कहि न सकउँ निज पुन्य प्रभाऊ ॥
सुंदर स्याम गौर दोउ भ्राता ।
आनँदहू के आनँद दाता ॥

२ इन्ह कै प्रीति परसपर पावनि ।
कहि न जाइ मन भाव सुहावनि ॥
सुनहु नाथ कह मुदित बिदेहू ।
ब्रह्म जीव इव सहज सनेहू ॥

३ पुनि पुनि प्रभुहि चितव नरनाहू ।
पुलक गात उर अधिक उछाहू ॥
मुनिहि प्रसंसि नाइ पद सीसू ।
चलेउ लवाइ नगर अवनीसू ॥

४ सुंदर सदनु सुखद सब काला ।
तहाँ बासु लै दीन्ह भुआला ॥
करि पूजा सब बिधि सेवकाई ।
गयउ राउ गृह बिदा कराई ॥

२१७ रिषय संग रघुबंस मनि करि भोजनु बिश्रामु ।
बैठे प्रभु भ्राता सहित दिवसु रहा भरि जामु ॥

१ लखन हृदयँ लालसा बिसेषी ।
जाइ जनकपुर आइअ देखी ॥
प्रभु भय बहुरि मुनिहि सकुचाहीं ।
प्रगट न कहहिं मनहिं मुसुकाहीं ॥

84

The king said, "Beholding your feet, sage,   1
I marvel at the fruit of my merit.
These two comely brothers, dark and fair,
would bestow bliss on bliss itself!
Their pure love for one another   2
brings inexpressible joy to my heart."
Then the delighted king added, "Lord,
it is like the innate love of God and soul."
Glancing repeatedly at Ram, the king felt   3
a bodily thrill, while zeal flooded his heart.
Praising the sage and bowing at his feet,
the lord of earth conducted him into the city,
to a splendid, ever pleasant abode   4
where the king invited him to reside.
Having honored and served him in every way,
the monarch took his leave and went home.

Lord Ram, jewel of the Raghus, took food   217
and rest with the seers,
and then sat with his brother
while one watch of day remained.[29]

Lakshman had a heartfelt desire   1
to go and see the sights of Janakpur,
but in awe of his brother and shy before the sage,
he did not reveal it and only smiled wistfully.

२ राम अनुज मन की गति जानी ।
भगत बछलता हियँ हुलसानी ॥
परम बिनीत सकुचि मुसुकाई ।
बोले गुर अनुसासन पाई ॥

३ नाथ लखनु पुरु देखन चहहीं ।
प्रभु सकोच डर प्रगट न कहहीं ॥
जौं राउर आयसु मैं पावौं ।
नगर देखाइ तुरत लै आवौं ॥

४ सुनि मुनीसु कह बचन सप्रीती ।
कस न राम तुम्ह राखहु नीती ॥
धरम सेतु पालक तुम्ह ताता ।
प्रेम बिबस सेवक सुखदाता ॥

२१८ जाइ देखि आवहु नगरु सुख निधान दोउ भाइ ।
करहु सुफल सब के नयन सुंदर बदन देखाइ ॥

१ मुनि पद कमल बंदि दोउ भ्राता ।
चले लोक लोचन सुख दाता ॥
बालक बृंद देखि अति सोभा ।
लगे संग लोचन मनु लोभा ॥

२ पीत बसन परिकर कटि भाथा ।
चारु चाप सर सोहत हाथा ॥
तन अनुहरत सुचंदन खोरी ।
स्यामल गौर मनोहर जोरी ॥

Knowing his brother's inner state, Ram   2
was filled with affection for his devotee.
Smiling shyly and with utmost politeness,
he obtained the guru's leave to speak:
"Master, Lakshman longs to see the city,   3
but in awe of you, sir, dares not express this.
If I may have your permission,
I will show him the town and soon return."
Hearing this, the sage said with affection: 4
"Ram, you can but uphold right conduct,
for you guard dharma's boundary wall,[30] son,
yet yield to love to satisfy your servants.

Go see the town and then return—   218
you two are a treasury of joy!
Reward everyone's eyes with the sight
of your handsome faces."

Saluting the sage's holy feet, the two brothers,   1
who delight the eyes of all people, went forth.
Beholding their beauty, a crowd of children
fell in with them, eyes and hearts captivated.
They were clad in yellow, quivers cinched at the waist,   2
with fine bows and arrows in hand
and bodies adorned with sandalwood paste,
dusky and fair, an enchanting pair!—

३ केहरि कंधर बाहु बिसाला ।
उर अति रुचिर नागमनि माला ॥
सुभग सोन सरसीरुह लोचन ।
बदन मयंक तापत्रय मोचन ॥

४ कानन्हि कनक फूल छबि देहीं ।
चितवत चितहि चोरि जनु लेहीं ॥
चितवनि चारु भृकुटि बर बाँकी ।
तिलक रेख सोभा जनु चाँकी ॥

२१९ रुचिर चौतनीं सुभग सिर मेचक कुंचित केस ।
नख सिख सुंदर बंधु दोउ सोभा सकल सुदेस ॥

१ देखन नगरु भूपसुत आए ।
समाचार पुरबासिन्ह पाए ॥
धाए धाम काम सब त्यागी ।
मनहुँ रंक निधि लूटन लागी ॥

२ निरखि सहज सुंदर दोउ भाई ।
होहिं सुखी लोचन फल पाई ॥
जुबतीं भवन झरोखन्हि लागीं ।
निरखहिं राम रूप अनुरागीं ॥

३ कहहिं परसपर बचन सप्रीती ।
सखि इन्ह कोटि काम छबि जीती ॥
सुर नर असुर नाग मुनि माहीं ।
सोभा असि कहुँ सुनिअति नाहीं ॥

lion-shouldered and long-armed,   3
chests hung with strands of giant pearls,
with radiant, red-lotus eyes, and faces
like the moon, which quenches the three fires.[31]
Gold ear pendants so enhanced their beauty   4
that a mere glimpse stole away the mind.
Their glances were charming, eyebrows arched,
and their forehead marks set the seal on splendor.[32]

With charming square caps on lovely heads   219
over blue-black, curly locks,
the two brothers were, from head to toe,
the epitome of all beauty.

"The princes have come to see the city!"   1
When this news reached the townspeople,
they rushed out, leaving homes and chores,
like paupers bent on looting a treasury.
Seeing the unaffected grace of the brothers   2
they were overjoyed, their eyes rewarded.
Girls pressed against latticed house windows,
gazing with infatuation at Ram's handsome form.
They spoke lovingly to one another,   3
"Friend, he has bested a billion Kamas.[33]
Not among gods, demons, divine serpents, or sages
has one even heard of such splendor.

४ बिष्नु चारि भुज बिधि मुख चारी ।
बिकट बेष मुख पंच पुरारी ॥
अपर देउ अस कोउ न आही ।
यह छबि सखी पटतरिअ जाही ॥

२२० बय किसोर सुषमा सदन स्याम गौर सुख धाम ।
अंग अंग पर वारिअहिं कोटि कोटि सत काम ॥

१ कहहु सखी अस को तनु धारी ।
जो न मोह यह रूप निहारी ॥
कोउ सप्रेम बोली मृदु बानी ।
जो मैं सुना सो सुनहु सयानी ॥

२ ए दोऊ दसरथ के ढोटा ।
बाल मरालन्हि के कल जोटा ॥
मुनि कौसिक मख के रखवारे ।
जिन्ह रन अजिर निसाचर मारे ॥

३ स्याम गात कल कंज बिलोचन ।
जो मारीच सुभुज मदु मोचन ॥
कौसल्या सुत सो सुख खानी ।
नामु रामु धनु सायक पानी ॥

४ गौर किसोर बेषु बर काछें ।
कर सर चाप राम के पाछें ॥
लछिमनु नामु राम लघु भ्राता ।
सुनु सखि तासु सुमित्रा माता ॥

Vishnu has four arms, Brahma four heads,   4
Shiva sports five faces and a fearful getup—
there is simply no other god, dear friend,
who could suggest a simile for this beauty.

Strapping youths, dark and fair, the epitome of good looks   220
and such embodiments of joy,
that a thousand billion love gods could offer their lives
for their every limb!

Tell me, my dear, is there anyone alive   1
who would not be smitten by their sight?"
Then one spoke up in a sweet voice,
  "Clever girls, listen to what I've heard:
These two are the sons of Dasarath,   2
a pretty pair of royal fledglings.[34]
They guarded the rites of Sage Kaushik,
slaying demons on the field of war.
The dark-limbed one with lotus eyes,   3
who relieved Marich and Subahu of pride,
the son of Kausalya and treasury of joy,
is named Ram, bearing bow and arrow.
That fair-skinned youth, smartly attired,   4
holding arrow and bow, just behind Ram,
is called Lakshman, Ram's young brother,
and his mother, friend, is Queen Sumitra.

२२१ बिप्रकाजु करि बंधु दोउ मग मुनिबधू उधारि ।
आए देखन चापमख सुनि हरषीं सब नारि ॥

१ देखि राम छबि कोउ एक कहई ।
जोगु जानकिहि यह बरु अहई ॥
जौं सखि इन्हहि देख नरनाहू ।
पन परिहरि हठि करइ बिबाहू ॥

२ कोउ कह ए भूपति पहिचाने ।
मुनि समेत सादर सनमाने ॥
सखि परंतु पनु राउ न तजई ।
बिधि बस हठि अबिबेकहि भजई ॥

३ कोउ कह जौं भल अहइ बिधाता ।
सब कहँ सुनिअ उचित फल दाता ॥
तौ जानकिहि मिलिहि बरु एहू ।
नाहिन आलि इहाँ संदेहू ॥

४ जौं बिधि बस अस बनै सँजोगू ।
तौ कृतकृत्य होइ सब लोगू ॥
सखि हमरें आरति अति तातें ।
कबहुँक ए आवहिं एहि नातें ॥

२२२ नाहिं त हम कहुँ सुनहु सखि इन्ह कर दरसनु दूरि ।
यह संघटु तब होइ जब पुन्य पुराकृत भूरि ॥

The two brothers, having served the Brahman 221
and saved the sage's wife,
have come to witness the bow rite." On hearing this,
the women were overjoyed.

Seeing Ram's grace, one of them said, 1
"This one is a groom befitting Janaki.
If, my dears, the lord of men should see him,
he'd cancel his vow and insist on a wedding!"[35]
Another said, "The king did meet him 2
and honored him along with the sage.
But, friend, he still won't give up his vow,
for he is fated to cling to bad judgment."
"If the creator be kind," declared another, 3
"and give, as we hear, rightful fruits to all,
then Janaki will get this lad as her mate,
there's no doubt of it, my dears.
If, by divine grace, such a union occurs, 4
everyone's wishes will be fulfilled.
Oh friend, I feel terribly anxious
that this match somehow be made,

for otherwise—mark my words, girls— 222
we are unlikely to see him again.
But this union will only occur if we ourselves
have abundant stores of past merit."

१ बोली अपर कहेहु सखि नीका ।
एहिं बिआह अति हित सबही का ॥
कोउ कह संकर चाप कठोरा ।
ए स्यामल मृदु गात किसोरा ॥

२ सबु असमंजस अहइ सयानी ।
यह सुनि अपर कहइ मृदु बानी ॥
सखि इन्ह कहँ कोउ कोउ अस कहहीं ।
बड़ प्रभाउ देखत लघु अहहीं ॥

३ परसि जासु पद पंकज धूरी ।
तरी अहल्या कृत अघ भूरी ॥
सो कि रहिहि बिनु सिव धनु तोरें ।
यह प्रतीति परिहरिअ न भोरें ॥

४ जेहिं बिरंचि रचि सीय सँवारी ।
तेहिं स्यामल बरु रचेउ बिचारी ॥
तासु बचन सुनि सब हरषानीं ।
ऐसेइ होउ कहहिं मृदु बानीं ॥

२२३ हियँ हरषहिं बरषहिं सुमन सुमुखि सुलोचनि बृंद ।
जाहिं जहाँ जहँ बंधु दोउ तहँ तहँ परमानंद ॥

१ पुर पूरब दिसि गे दोउ भाई ।
जहँ धनुमख हित भूमि बनाई ॥
अति बिस्तार चारु गच ढारी ।
बिमल बेदिका रुचिर सँवारी ॥

Another said, "Friend, you've said it well: 1
this marriage will be best for everyone."
But then one said, "Shiva's bow is unyielding,
and this dark lad but a tender stripling.
It's all so vexatious, my dears!"   2
Hearing this, another girl said softly,
"Friends, there are some who say
that though he looks slight, he is powerful,
and a touch of the dust of his tender feet   3
freed Ahalya, though she had greatly sinned.
How can he fail to shatter Shiva's bow?[36]
Let us hold fast to this conviction,
that the creator who crafted Sita's charms   4
deliberately designed this dark lad as her groom."
Her speech delighted all the women,
who sweetly chorused, "So be it!"

Their hearts rejoicing, bevies of pretty-eyed girls   223
showered blossoms,
and wherever the two brothers went
there reigned supreme delight.

They proceeded to the eastern part of the city,   1
where a stadium[37] was built for the bow rite.
In a vast, sloping ground, beautifully paved,
a flawless fire altar had been attractively set.

२ चहुँ दिसि कंचन मंच बिसाला ।
   रचे जहाँ बैठहिं महिपाला ॥
   तेहि पाछें समीप चहुँ पासा ।
   अपर मंच मंडली बिलासा ॥

३ कछुक ऊँचि सब भाँति सुहाई ।
   बैठहिं नगर लोग जहँ जाई ॥
   तिन्ह के निकट बिसाल सुहाए ।
   धवल धाम बहुबरन बनाए ॥

४ जहँ बैठें देखहिं सब नारी ।
   जथाजोगु निज कुल अनुहारी ॥
   पुर बालक कहि कहि मृदु बचना ।
   सादर प्रभुहि देखावहिं रचना ॥

२२४ सब सिसु एहि मिस प्रेमबस परसि मनोहर गात ।
     तन पुलकहिं अति हरषु हियँ देखि देखि दोउ भ्रात ॥

१ सिसु सब राम प्रेमबस जाने ।
   प्रीति समेत निकेत बखाने ॥
   निज निज रुचि सब लेहिं बोलाई ।
   सहित सनेह जाहिं दोउ भाई ॥

२ राम देखावहिं अनुजहि रचना ।
   कहि मृदु मधुर मनोहर बचना ॥
   लव निमेष महुँ भुवन निकाया ।
   रचइ जासु अनुसासन माया ॥

On four sides were great gilded platforms   2
designed to seat the attending kings.
Just behind these, in each direction,
other daises formed a splendid circle,
a little higher and very lovely,   3
to seat the townsmen who would come.
Near to these, vast and beautiful,
was a white mansion with colorful decor
to suitably seat all women spectators   4
according to their respective lineages.
Chattering sweetly, the city's children
politely showed the arrangements to the Lord.

On this pretext, all the love-struck children   224
tried to touch his lovely limbs.
Bodies thrilling with pleasure, they kept gazing
blissfully at both brothers.

Knowing the children were lost in love, Ram   1
affectionately praised all the buildings.
As each child called to them excitedly
the brothers would kindly go to him.
Ram showed it all to his younger brother,   2
speaking sweet and charming words.
He at whose command, in the blink
of an eye, Maya crafts countless worlds,

३ भगति हेतु सोइ दीनदयाला ।
चितवत चकित धनुष मखसाला ॥
कौतुक देखि चले गुरु पाहीं ।
जानि बिलंबु त्रास मन माहीं ॥

४ जासु त्रास डर कहुँ डर होई ।
भजन प्रभाउ देखावत सोई ॥
कहि बातें मृदु मधुर सुहाई ।
किए बिदा बालक बरिआई ॥

२२५ सभय सप्रेम बिनीत अति सकुच सहित दोउ भाइ ।
गुर पद पंकज नाइ सिर बैठे आयसु पाइ ॥

१ निसि प्रबेस मुनि आयसु दीन्हा ।
सबहीं संध्याबंदनु कीन्हा ॥
कहत कथा इतिहास पुरानी ।
रुचिर रजनि जुग जाम सिरानी ॥

२ मुनिबर सयन कीन्हि तब जाई ।
लगे चरन चापन दोउ भाई ॥
जिन्ह के चरन सरोरुह लागी ।
करत बिबिध जप जोग बिरागी ॥

३ तेइ दोउ बंधु प्रेम जनु जीते ।
गुर पद कमल पलोटत प्रीते ॥
बार बार मुनि अग्या दीन्ही ।
रघुबर जाइ सयन तब कीन्ही ॥

that friend of the lowly, for devotion's sake,   3
gazed in awe at the bow-sacrifice ground.
Having seen it all, they started back to the guru
timid at heart, knowing they were late.
He, in fear of whom fear itself is afraid,   4
thus displayed the power of devotion
and with sweet and gentle words
firmly bade the children farewell.

Then, with apprehension, love, humility,   225
and great timidity, the two brothers
bowed their heads at the teacher's holy feet
and sat down at his command.

As night fell, at the guru's order   1
they all performed the evening worship.
In the telling of ancient tales and lore
two watches of sweet night were spent.
The great sage then lay down to rest   2
as the brothers began massaging his feet.
They—for the sake of whose lotus-like feet
ascetics undertake all kinds of disciplines—
those two brothers, as if conquered by love,   3
fondly pressed the feet of their guru.
Only upon the sage's repeated order
did the best of Raghus go and lie down.

४   चापत चरन लखनु उर लाएँ ।
सभय सप्रेम परम सचु पाएँ ॥
पुनि पुनि प्रभु कह सोवहु ताता ।
पौढ़े धरि उर पद जलजाता ॥

२२६   उठे लखनु निसि बिगत सुनि अरुनसिखा धुनि कान ।
गुर तें पहिलेहिं जगतपति जागे रामु सुजान ॥

१   सकल सौच करि जाइ नहाए ।
नित्य निबाहि मुनिहि सिर नाए ॥
समय जानि गुर आयसु पाई ।
लेन प्रसून चले दोउ भाई ॥

२   भूप बागु बर देखेउ जाई ।
जहँ बसंत रितु रही लोभाई ॥
लागे बिटप मनोहर नाना ।
बरन बरन बर बेलि बिताना ॥

३   नव पल्लव फल सुमन सुहाए ।
निज संपति सुर रूख लजाए ॥
चातक कोकिल कीर चकोरा ।
कूजत बिहग नटत कल मोरा ॥

४   मध्य बाग सरु सोह सुहावा ।
मनि सोपान बिचित्र बनावा ॥
बिमल सलिलु सरसिज बहुरंगा ।
जलखग कूजत गुंजत भृंगा ॥

Lakshman pressed his feet, holding them to his heart   4
reverently and lovingly, feeling supreme joy.
Again and again the Lord said, "Go to sleep, dear brother,"
and so he lay, with those blessed feet on his breast.

When night had passed, Lakshman arose   226
at the crowing of the cock,
and well before his teacher, noble Ram,
master of the world, awakened too.

Purifying themselves,[38] they went to bathe,   1
finished the daily rites, and bowed to the sage.
Mindful of the hour, with their guru's leave
the two brothers left to gather flowers.[39]
They beheld the king's splendid garden,   2
where spring's enchantment forever reigned,
countless charming trees were planted,
and varicolored vines formed a lovely canopy.
Abounding in fresh buds, blossoms, and fruit,   3
those trees put heaven's wishing tree to shame.
Black and pied cuckoos, parrot and *cakor*
called sweetly there, and peacocks danced.
At the garden's center was a beautiful pool   4
with bejeweled steps artfully designed.
In its clear water grew multicolored lotuses.
Waterfowl cooed there and bees hummed.

२२७ बागु तड़ागु बिलोकि प्रभु हरषे बंधु समेत ।
परम रम्य आरामु यहु जो रामहि सुख देत ॥

१ चहुँ दिसि चितइ पूँछि मालीगन ।
लगे लेन दल फूल मुदित मन ॥
तेहि अवसर सीता तहँ आई ।
गिरिजा पूजन जननि पठाई ॥

२ संग सखीं सब सुभग सयानीं ।
गावहिं गीत मनोहर बानीं ॥
सर समीप गिरिजा गृह सोहा ।
बरनि न जाइ देखि मनु मोहा ॥

३ मज्जनु करि सर सखिन्ह समेता ।
गई मुदित मन गौरि निकेता ॥
पूजा कीन्हि अधिक अनुरागा ।
निज अनुरूप सुभग बरु मागा ॥

४ एक सखी सिय संगु बिहाई ।
गई रही देखन फुलवाई ॥
तेहिं दोउ बंधु बिलोके जाई ।
प्रेम बिबस सीता पहिं आई ॥

२२८ तासु दसा देखी सखिन्ह पुलक गात जलु नैन ।
कहु कारनु निज हरष कर पूछहिं सब मृदु बैन ॥

Beholding garden and pool, the Lord   227
and his brother were delighted.
Supremely pleasant was this park that so pleased Ram,
who pleases all.[40]

They looked around, and with the gardeners' consent   1
began happily gathering leaves and blossoms.
Just then, Sita came there,
sent by her mother[41] to worship goddess Girija,
with her friends, all lovely and clever,   2
singing songs in enchanting voices.
Near the pond, the goddess's radiant home
captivated the gaze with indescribable beauty.
After bathing in the pool with her friends,   3
Sita joyously entered Gauri's sanctuary.
Performing her worship with great fervor,
she asked for a handsome and suitable mate.
But one friend left Sita's company   4
and wandered off to see the garden.
She spied the two brothers there
and, overcome by love, came back to Sita.

Seeing her state, her body flushed   228
and eyes tear-filled, the girls
all sweetly inquired, "Tell us
the cause of your great delight!"

१ देखन बागु कुअँर दुइ आए ।
बय किसोर सब भाँति सुहाए ॥
स्याम गौर किमि कहौं बखानी ।
गिरा अनयन नयन बिनु बानी ॥

२ सुनि हरषीं सब सखीं सयानी ।
सिय हियँ अति उतकंठा जानी ॥
एक कहइ नृपसुत तेइ आली ।
सुने जे मुनि सँग आए काली ॥

३ जिन्ह निज रूप मोहनी डारी ।
कीन्हे स्वबस नगर नर नारी ॥
बरनत छबि जहँ तहँ सब लोगू ।
अवसि देखिअहिं देखन जोगू ॥

४ तासु बचन अति सियहि सोहाने ।
दरस लागि लोचन अकुलाने ॥
चली अग्र करि प्रिय सखि सोई ।
प्रीति पुरातन लखइ न कोई ॥

२२९ सुमिरि सीय नारद बचन उपजी प्रीति पुनीत ।
चकित बिलोकति सकल दिसि जनु सिसु मृगी
सभीत ॥

She said, "Two princes have come to see the park, 1
handsome youths, pleasing in every way,
one dark, one fair. But how can I describe them?
Speech lacks eyes and the eyes are speechless!"
Hearing her, those clever girls were delighted, 2
knowing the great longing in Sita's heart.
One said, "Dears, they must be the very princes
who came yesterday, so we hear, with the sage,
and with their beauty cast such a spell 3
that they brought all the townsfolk under their sway
and everywhere, everyone recounts their glory.
Surely we must see them, for they deserve to be seen!"
Her words were most welcome to Sita, 4
for her eyes were restless for that sight.
She went, led by that dear companion,
her immemorial love perceived by none.[42]

Recalling Narad's words,[43] Sita felt 229
a surge of the purest love
and looked anxiously in all directions
like a frightened little doe.

१ कंकन किंकिनि नूपुर धुनि सुनि ।
कहत लखन सन रामु हृदयँ गुनि ॥
मानहुँ मदन दुंदुभी दीन्ही ।
मनसा बिस्व बिजय कहँ कीन्ही ॥

२ अस कहि फिरि चितए तेहि ओरा ।
सिय मुख ससि भए नयन चकोरा ॥
भए बिलोचन चारु अचंचल ।
मनहुँ सकुचि निमि तजे दिगंचल ॥

३ देखि सीय सोभा सुखु पावा ।
हृदयँ सराहत बचनु न आवा ॥
जनु बिरंचि सब निज निपुनाई ।
बिरचि बिस्व कहँ प्रगटि देखाई ॥

४ सुंदरता कहुँ सुंदर करई ।
छबिगृहँ दीपसिखा जनु बरई ॥
सब उपमा कबि रहे जुठारी ।
केहिं पटतरौं बिदेहकुमारी ॥

२३० सिय सोभा हियँ बरनि प्रभु आपनि दसा बिचारि ।
बोले सुचि मन अनुज सन बचन समय अनुहारि ॥

१ तात जनकतनया यह सोई ।
धनुषजग्य जेहि कारन होई ॥
पूजन गौरि सखीं लै आई ।
करत प्रकासु फिरइ फुलवाई ॥

At the sound of bracelets, waistband, and anklets,   1
Ram mused to himself, then said to Lakshman,
"It seems the love god sounds his drums,
setting his mind on world domination."
Then he turned in that direction, his eyes   2
cakor birds for the moon of Sita's face.
His lovely eyes became as still
as if Nimi, embarrassed, had fled their lids.[44]
Seeing Sita's beauty gave him joy   3
and he silently praised her in his heart.
"It is as if the creator, using all his skills,
had crafted her to show off to the world.
She beautifies beauty itself,   4
like a flame illumining the abode of splendor.
But all similes are the stale leavings of poets,[45]
and to what may I liken Videha's daughter?"

Having described Sita's beauty in his heart,   230
the Lord, mindful of his own condition,
addressed his younger brother with a pure mind
in words suited to the occasion.

"Brother, this must be that daughter of Janak   1
for whose sake the bow rite is being held.
Brought by her friends to worship Gauri,
she now ambles, lighting up the garden.

२ जासु बिलोकि अलौकिक सोभा ।
सहज पुनीत मोर मनु छोभा ॥
सो सबु कारन जान बिधाता ।
फरकहिं सुभद अंग सुनु भ्राता ॥

३ रघुबंसिन्ह कर सहज सुभाऊ ।
मनु कुपंथ पगु धरइ न काऊ ॥
मोहि अतिसय प्रतीति मन केरी ।
जेहिं सपनेहुँ परनारि न हेरी ॥

४ जिन्ह कै लहहिं न रिपु रन पीठी ।
नहिं पावहिं परतिय मनु डीठी ॥
मंगन लहहिं न जिन्ह कै नाहीं ।
ते नरबर थोरे जग माहीं ॥

२३१ करत बतकही अनुज सन मन सिय रूप लोभान ।
मुख सरोज मकरंद छबि करइ मधुप इव पान ॥

१ चितवति चकित चहूँ दिसि सीता ।
कहँ गए नृप किसोर मनु चिंता ॥
जहँ बिलोक मृग सावक नैनी ।
जनु तहँ बरिस कमल सित श्रेनी ॥

२ लता ओट तब सखिन्ह लखाए ।
स्यामल गौर किसोर सुहाए ॥
देखि रूप लोचन ललचाने ।
हरषे जनु निज निधि पहिचाने ॥

Seeing her unearthly beauty,   2
my normally pure heart is perturbed.
God alone knows why, brother,
but my right side is throbbing.[46]
It is the firm nature of Raghu men   3
never to let their minds go astray.
Indeed, it is my heartfelt conviction
that those who never dream of gazing at another's wife,
who never show their backs to foes in battle,   4
or give another's woman a glance or thought,
and who never say no to a suppliant—
such ideal men are rare in this world."

He spoke casually to his younger brother,   231
but his heart, enticed by Sita's beauty,
drank in, like a honeybee,
the nectar of her lotus face.[47]

Sita was looking about, greatly perplexed,   1
wondering where the young princes had gone.
Wherever her large, fawn-like eyes glanced
there seemed to rain a chain of white lotuses.
Then her friends pointed out, in a bower of vines,   2
the handsome youths, dark and fair.
Seeing his beauty, her eyes were drawn there
and she rejoiced as one finding her own treasure.

३ थके नयन रघुपति छबि देखें ।
   पलकन्हिहूँ परिहरीं निमेषें ॥
   अधिक सनेहँ देह भै भोरी ।
   सरद ससिहि जनु चितव चकोरी ॥
४ लोचन मग रामहि उर आनी ।
   दीन्हे पलक कपाट सयानी ॥
   जब सिय सखिन्ह प्रेमबस जानी ।
   कहि न सकहिं कछु मन सकुचानी ॥

२३२ लताभवन तें प्रगट भे तेहि अवसर दोउ भाइ ।
     निकसे जनु जुग बिमल बिधु जलद पटल बिलगाइ ॥

१ सोभा सीवँ सुभग दोउ बीरा ।
   नील पीत जलजाभ सरीरा ॥
   मोरपंख सिर सोहत नीके ।
   गुच्छ बीच बिच कुसुम कली के ॥
२ भाल तिलक श्रमबिंदु सुहाए ।
   श्रवन सुभग भूषन छबि छाए ॥
   बिकट भृकुटि कच घूघरवारे ।
   नव सरोज लोचन रतनारे ॥
३ चारु चिबुक नासिका कपोला ।
   हास बिलास लेत मनु मोला ॥
   मुखछबि कहि न जाइ मोहि पाहीं ।
   जो बिलोकि बहु काम लजाहीं ॥

Her eyes were stunned by Ram's splendor   3
and their lids quit the task of blinking.
Overcome by love, she forgot herself
like a *cakor* hen gazing at the autumn moon.[48]
Bringing Ram into her heart by her eyes' path,   4
the wise girl shut the doors of their lids.[49]
When they realized that Sita was overcome by love,
her friends were embarrassed and could say nothing.

At that moment, the two brothers   232
came out of the bower
like two brilliant moons emerging
from a bank of clouds.

"Both heroes are the epitome of charm[50]   1
with bodies like blue and golden lotuses.
Peacock feathers shimmer on their heads
interspersed with bunches of flower buds.
Their brow-marks shine with beads of sweat   2
and their ears are beautifully adorned.
Their eyebrows are curved, their hair curly,
and their eyes tinged with the red of young lotus petals.[51]
Their chins, noses, and cheeks are lovely   3
and the play of their smiles steals the heart.
But I cannot describe the luster of their faces:
to see them puts hosts of Kamas to shame!

४ उर मनि माल कंबु कल गीवा ।
काम कलभ कर भुज बलसींवा ॥
सुमन समेत बाम कर दोना ।
साँवर कुअँर सखी सुठि लोना ॥

२३३ केहरि कटि पट पीत धर सुषमा सील निधान ।
देखि भानुकुलभूषनहि बिसरा सखिन्ह अपान ॥

१ धरि धीरजु एक आलि सयानी ।
सीता सन बोली गहि पानी ॥
बहुरि गौरि कर ध्यान करेहू ।
भूपकिसोर देखि किन लेहू ॥

२ सकुचि सीयँ तब नयन उघारे ।
सनमुख दोउ रघुसिंघ निहारे ॥
नख सिख देखि राम कै सोभा ।
सुमिरि पिता पनु मनु अति छोभा ॥

३ परबस सखिन्ह लखी जब सीता ।
भयउ गहरु सब कहहिं सभीता ॥
पुनि आउब एहि बेरिआँ काली ।
अस कहि मन बिहसी एक आली ॥

४ गूढ़ गिरा सुनि सिय सकुचानी ।
भयउ बिलंबु मातु भय मानी ॥
धरि बड़ि धीर रामु उर आने ।
फिरी अपनपउ पितुबस जाने ॥

Gem strands on their chests, conch-like necks,   4
arms strong and supple as young elephants' trunks.[52]
And the one with a leaf cup of blossoms in his left hand—
that dark youth, my dear—is totally ravishing![53]

His lion-like waist bound in yellow cloth,   233
he is a treasury of beauty and nobility."
Seeing the jewel of the solar lineage,
the girls forgot themselves completely.

Composing herself, one clever girl   1
addressed Sita, taking her hand.
"Meditate on Gauri later,
why not take a look at the king's sons?"
Then Sita shyly opened her eyes   2
and saw before her the two Raghu lions.
Beholding Ram's beauty from head to foot
she recalled her father's vow and grew anxious.
When her friends saw Sita so enthralled,[54]   3
they all said nervously, "It's getting late."
"And we'll come back, same time tomorrow,"
one said with a knowing smile.
At her allusive speech, Sita grew abashed,   4
for it was late and she was fearful of her mother.
She composed herself, took Ram into her heart,
and turned away, knowing she was her father's ward.

२३४ देखन मिस मृग बिहग तरु फिरइ बहोरि बहोरि ।
निरखि निरखि रघुबीर छबि बाढ़इ प्रीति न थोरि ॥

१ जानि कठिन सिवचाप बिसूरति ।
चली राखि उर स्यामल मूरति ॥
प्रभु जब जात जानकी जानी ।
सुख सनेह सोभा गुन खानी ॥

२ परम प्रेममय मृदु मसि कीन्ही ।
चारु चित्त भीतीं लिखि लीन्ही ॥
गई भवानी भवन बहोरी ।
बंदि चरन बोली कर जोरी ॥

३ जय जय गिरिबरराज किसोरी ।
जय महेस मुख चंद चकोरी ॥
जय गजबदन षडानन माता ।
जगत जननि दामिनि दुति गाता ॥

४ नहिं तव आदि मध्य अवसाना ।
अमित प्रभाउ बेदु नहिं जाना ॥
भव भव बिभव पराभव कारिनि ।
बिस्व बिमोहनि स्वबस बिहारिनि ॥

२३५ पतिदेवता सुतीय महुँ मातु प्रथम तव रेख ।
महिमा अमित न सकहिं कहि सहस सारदा सेष ॥

Yet on the pretext of looking at an animal, bird, 234
or tree, she turned time and again
to gaze repeatedly at the Raghu hero's beauty
and her love grew ever stronger.

Worried by the weight of Shiva's bow, 1
she went, holding Ram's dark form within.
When the Lord saw Janaki leaving,
a treasury of joy, affection, grace, and virtue,
he made, of supreme love, a fine ink 2
and inscribed her on the tablet of his mind.
Sita returned to Bhavani's abode,*
saluted her feet, and spoke, hands joined in prayer.
"Hail to you! Daughter of the monarch of mountains, 3
Hail! *Cakor* hen to the moon of Mahesh's face,
Hail! Mother of elephant-headed and six-faced gods
and mother of the world, with body bright as lightning!
You have no beginning, middle, or end 4
and even the Veda does not know your infinite sway.
Cause of cosmic origin, existence, and dissolution,
you enchant the world and play at your own whim,

and among good, husband-worshiping wives, 235
mother, you are reckoned first.
Your endless glory cannot be told
even by a thousand Sharadas and Sheshas!

---

* The temple of Parvati.

१ सेवत तोहि सुलभ फल चारी ।
बरदायनी पुरारि पिआरी ॥
देबि पूजि पद कमल तुम्हारे ।
सुर नर मुनि सब होहिं सुखारे ॥

२ मोर मनोरथु जानहु नीकें ।
बसहु सदा उर पुर सबही कें ॥
कीन्हेउँ प्रगट न कारन तेहीं ।
अस कहि चरन गहे बैदेहीं ॥

३ बिनय प्रेम बस भई भवानी ।
खसी माल मूरति मुसुकानी ॥
सादर सियँ प्रसादु सिर धरेऊ ।
बोली गौरि हरषु हियँ भरेऊ ॥

४ सुनु सिय सत्य असीस हमारी ।
पूजिहि मन कामना तुम्हारी ॥
नारद बचन सदा सुचि साचा ।
सो बरु मिलिहि जाहिं मनु राचा ॥

५ मनु जाहिं राचेउ मिलिहि सो बरु
सहज सुंदर साँवरो ।
करुना निधान सुजान सीलु
सनेहु जानत रावरो ॥
एहि भाँति गौरि असीस सुनि सिय
सहित हियँ हरषीं अली ।

116

Serving you, the four goals are easily secured,   1
boon-granting beloved of the triple cities' foe!
Adoring your lotus-like feet, goddess,
gods, men, and sages all find satisfaction.
You well know my heart's longing,   2
for you dwell eternally in the city of every soul,
and for this reason, I have not revealed it."
So saying, Vaidehi clasped the Mother's feet.
Bhavani was moved by her loving supplication.   3
A garland slipped from her image, and it smiled.
Sita reverently placed the gift on her head,
and then Gauri spoke, her heart filled with joy.
"Hear, Sita, my unfailing blessing.   4
Your heart's yearning will be fulfilled!
Narad's words are ever clear and true.
You will get the groom your heart adores.

He who is adored by your heart,   5
that handsome dark bridegroom will be yours.
Mercy's treasury, all-comprehending,
he knows your virtue and your love."
When they heard Gauri's blessing,
Sita and her friends were overjoyed,

तुलसी भवानिहि पूजि पुनि पुनि
मुदित मन मंदिर चली ॥

२३६ जानि गौरि अनुकूल सिय हिय हरषु न जाइ कहि ।
मंजुल मंगल मूल बाम अंग फरकन लगे ॥

१ हृदयँ सराहत सीय लोनाई ।
गुर समीप गवने दोउ भाई ॥
राम कहा सबु कौसिक पाहीं ।
सरल सुभाउ छुअत छल नाहीं ॥

२ सुमन पाइ मुनि पूजा कीन्ही ।
पुनि असीस दुहु भाइन्ह दीन्ही ॥
सुफल मनोरथ होहुँ तुम्हारे ।
रामु लखनु सुनि भए सुखारे ॥

३ करि भोजनु मुनिबर बिग्यानी ।
लगे कहन कछु कथा पुरानी ॥
बिगत दिवसु गुरु आयसु पाई ।
संध्या करन चले दोउ भाई ॥

४ प्राची दिसि ससि उयउ सुहावा ।
सिय मुख सरिस देखि सुखु पावा ॥
बहुरि बिचारु कीन्ह मन माहीं ।
सीय बदन सम हिमकर नाहीं ॥

Tulsi says, and after bowing to her time and again,
they turned homeward.

Knowing Gauri to be favorable,   236
Sita's heart felt unutterable happiness
and her lovely left side began to tremble,
betokening all auspiciousness.

Inwardly praising Sita's charms,   1
the brothers returned to their teacher.
Ram told Vishvamitra everything,
being innately pure and untouched by guile.
Taking the flowers, the sage did his worship   2
and then blessed the two brothers:
"May your hearts' desires bear fruit."
At this, Ram and Lakshman were overjoyed.
After having his meal, the learned sage   3
began expounding ancient tales.
When day was spent, with his leave
the brothers went to do the evening rites.
To the east rose the lovely moon,   4
which, to Ram's glad eyes, resembled Sita's face.
But then he thought to himself,
"No, that icy one[55] has no semblance to Sita.

२३७ जनमु सिंधु पुनि बंधु बिषु दिन मलीन सकलंक।
सिय मुख समता पाव किमि चंदु बापुरो रंक ॥

१ घटइ बढ़इ बिरहिनि दुखदाई।
ग्रसइ राहु निज संधिहिं पाई ॥
कोक सोकप्रद पंकज द्रोही।
अवगुन बहुत चंद्रमा तोही ॥

२ बैदेही मुख पटतर दीन्हे।
होइ दोषु बड़ अनुचित कीन्हे ॥
सिय मुख छबि बिधु ब्याज बखानी।
गुर पहिं चले निसा बड़ि जानी ॥

३ करि मुनि चरन सरोज प्रनामा।
आयसु पाइ कीन्ह बिश्रामा ॥
बिगत निसा रघुनायक जागे।
बंधु बिलोकि कहन अस लागे ॥

४ उयउ अरुन अवलोकहु ताता।
पंकज कोक लोक सुखदाता ॥
बोले लखनु जोरि जुग पानी।
प्रभु प्रभाउ सूचक मृदु बानी ॥

२३८ अरुनोदयँ सकुचे कुमुद उडगन जोति मलीन।
जिमि तुम्हार आगमन सुनि भए नृपति बलहीन ॥

Born of the salty sea, with poison for a brother,   237
all blemished, and dingy by day—
how can that poor wretch of a moon
be compared to Sita's countenance?

He waxes and wanes, brings woe to lovesick women,   1
and Rahu, when nearby, gobbles him up.[56]
Tormenter of cuckoos, foe of lotuses—
Moon, you have a legion of flaws!
To make a metaphor for Vaidehi's face   2
is most inappropriate and simply wrong."
Praising Sita's beauty with the moon as pretext,
he went to his guru, for night had come on.
He saluted the sage's holy feet   3
and with his leave, lay down to rest.
When night had passed, the Raghu lord awoke,
looked at his brother, and spoke thus,
"Just see the rosy dawn, brother,   4
that delights birds, lotus buds, and all beings."
Lakshman replied with reverent salute,
sweetly proclaiming his master's might,

"Just as, at sun's rise, night lilies are abashed   238
and the lamps of the stars grow dim,
so when they hear of your approach,
the lords of men will become powerless.

१ नृप सब नखत करहिं उजिआरी ।
टारि न सकहिं चाप तम भारी ॥
कमल कोक मधुकर खग नाना ।
हरषे सकल निसा अवसाना ॥

२ ऐसेहिं प्रभु सब भगत तुम्हारे ।
होइहहिं टूटें धनुष सुखारे ॥
उयउ भानु बिनु श्रम तम नासा ।
दुरे नखत जग तेजु प्रकासा ॥

३ रबि निज उदय ब्याज रघुराया ।
प्रभु प्रतापु सब नृपन्ह दिखाया ॥
तव भुज बल महिमा उदघाटी ।
प्रगटी धनु बिघटन परिपाटी ॥

४ बंधु बचन सुनि प्रभु मुसुकाने ।
होइ सुचि सहज पुनीत नहाने ॥
नित्यक्रिया करि गुरु पहिं आए ।
चरन सरोज सुभग सिर नाए ॥

५ सतानंदु तब जनक बोलाए ।
कौसिक मुनि पहिं तुरत पठाए ॥
जनक बिनय तिन्ह आइ सुनाई ।
हरषे बोलि लिए दोउ भाई ॥

२३९ सतानंद पद बंदि प्रभु बैठे गुर पहिं जाइ ।
चलहु तात मुनि कहेउ तब पठवा जनक बोलाइ ॥

Those kings, constellations of little light,   1
cannot dispel the bow's dense darkness.
But as hosts of lotuses, cuckoos, bees, and birds
all rejoice at night's passing away,
just so, Lord, will all your adherents   2
delight in the breaking of the bow.
At the sun's rise, darkness effortlessly ends,
stars are obscured and the world is lit up.
By the ruse of his rising, Raghu Lord,   3
the sun has shown the kings your splendor.
To proclaim the famed might of your arms
this bow-breaking has been contrived."
The Lord smiled at his brother's speech   4
and, though always pure, took a cleansing bath,
did obligatory rites, and went to the teacher,
bowing his lovely head at his feet.
Then King Janak summoned Shatanand*   5
and sent him at once to Sage Kaushik.
He came and delivered the king's request,
and the sage gladly called the two brothers.

Touching Shatanand's feet, the Lord went   239
and sat near his teacher.
Then the sage said, "Come along, son,
for King Janak has summoned us.

---

* Janak's family priest.

१ सीय स्वयंबरु देखिअ जाई ।
ईसु काहि धौं देइ बड़ाई ॥
लखन कहा जस भाजनु सोई ।
नाथ कृपा तव जापर होई ॥

२ हरषे मुनि सब सुनि बर बानी ।
दीन्हि असीस सबहिं सुखु मानी ॥
पुनि मुनिबृंद समेत कृपाला ।
देखन चले धनुषमख साला ॥

३ रंगभूमि आए दोउ भाई ।
असि सुधि सब पुरबासिन्ह पाई ॥
चले सकल गृह काज बिसारी ।
बाल जुबान जरठ नर नारी ॥

४ देखी जनक भीर भै भारी ।
सुचि सेवक सब लिए हँकारी ॥
तुरत सकल लोगन्ह पहिं जाहू ।
आसन उचित देहु सब काहू ॥

२४० कहि मृदु बचन बिनीत तिन्ह बैठारे नर नारि ।
उत्तम मध्यम नीच लघु निज निज थल अनुहारि ॥

१ राजकुअँर तेहि अवसर आए ।
मनहुँ मनोहरता तन छाए ॥
गुन सागर नागर बर बीरा ।
सुंदर स्यामल गौर सरीरा ॥

Let us go and see Sita's bridegroom choice 1
and whom God will endow with glory."
Lakshman said, "Fame's favored recipient,
lord, can only be he whom you favor."
This apt speech pleased all the sages 2
and they happily gave their blessings.
Then, along with the ascetics, the gracious one
went to see the place of the bow sacrifice.
"The two brothers are coming to the arena!" 3
When this news reached the townspeople,
they all went, forgetting household chores—
children and youths, the aged, men and women.
When Janak saw the multitude assembling 4
he sent for his trusted servants and said,
"Go at once to all the people
and offer each one a suitable seat."

With gentle words, they politely seated 240
all the men and women
in places befitting their station—
high, middle, low, and least.[57]

At that moment, the two princes arrived, 1
as if enchantment had suffused two forms.
Vastly noble and urbane, ideal champions,
with handsome dark and golden bodies,

२ राज समाज बिराजत रूरे ।
उडगन महुँ जनु जुग बिधु पूरे ॥
जिन्ह के रही भावना जैसी ।
प्रभु मूरति तिन्ह देखी तैसी ॥

३ देखहिं रूप महा रनधीरा ।
मनहुँ बीर रसु धरें सरीरा ॥
डरे कुटिल नृप प्रभुहि निहारी ।
मनहुँ भयानक मूरति भारी ॥

४ रहे असुर छल छोनिप बेषा ।
तिन्ह प्रभु प्रगट काल सम देखा ॥
पुरबासिन्ह देखे दोउ भाई ।
नर भूषन लोचन सुखदाई ॥

२४१ नारि बिलोकहिं हरषि हियँ निज निज रुचि अनुरूप ।
जनु सोहत सिंगार धरि मूरति परम अनूप ॥

१ बिदुषन्ह प्रभु बिराटमय दीसा ।
बहु मुख कर पग लोचन सीसा ॥
जनक जाति अवलोकहिं कैसें ।
सजन सगे प्रिय लागहिं जैसें ॥

२ सहित बिदेह बिलोकहिं रानी ।
सिसु सम प्रीति न जाति बखानी ॥
जोगिन्ह परम तत्त्वमय भासा ।
सांत सुद्ध सम सहज प्रकासा ॥

126

in that assembly of kings they shone   2
like two full moons amid a mass of stars.
Depending on their temperament, the viewers
perceived the Lord's form accordingly.
To great warriors, his body appeared   3
as if the martial spirit itself had incarnated.[58]
Wicked kings looked at him in fear,
as though at a most terrifying manifestation,
and to demons hiding in the guise of kings,   4
the Lord looked like death itself.
The townsmen saw the two brothers
as exemplary men, delighting the eyes.

The women gazed at him with glad hearts,   241
each according to her own liking,
as if love's tenderest mood had taken
a supremely incomparable form.

To the learned, the Lord appeared in cosmic form   1
with countless faces, hands, feet, heads, and eyes.
When those of Janak's clan beheld him,
he seemed noble and dear as a kinsman.
King Videha and his queens saw him   2
with indescribable love, as a darling child.
Yogis saw him imbued with ultimate qualities—
tranquility, purity, self-control, and inner light.

३ हरिभगतन्ह देखे दोउ भ्राता ।
इष्टदेव इव सब सुख दाता ॥
रामहि चितव भायँ जेहि सीया ।
सो सनेहु सुखु नहिं कथनीया ॥

४ उर अनुभवति न कहि सक सोऊ ।
कवन प्रकार कहै कबि कोऊ ॥
एहि बिधि रहा जाहि जस भाऊ ।
तेहिं तस देखेउ कोसलराऊ ॥

२४२ राजत राज समाज महुँ कोसलराज किसोर ।
सुंदर स्यामल गौर तन बिस्व बिलोचन चोर ॥

१ सहज मनोहर मूरति दोऊ ।
कोटि काम उपमा लघु सोऊ ॥
सरद चंद निंदक मुख नीके ।
नीरज नयन भावते जी के ॥

२ चितवनि चारु मार मनु हरनी ।
भावति हृदय जाति नहिं बरनी ॥
कल कपोल श्रुति कुंडल लोला ।
चिबुक अधर सुंदर मृदु बोला ॥

३ कुमुदबंधु कर निंदक हाँसा ।
भृकुटी बिकट मनोहर नासा ॥
भाल बिसाल तिलक झलकाहीं ।
कच बिलोकि अलि अवलि लजाहीं ॥

Hari's devotees perceived the pair of brothers   3
as their own personal deity, giver of all happiness.
But the way in which Sita looked at Ram—
that love and joy cannot be expressed.
Feeling it within, she too could not speak,   4
so how could any poet tell of it?
In this way, according to their particular natures
each one saw the Lord of Kosala.

The sons of Kosala's king were resplendent   242
amid that royal assembly,
their lovely forms, dark and fair,
stealing the eyes of all the world.

So innately charming were their forms   1
that a million Kamas make a paltry metaphor.
Their faces put the autumn moon to shame,
their lotus eyes delight the soul,
their glances bemuse the love god's mind,   2
and please the heart in indescribable ways.
With tender cheeks, shimmering earrings,
handsome chins and lips, sweet speech,
smiles that put moonbeams to shame,   3
arched eyebrows and lovely noses,
broad foreheads with gleaming marks,
black curls to make bee-swarms abashed,

४   पीत चौतनीं सिरन्हि सुहाईं ।
     कुसुम कलीं बिच बीच बनाईं ॥
     रेखें रुचिर कंबु कल गीवाँ ।
     जनु त्रिभुवन सुषमा की सीवाँ ॥

२४३   कुंजर मनि कंठा कलित उरन्हि तुलसिका माल ।
     बृषभ कंध केहरि ठवनि बल निधि बाहु बिसाल ॥

१   कटि तूनीर पीत पट बाँधें ।
     कर सर धनुष बाम बर काँधें ॥
     पीत जग्य उपबीत सुहाए ।
     नख सिख मंजु महाछबि छाए ॥

२   देखि लोग सब भए सुखारे ।
     एकटक लोचन चलत न तारे ॥
     हरषे जनकु देखि दोउ भाई ।
     मुनि पद कमल गहे तब जाई ॥

३   करि बिनती निज कथा सुनाई ।
     रंग अवनि सब मुनिहि देखाई ॥
     जहँ जहँ जाहिं कुअँर बर दोऊ ।
     तहँ तहँ चकित चितव सबु कोऊ ॥

४   निज निज रुख रामहि सबु देखा ।
     कोउ न जान कछु मरमु बिसेषा ॥
     भलि रचना मुनि नृप सन कहेऊ ।
     राजाँ मुदित महासुख लहेऊ ॥

yellow caps adorning their heads,   4
decorated with sprays of flower buds,
lovely necks lined like smooth conchs,
as if encompassing the beauty of the three worlds,

with necklaces of huge pearls   243
and tulsi-leaf garlands on their breasts,
bull-like shoulders, lion-like stance,
and great arms endowed with might,

with quivers and cinched yellow waistcloths,   1
arrows in hand, bows on left shoulders,
and lovely sacred threads of saffron hue,
they were suffused with beauty from head to toe.
Everyone was overjoyed to see them   2
and gazed with steady, unblinking eyes.
Delighted by the sight of the two brothers,
Janak went to bow at the sage's holy feet.
After humbly relating his own story,[59]   3
he showed him all the sacred ground.
Wherever the two fair princes went
everyone stood staring, wonderstruck.
They each thought to have caught Ram's eye,   4
yet no one grasped the hidden import.
"Fine arrangements," said sage to ruler,
and the king was pleased and felt elated.

२४४ सब मंचन्ह तें मंचु एक सुंदर बिसद बिसाल ।
मुनि समेत दोउ बंधु तहँ बैठारे महिपाल ॥

१ प्रभुहि देखि सब नृप हियँ हारे ।
जनु राकेस उदय भएँ तारे ॥
असि प्रतीति सब के मन माहीं ।
राम चाप तोरब सक नाहीं ॥
२ बिनु भंजेहुँ भव धनुषु बिसाला ।
मेलिहि सीय राम उर माला ॥
अस बिचारि गवनहु घर भाई ।
जसु प्रतापु बलु तेजु गवाँई ॥
३ बिहसे अपर भूप सुनि बानी ।
जे अबिबेक अंध अभिमानी ॥
तोरेहुँ धनुषु ब्याहु अवगाहा ।
बिनु तोरें को कुआँरि बिआहा ॥
४ एक बार कालउ किन होऊ ।
सिय हित समर जितब हम सोऊ ॥
यह सुनि अवर महिप मुसुकाने ।
धरमसील हरिभगत सयाने ॥

२४५ सीय बिआहबि राम गरब दूरि करि नृपन्ह के ।
जीति को सक संग्राम दसरथ के रन बाँकुरे ॥

132

Upon a dais grander, more spotless,   244
and more lovely than all others,
the lord of the realm seated the great sage
along with the two brothers.

Seeing the Lord, all the rulers felt as lost   1
as stars when the full moon rises.
They all felt the inner conviction,
"Ram will break the bow, no doubt!
But even if Shiva's weapon does not shatter,   2
Sita will lay the garland on Ram's breast.
Musing on this, let's go home, brothers,
for we waste our fame, glory, and might here."
But hearing this, other kings guffawed,   3
blinded by ignorance and egoism, and said,
"Even breaking the bow won't ensure marriage,
and without snapping it, who can wed the maid?
Even if Death himself should show up,   4
we will best him in battle for Sita's sake!"
Hearing this, other kings smiled,
those devoted to Hari, righteous and wise,

and said, "Ram will surely wed Sita,   245
dispelling the arrogance of the kings.
For who can conquer in combat
the valiant sons of King Dasarath?

१ ब्यर्थ मरहु जनि गाल बजाई ।
मन मोदकन्हि कि भूख बुताई ॥
सिख हमारि सुनि परम पुनीता ।
जगदंबा जानहु जियँ सीता ॥

२ जगत पिता रघुपतिहि बिचारी ।
भरि लोचन छबि लेहु निहारी ॥
सुंदर सुखद सकल गुन रासी ।
ए दोउ बंधु संभु उर बासी ॥

३ सुधा समुद्र समीप बिहाई ।
मृगजलु निरखि मरहु कत धाई ॥
करहु जाइ जा कहुँ जोइ भावा ।
हम तौ आजु जनम फलु पावा ॥

४ अस कहि भले भूप अनुरागे ।
रूप अनूप बिलोकन लागे ॥
देखहिं सुर नभ चढ़े बिमाना ।
बरषहिं सुमन करहिं कल गाना ॥

२४६ जानि सुअवसरु सीय तब पठई जनक बोलाइ ।
चतुर सखीं सुंदर सकल सादर चलीं लवाइ ॥

१ सिय सोभा नहिं जाइ बखानी ।
जगदंबिका रूप गुन खानी ॥
उपमा सकल मोहि लघु लागीं ।
प्राकृत नारि अंग अनुरागीं ॥

Do not die in vain, spewing bombast.   1
Do imagined sweets ever sate one's hunger?
Listen to our most holy instruction
and know in your soul: Sita is mother of the universe,
and its father, the Raghu lord. Consider this,   2
and fill your eyes with their beauty!
Beautiful, bliss-giving mines of merit,
these two brothers abide in Shiva's heart.
Why leave an ocean of nectar, near at hand,   3
to die chasing a glimpse of mirage?
Do whatever pleases you, but as for us,
today we have reaped this life's reward!"
With this, the good kings fell entranced   4
and began gazing at those matchless forms,
as the gods watched from celestial carriages,
showering blossoms and singing sweetly.

Then, knowing the moment to be right,   246
King Janak called for Sita,
and she came, reverently guided
by skillful and lovely companions.

Sita's splendor cannot be described,   1
for she is creation's mother, mine of beauty and merit.
All similes seem trifling to me,
attached to the limbs of worldly women.

२ सिय बरनिअ तेइ उपमा देई ।
कुकबि कहाइ अजसु को लेई ॥
जौं पटतरिअ तीय सम सीया ।
जग असि जुबति कहाँ कमनीया ॥

३ गिरा मुखर तन अरध भवानी ।
रति अति दुखित अतनु पति जानी ॥
बिष बारुनी बंधु प्रिय जेही ।
कहिअ रमासम किमि बैदेही ॥

४ जौं छबि सुधा पयोनिधि होई ।
परम रूपमय कच्छपु सोई ॥
सोभा रजु मंदरु सिंगारू ।
मथै पानि पंकज निज मारू ॥

२४७ एहि बिधि उपजै लच्छि जब सुंदरता सुख मूल ।
तदपि सकोच समेत कबि कहहिं सीय समतूल ॥

१ चलीं संग लै सखीं सयानी ।
गावत गीत मनोहर बानी ॥
सोह नवल तनु सुंदर सारी ।
जगत जननि अतुलित छबि भारी ॥

२ भूषन सकल सुदेस सुहाए ।
अंग अंग रचि सखिन्ह बनाए ॥
रंगभूमि जब सिय पगु धारी ।
देखि रूप मोहे नर नारी ॥

Who would dare offer them to describe Sita   2
and win infamy as a bad poet?
Were any woman to be compared to Sita,
where on earth would such a beauty be?
Sarasvati talks too much, Bhavani has but half a body,   3
Rati mopes over her disembodied spouse,
and, as for the dear sister of venom and liquor—
how can Lakshmi be likened to Videha's daughter?[60]
Were the milk-ocean the nectar of beauty,   4
the cosmic tortoise transcendently fair,
were loveliness the rope, eros Mount Mandara,
and were Kama himself to churn with lotus hands—

when, from all this, a Lakshmi arose,   247
root-source of beauty and delight,
even then, it would give a poet pause
to dare compare her to Sita.

She was brought in by astute friends   1
who were singing in charming voices.
Her young body adorned by an exquisite sari,
creation's mother was incomparably splendid.
Many pieces of jewelry, artfully arrayed,   2
had been placed on her limbs by her companions.
When Sita stepped onto the sacred ground,
the sight of her beauty transfixed all men and women.

३ हरषि सुरन्ह दुंदुभीं बजाईं ।
बरषि प्रसून अपछरा गाईं ॥
पानि सरोज सोह जयमाला ।
अवचट चितए सकल भुआला ॥
४ सीय चकित चित रामहि चाहा ।
भए मोहबस सब नरनाहा ॥
मुनि समीप देखे दोउ भाई ।
लगे ललकि लोचन निधि पाई ॥

२४८ गुरजन लाज समाजु बड़ देखि सीय सकुचानि ।
लागि बिलोकन सखिन्ह तन रघुबीरहि उर आनि ॥

१ राम रूपु अरु सिय छबि देखें ।
नर नारिन्ह परिहरीं निमेषें ॥
सोचहिं सकल कहत सकुचाहीं ।
बिधि सन बिनय करहिं मन माहीं ॥
२ हरु बिधि बेगि जनक जड़ताई ।
मति हमारि असि देहि सुहाई ॥
बिनु बिचार पनु तजि नरनाहू ।
सीय राम कर करै बिबाहू ॥
३ जगु भल कहिहि भाव सब काहू ।
हठ कीन्हें अंतहुँ उर दाहू ॥
एहिं लालसाँ मगन सब लोगू ।
बरु साँवरो जानकी जोगू ॥

138

Rejoicing, the gods sounded their great drums   3
and heavenly courtesans sang, raining down blossoms.
In her delicate hands shone the victory garland,
arresting the gaze of all the kings.
As Sita's questing glance sought Ram   4
all those lords of men fell spellbound.
Seeing the two brothers near the sage,
her longing eyes found their treasure.

But at the sight of the assembled elders   248
and the great crowd, Sita was embarrassed,
and looked at her friends,
having taken the Raghu hero into her heart.

To behold Ram's form and Sita's glory,   1
men and women gazed wide-eyed.
All had one thought that none dared utter
and inwardly petitioned the maker of fate.
"Oh God, quickly dispel Janak's dull-wittedness   2
and give him our own good sense.
Without a thought, let the king renounce his vow
and just marry Sita to Ram!
The world will approve, everyone will be pleased,   3
and obstinacy will bring only remorse in the end."
They were all lost in a single longing:
"The dark lad alone is the groom fit for Janaki!"

४ तब बंदीजन जनक बोलाए ।
बिरिदावली कहत चलि आए ॥
कह नृपु जाइ कहहु पन मोरा ।
चले भाट हियँ हरषु न थोरा ॥

२४९ बोले बंदी बचन बर सुनहु सकल महिपाल ।
पन बिदेह कर कहहिं हम भुजा उठाइ बिसाल ॥

१ नृप भुजबलु बिधु सिवधनु राहू ।
गरुअ कठोर बिदित सब काहू ॥
रावनु बानु महाभट भारे ।
देखि सरासन गवँहिं सिधारे ॥

२ सोइ पुरारि कोदंडु कठोरा ।
राज समाज आजु जोइ तोरा ॥
त्रिभुवन जय समेत बैदेही ।
बिनहिं बिचार बरइ हठि तेही ॥

३ सुनि पन सकल भूप अभिलाषे ।
भटमानी अतिसय मन माखे ॥
परिकर बाँधि उठे अकुलाई ।
चले इष्टदेवन्ह सिर नाई ॥

४ तमकि ताकि तकि सिवधनु धरहीं ।
उठइ न कोटि भाँति बलु करहीं ॥
जिन्ह के कछु बिचारु मन माहीं ।
चाप समीप महीप न जाहीं ॥

Then Janak summoned the royal bards   4
and they came, glorifying his lineage.
The king said, "Go and announce my vow,"
and the bards went forth with glad hearts.

With noble speech the singers declared,   249
"Listen, all you guardians of earth:
upraising our arms, we pronounce
the solemn vow of Lord Videha.

To the moon of royal might, Shiva's bow is Rahu,   1
its weight and stiffness known to all.
Even mighty warriors like Ravan[61] and Bana,
beholding this bow, went quietly away.
This awful weapon of the triple cities' foe—   2
whoever breaks it today in the royal assembly
wins universal victory, and Vaidehi too
will perforce wed him without a thought."
Hearing the oath, all the kings felt desire   3
and arrogant warriors were highly aroused.
Girding their waists, they got up excitedly,
saluted their personal gods, and came forward.
Glowering at the bow, they grasped it   4
yet could not lift it even with endless efforts.
Those earth-protectors who had a little sense
did not so much as approach the great bow.

२५० तमकि धरहिं धनु मूढ़ नृप उठइ न चलहिं लजाइ ।
मनहुँ पाइ भट बाहुबलु अधिकु अधिकु गरुआइ ॥

१ भूप सहस दस एकहि बारा ।
लगे उठावन टरइ न टारा ॥
डगइ न संभु सरासनु कैसें ।
कामी बचन सती मनु जैसें ॥

२ सब नृप भए जोगु उपहासी ।
जैसें बिनु बिराग संन्यासी ॥
कीरति बिजय बीरता भारी ।
चले चाप कर बरबस हारी ॥

३ श्रीहत भए हारि हियँ राजा ।
बैठे निज निज जाइ समाजा ॥
नृपन्ह बिलोकि जनकु अकुलाने ।
बोले बचन रोष जनु साने ॥

४ दीप दीप के भूपति नाना ।
आए सुनि हम जो पनु ठाना ॥
देव दनुज धरि मनुज सरीरा ।
बिपुल बीर आए रनधीरा ॥

२५१ कुअँरि मनोहर बिजय बड़ि कीरति अति कमनीय ।
पावनिहार बिरंचि जनु रचेउ न धनु दमनीय ॥

Foolish kings seized the bow in a rage,   250
but left in shame without lifting it,
for it seemed to drain the might
of heroes' arms and grow ever heavier.

Then ten thousand monarchs together   1
tried to lift it, but could not make it budge.
Shiva's bow was as immovable as the mind
of a faithful wife propositioned by a lecher.
All those kings became fit objects of derision,   2
like renunciates without detachment.
Their fame, victory, and proud virility
vanished, overthrown by the bow.
Lusterless and inwardly beaten, the kings   3
retreated to sit among their retainers.
Looking in dismay at those rulers of men,
King Janak spoke as though in anger.[62]
"Countless kings from every continent   4
have come, hearing of my firm resolve.
Gods and demon lords, taking human guise,
and war-hardened heroes—all have come.

An alluring maid, vast victory,   251
and most desirable fame—
yet it seems the creator has not crafted anyone
fit to win these by breaking the bow.

१ कहहु काहि यहु लाभु न भावा ।
काहुँ न संकर चाप चढ़ावा ॥
रहउ चढ़ाउब तोरब भाई ।
तिलु भरि भूमि न सके छड़ाई ॥

२ अब जनि कोउ माखै भट मानी ।
बीर बिहीन मही मैं जानी ॥
तजहु आस निज निज गृह जाहू ।
लिखा न बिधि बैदेहि बिबाहू ॥

३ सुकृतु जाइ जौं पनु परिहरऊँ ।
कुअँरि कुआरि रहउ का करऊँ ॥
जौं जनतेउँ बिनु भट भुबि भाई ।
तौ पनु करि होतेउँ न हँसाई ॥

४ जनक बचन सुनि सब नर नारी ।
देखि जानकिहि भए दुखारी ॥
माखे लखनु कुटिल भईँ भौंहें ।
रदपट फरकत नयन रिसौंहें ॥

२५२ कहि न सकत रघुबीर डर लगे बचन जनु बान ।
नाइ राम पद कमल सिरु बोले गिरा प्रमान ॥

१ रघुबंसिन्ह महुँ जहँ कोउ होई ।
तेहिं समाज अस कहइ न कोई ॥
कही जनक जसि अनुचित बानी ।
बिद्यमान रघुकुलमनि जानी ॥

144

Tell me, who would not covet these prizes?   1
Yet none has lifted Shankar's weapon.
Never mind hefting and breaking it, brothers,
no one could move it even a micron![63]
Now, let no self-styled hero be annoyed   2
that I find earth to be bereft of brave men.
Abandon your hopes and go to your homes,
for fate has not written marriage for Vaidehi!
My merit will depart if I give up my vow.   3
Let the girl stay a virgin. What can I do?
Brothers, had I known the world to lack warriors,
I would not have risked mockery with my oath."
Hearing Janak's speech, all men and women   4
looked at Janaki and felt deep sorrow.
But Lakshman seethed, his brows arched,
lips trembled, and his eyes reddened with rage.

He could not speak for fear of the Raghu hero,   252
yet the king's words stung like arrows.
Then, bowing his head at Ram's lovely feet,
he declared with grave authority:

"When one from the Raghu clan is present   1
in an assembly, no one talks like this.
Yet Janak has uttered these improper words
knowing the jewel of Raghus to be here.

२ सुनहु भानुकुल पंकज भानू ।
कहउँ सुभाउ न कछु अभिमानू ॥
जौं तुम्हारि अनुसासन पावौं ।
कंदुक इव ब्रह्मांड उठावौं ॥

३ काचे घट जिमि डारौं फोरी ।
सकउँ मेरु मूलक जिमि तोरी ॥
तव प्रताप महिमा भगवाना ।
को बापुरो पिनाक पुराना ॥

४ नाथ जानि अस आयसु होऊ ।
कौतुकु करौं बिलोकिअ सोऊ ॥
कमल नाल जिमि चाप चढ़ावौं ।
जोजन सत प्रमान लै धावौं ॥

२५३ तोरौं छत्रक दंड जिमि तव प्रताप बल नाथ ।
जौं न करौं प्रभु पद सपथ कर न धरौं धनु भाथ ॥

१ लखन सकोप बचन जे बोले ।
डगमगानि महि दिग्गज डोले ॥
सकल लोग सब भूप डेराने ।
सिय हियँ हरषु जनकु सकुचाने ॥

२ गुर रघुपति सब मुनि मन माहीं ।
मुदित भए पुनि पुनि पुलकाहीं ॥
सयनहिं रघुपति लखनु नेवारे ।
प्रेम समेत निकट बैठारे ॥

Sun to the lotuses of the solar line—   2
I speak my heart, without self-pride.
Were I to gain your leave,
I would lift the world like a toy ball
and break it like a raw clay pot.   3
I can snap Mount Meru like a radish root,
divine one, thanks to your power and glory.
What, then, of this wretched old bow?
Lord, if I knew it were your command,   4
just see what I would do in sport:
I would lift the bow like a lotus stalk
and run with it for a hundred leagues.

I would break it, master, like a mushroom's stem,   253
by your glorious might.
If I do not do this, I swear by your feet
to never touch bow and quiver again."

When Lakshman spoke these words in anger,   1
the earth shook, the cosmic elephants trembled,
and the kings and people were all terrified,
Sita was glad at heart, and Janak abashed.
The guru, Ram, and the sages inwardly rejoiced,   2
their limbs shivering with pleasure.
The Raghu lord checked Lakshman with a sign,
and lovingly bade him sit near himself.

३ बिस्वामित्र समय सुभ जानी ।
बोले अति सनेहमय बानी ॥
उठहु राम भंजहु भवचापा ।
मेटहु तात जनक परितापा ॥

४ सुनि गुरु बचन चरन सिरु नावा ।
हरषु बिषादु न कछु उर आवा ॥
ठाढ़े भए उठि सहज सुभाएँ ।
ठवनि जुबा मृगराजु लजाएँ ॥

२५४ उदित उदय गिरि मंच पर रघुबर बालपतंग ।
बिकसे संत सरोज सब हरषे लोचन भृंग ॥

१ नृपन्ह केरि आसा निसि नासी ।
बचन नखत अवली न प्रकासी ॥
मानी महिप कुमुद सकुचाने ।
कपटी भूप उलूक लुकाने ॥

२ भए बिसोक कोक मुनि देवा ।
बरिसहिं सुमन जनावहिं सेवा ॥
गुर पद बंदि सहित अनुरागा ।
राम मुनिन्ह सन आयसु मागा ॥

३ सहजहिं चले सकल जग स्वामी ।
मत्त मंजु बर कुंजर गामी ॥
चलत राम सब पुर नर नारी ।
पुलक पूरि तन भए सुखारी ॥

Vishvamitra, knowing the time to be propitious,   3
spoke in words suffused with affection.
"Rise up, Ram. Shatter Shiva's bow,
son, and relieve King Janak's distress."
Hearing his guru's order, Ram saluted his feet,   4
neither elation nor anxiety in his heart.
He stood up with inborn dignity
and a bearing to shame a young lion.

At the rising, over the sunrise-summit of that dais,   254
of the young sun of the Raghus,
the lotuses of holy ones bloomed and their eyes
became happy honeybees.

The night of the kings' hopes was ended   1
and the stars of their boasting went out.
Arrogant monarchs wilted like night lilies
and devious ones disappeared, owl-like.
The songbirds of sages and gods grew carefree.   2
Raining blossoms, they stood ready to worship.
Saluting his guru's feet with adoration,
Ram sought the permission of the sages.
And then, the Lord of all worlds strode easily   3
with the gait of a majestic elephant bull.
As Ram walked, all the people of the city
became joyful, trembling in every limb.

४   बंदि पितर सुर सुकृत सँभारे ।
     जौं कछु पुन्य प्रभाउ हमारे ॥
     तौ सिवधनु मृनाल की नाईं ।
     तोरहुँ रामु गनेस गोसाईं ॥

२५५ रामहि प्रेम समेत लखि सखिन्ह समीप बोलाइ ।
     सीता मातु सनेह बस बचन कहइ बिलखाइ ॥

१   सखि सब कौतुकु देखनिहारे ।
     जेउ कहावत हितू हमारे ॥
     कोउ न बुझाइ कहइ गुर पाहीं ।
     ए बालक असि हठ भलि नाहीं ॥

२   रावन बान छुआ नहिं चापा ।
     हारे सकल भूप करि दापा ॥
     सो धनु राजकुअँर कर देहीं ।
     बाल मराल कि मंदर लेहीं ॥

३   भूप सयानप सकल सिरानी ।
     सखि बिधि गति कछु जाति न जानी ॥
     बोली चतुर सखी मृदु बानी ।
     तेजवंत लघु गनिअ न रानी ॥

४   कहँ कुंभज कहँ सिंधु अपारा ।
     सोषेउ सुजसु सकल संसारा ॥
     रबि मंडल देखत लघु लागा ।
     उदयँ तासु तिभुवन तम भागा ॥

They petitioned ancestors and gods, recalling good deeds,   4
"If our merit has any effect at all,
then let Shiva's bow, like a lotus stem,
be broken by Ram, Lord Ganesh!"

Looking at Ram with maternal love   255
and summoning her women friends,
Sita's mother, overwhelmed by affection,
uttered words of lamentation.

"Friends, all the onlookers at this travesty   1
call themselves our well-wishers,
so why does someone not explain to the sage
that such resolve is no good for this child?
That which Ravan and Bana would not touch,   2
which trounced all of the prideful kings—
that bow is to go in the hand of this princeling?
Can a gosling lift up Mount Mandara?
All the king's wit has been spent, my dears,   3
and fate's ways elude understanding!"
But one wise companion sweetly replied,
"Do not reckon the mighty as meek, my queen.
How to compare the pot-born sage to the vast ocean?   4
Yet he drained it, as is famed throughout creation.[64]
The sun's circle looks small, and yet
at his rising, darkness flees the three worlds.

२५६ मंत्र परम लघु जासु बस बिधि हरि हर सुर सर्ब ।
महामत्त गजराज कहुँ बस कर अंकुस खर्ब ॥

१ काम कुसुम धनु सायक लीन्हे ।
सकल भुवन अपने बस कीन्हे ॥
देबि तजिअ संसउ अस जानी ।
भंजब धनुषु राम सुनु रानी ॥

२ सखी बचन सुनि भै परतीती ।
मिटा बिषादु बढ़ी अति प्रीती ॥
तब रामहि बिलोकि बैदेही ।
सभय हृदयँ बिनवति जेहि तेही ॥

३ मनहीं मन मनाव अकुलानी ।
होहु प्रसन्न महेस भवानी ॥
करहु सफल आपनि सेवकाई ।
करि हितु हरहु चाप गरुआई ॥

४ गननायक बर दायक देवा ।
आजु लगें कीन्हिउँ तुअ सेवा ॥
बार बार बिनती सुनि मोरी ।
करहु चाप गुरुता अति थोरी ॥

२५७ देखि देखि रघुबीर तन सुर मनाव धरि धीर ।
भरे बिलोचन प्रेम जल पुलकावली सरीर ॥

A mantra is most minute, but it sways 256
Brahma, Hari, Hara, and all gods,
and a rampaging bull elephant may be subdued
by a tiny little goad.

Kama merely lifts his flower-bow and arrows 1
and takes control of the whole cosmos.
Knowing this, revered one, discard doubt.
Ram will break the bow, dear queen!"
At her companion's words, she took heart. 2
Her sorrow effaced, her love grew even greater.
Then Vaidehi looked at Ram
and nervously petitioned any god who came to mind.
Distressed, she inwardly pleaded with them, 3
"Be pleased with me, Shiva and Bhavani!
Let my worshipful service bear fruit,
and kindly reduce the weight of the bow.
Lord of legions, boon-giving Ganesh, 4
until this day I have always served you.
Now hear my repeated plea
and lessen the heaviness of that bow!"

Glancing again and again at Ram, she invoked the gods 257
and took courage,
her eyes filling with tears of love
and her body flushed with emotion.

१   नीकें निरखि नयन भरि सोभा ।
  पितु पनु सुमिरि बहुरि मनु छोभा ॥
  अहह तात दारुनि हठ ठानी ।
  समुझत नहिं कछु लाभु न हानी ॥

२   सचिव सभय सिख देइ न कोई ।
  बुध समाज बड़ अनुचित होई ॥
  कहँ धनु कुलिसहु चाहि कठोरा ।
  कहँ स्यामल मृदुगात किसोरा ॥

३   बिधि केहि भाँति धरौं उर धीरा ।
  सिरस सुमन कन बेधिअ हीरा ॥
  सकल सभा कै मति भै भोरी ।
  अब मोहि संभुचाप गति तोरी ॥

४   निज जड़ता लोगन्ह पर डारी ।
  होहि हरुअ रघुपतिहि निहारी ॥
  अति परिताप सीय मन माहीं ।
  लव निमेष जुग सय सम जाहीं ॥

२५८   प्रभुहि चितइ पुनि चितव महि राजत लोचन लोल ।
  खेलत मनसिज मीन जुग जनु बिधु मंडल डोल ॥

१   गिरा अलिनि मुख पंकज रोकी ।
  प्रगट न लाज निसा अवलोकी ॥
  लोचन जलु रह लोचन कोना ।
  जैसें परम कृपन कर सोना ॥

Sating her eyes on his beauty, she again 1
recalled her father's pledge, and grew anxious.
"Alas! Father is bent on a most awful vow
with no consideration of gain or loss.
His timid ministers give no guidance, 2
which ill suits an assembly of the learned.
Before that bow, stronger than adamant,
what is the tender frame of this dark youth?
Oh maker of fate, how am I to take heart? 3
Can a flower's tendril pierce a diamond?[65]
This whole assembly has lost its wits.
Now you, bow of Shambhu, are my only hope!
Cast your denseness over the crowd 4
and grow light, looking to the Raghu lord!"
So greatly did Sita suffer at heart
that each second seemed a hundred aeons.

Glancing at the Lord and then at the ground, 258
her shining eyes darted about
like a playful pair of Love's fish
swimming in a pail of moonbeams.[66]

Her voice, like a bee caught in the lotus of her face, 1
could not emerge, seeing the night of her modesty.[67]
Her tears stayed in the corners of her eyes,
hidden like an arch miser's gold.

२ सकुची ब्याकुलता बड़ि जानी ।
धरि धीरजु प्रतीति उर आनी ॥
तन मन बचन मोर पनु साचा ।
रघुपति पद सरोज चितु राचा ॥

३ तौ भगवानु सकल उर बासी ।
करिहि मोहि रघुबर कै दासी ॥
जेहि कें जेहि पर सत्य सनेहू ।
सो तेहि मिलइ न कछु संदेहू ॥

४ प्रभु तन चितइ प्रेम तन ठाना ।
कृपानिधान राम सबु जाना ॥
सियहि बिलोकि तकेउ धनु कैसें ।
चितव गरुरु लघु ब्यालहि जैसें ॥

२५९ लखन लखेउ रघुबंसमनि ताकेउ हर कोदंडु ।
पुलकि गात बोले बचन चरन चापि ब्रह्मांडु ॥

१ दिसिकुंजरहु कमठ अहि कोला ।
धरहु धरनि धरि धीर न डोला ॥
रामु चहहिं संकर धनु तोरा ।
होहु सजग सुनि आयसु मोरा ॥

२ चाप समीप रामु जब आए ।
नर नारिन्ह सुर सुकृत मनाए ॥
सब कर संसउ अरु अग्यानू ।
मंद महीपन्ह कर अभिमानू ॥

Knowing her great distress, she checked herself   2
and bravely took faith in her heart:
"If in deed, thought, and word, my aim is true,
my mind set on the feet of the Raghu Lord,
then God, residing in the hearts of all,   3
will make me the handmaid of Ram.
Anyone who loves someone truly
will find that one, without any doubt."
Looking at the Lord, she reaffirmed her love,   4
and Ram, abode of mercy, understood all.
Glancing at Sita, he surveyed the bow
as Garuda might glare at a tiny snake.[68]

When Lakshman saw the jewel of the Raghus   259
intent on Hara's bow,
he shivered with joy, and spoke, planting his feet
firmly on the cosmic sphere.

"World-elephants, tortoise, snake, and boar:[69]   1
brace yourselves. Do not let earth shake.
Ram wants to shatter Shankar's bow,
so be alert, heeding my command."
When Ram approached the bow, men and women   2
invoked the gods and their own good deeds.
The doubt and ignorance of them all,
the vanity of the oafish kings,

३ भृगुपति केरि गरब गरुआई ।
सुर मुनिबरन्ह केरि कदराई ॥
सिय कर सोचु जनक पछितावा ।
रानिन्ह कर दारुन दुख दावा ॥

४ संभुचाप बड़ बोहितु पाई ।
चढ़े जाइ सब संगु बनाई ॥
राम बाहुबल सिंधु अपारू ।
चहत पारु नहिं कोउ कड़हारू ॥

२६० राम बिलोके लोग सब चित्र लिखे से देखि ।
चितई सीय कृपायतन जानी बिकल बिसेषि ॥

१ देखी बिपुल बिकल बैदेही ।
निमिष बिहात कलप सम तेही ॥
तृषित बारि बिनु जो तनु त्यागा ।
मुएँ करइ का सुधा तड़ागा ॥

२ का बरषा सब कृषी सुखानें ।
समय चुकें पुनि का पछितानें ॥
अस जियँ जानि जानकी देखी ।
प्रभु पुलके लखि प्रीति बिसेषी ॥

३ गुरहि प्रनामु मनहिं मन कीन्हा ।
अति लाघवँ उठाइ धनु लीन्हा ॥
दमकेउ दामिनि जिमि जब लयऊ ।
पुनि नभ धनु मंडल सम भयऊ ॥

the pressure of Parashuram's pride,[70]   3
the fearfulness of gods and godly sages,
Sita's anxiety and Janak's regret,
the burning torment of the royal women—
reaching the great ship of Shiva's bow,   4
they all crowded aboard, wishing to cross
the boundless sea of Ram's strength,
though they had no oarsman.

Glancing at the people, Ram saw them all   260
frozen as in a painting.
Then the merciful Lord looked at Sita
and knew her inner suffering.

He saw Vaidehi's vast anguish, and how   1
each instant weighed on her like an aeon.
If one perishes thirsting for water,
what profit to the corpse even in a nectar pool?
What use is rain to a drought-parched crop?   2
What good regret for a lost opportunity?
Thus reflecting, the Lord looked at Janaki
and thrilled to perceive her profound love.
He inwardly saluted his guru   3
and swiftly snatched up the bow.
It flashed like lightning when he took it,
then shone like an arc in the sky.

४   लेत चढ़ावत खैंचत गाढ़ें ।
काहुँ न लखा देख सबु ठाढ़ें ॥
तेहि छन राम मध्य धनु तोरा ।
भरे भुवन धुनि घोर कठोरा ॥

५   भरे भुवन घोर कठोर रव रबि
बाजि तजि मारगु चले ।
चिक्करहिं दिग्गज डोल महि अहि
कोल कूरुम कलमले ॥
सुर असुर मुनि कर कान दीन्हें
सकल बिकल बिचारहीं ।
कोदंड खंडेउ राम तुलसी
जयति बचन उचारहीं ॥

२६१   संकर चापु जहाजु सागरु रघुबर बाहुबलु ।
बूड़ सो सकल समाजु चढ़ा जो प्रथमहिं मोह बस ॥

१   प्रभु दोउ चापखंड महि डारे ।
देखि लोग सब भए सुखारे ॥
कौसिकरूप पयोनिधि पावन ।
प्रेम बारि अवगाहु सुहावन ॥

२   रामरूप राकेसु निहारी ।
बढ़त बीचि पुलकावलि भारी ॥

How he grasped, lifted, and mightily bent it,　　　　4
no one marked—they but saw him stand there.
At that instant, Ram broke the bow in two
with an awful sound that filled the cosmos.

The world was filled with an awful sound　　　　5
that sent the sun's stallions off course.
World-elephants trumpeted, the earth shook,
and its serpent, boar, and tortoise writhed.
Gods, demons, and sages covered their ears
and pondered anxiously.
Realizing Ram had broken the bow, Tulsi says,
they broke into cheers of victory.

Shankar's bow was a ship, the ocean,　　　　261
the might of the Raghu lord's arms,
and that whole host, who had come aboard
in ignorance, was drowned.

The Lord flung the bow halves to the ground　　　　1
as all the onlookers rejoiced.
The holy sea of sage Kaushik,
filled with love's deep, clear water,
seeing the full moon of Ram's form,　　　　2
swelled with waves of tingling joy.

बाजे नभ गहगहे निसाना ।
देवबधू नाचहिं करि गाना ॥

३ ब्रह्मादिक सुर सिद्ध मुनीसा ।
प्रभुहि प्रसंसहिं देहिं असीसा ॥
बरिसहिं सुमन रंग बहु माला ।
गावहिं किंनर गीत रसाला ॥

४ रही भुवन भरि जय जय बानी ।
धनुष भंग धुनि जात न जानी ॥
मुदित कहहिं जहँ तहँ नर नारी ।
भंजेउ राम संभुधनु भारी ॥

२६२ बंदी मागध सूतगन बिरुद बदहिं मतिधीर ।
करहिं निछावरि लोग सब हय गय धन मनि चीर ॥

१ झाँझि मृदंग संख सहनाई ।
भेरि ढोल दुंदुभी सुहाई ॥
बाजहिं बहु बाजने सुहाए ।
जहँ तहँ जुबतिन्ह मंगल गाए ॥

२ सखिन्ह सहित हरषी अति रानी ।
सूखत धान परा जनु पानी ॥
जनक लहेउ सुखु सोचु बिहाई ।
पैरत थकें थाह जनु पाई ॥

३ श्रीहत भए भूप धनु टूटे ।
जैसें दिवस दीप छबि छूटे ॥

The kettledrums of heaven boomed
and divine women danced and sang.
Brahma and the gods, perfect ones, and sages   3
praised the Lord and proffered blessings,
showering colorful flowers and garlands,
while celestial musicians sang melodiously.
Cries of "Victory!" echoed through the cosmos,   4
over the fading echo of the bow's cracking.
Everywhere, men and women happily declared,
"Ram has broken the great bow of Shiva!"

Bards, genealogists, and poets   262
solemnly intoned victory songs,
and everyone gave grateful offerings
of horses, elephants, wealth, jewels, and fine clothes.

Cymbals, drums, conchs, and oboes,[71]   1
majestic bass drums of all sorts—
a multitude of instruments played sonorously
while everywhere young women sang auspicious songs.
The queen and her companions were as ecstatic   2
as drought-stricken rice fields receiving rain.
Janak found joy and ceased to worry,
like a tired swimmer touching solid ground.
With bow broken, the kings became lusterless,   3
like lamps losing their glow in daylight.

सीय सुखहि बरनिअ केहि भाँती ।
जनु चातकी पाइ जलु स्वाती ॥

४ रामहि लखनु बिलोकत कैसें ।
ससिहि चकोर किसोरकु जैसें ॥
सतानंद तब आयसु दीन्हा ।
सीताँ गमनु राम पहिं कीन्हा ॥

२६३ संग सखीं सुंदर चतुर गावहिं मंगलचार ।
गवनी बाल मराल गति सुषमा अंग अपार ॥

१ सखिन्ह मध्य सिय सोहति कैसें ।
छबिगन मध्य महाछबि जैसें ॥
कर सरोज जयमाल सुहाई ।
बिस्व बिजय सोभा जेहिं छाई ॥

२ तन सकोचु मन परम उछाहू ।
गूढ़ प्रेमु लखि परइ न काहू ॥
जाइ समीप राम छबि देखी ।
रहि जनु कुआँरि चित्र अवरेखी ॥

३ चतुर सखीं लखि कहा बुझाई ।
पहिरावहु जयमाल सुहाई ॥
सुनत जुगल कर माल उठाई ।
प्रेम बिबस पहिराइ न जाई ॥

४ सोहत जनु जुग जलज सनाला ।
ससिहि सभीत देत जयमाला ॥

164

But how to describe Sita's joy? She was like
a thirsty cuckoo gaining Svati's shower.[72]
And Lakshman looked at Ram   4
as a young *cakor* bird does the moon.
Then guru Shatanand gave the order
that Sita should approach Ram.

Accompanied by lovely and skilled companions   263
singing songs of blessing,
she moved with the gait of a young *haṃsa*,
matchless beauty in her every limb.

Amid her friends, Sita shone   1
like supreme beauty in a field of loveliness,
in her lotus hands, a glorious garland
aglow with the splendor of world triumph.
Her body was shy but her heart most eager,   2
with a secret love none could perceive.
Coming near Ram and seeing his beauty,
she stood still, like a princess in a painting.
Her knowing friend understood and said,   3
"Now place the garland of victory on him."
At this, her two hands lifted the garland,
yet, overcome by love, could not bestow it,
looking as lovely as two long-stemmed lotuses   4
timidly offering a marriage garland to the moon.

गावहिं छबि अवलोकि सहेली ।
सियँ जयमाल राम उर मेली ॥

२६४ रघुबर उर जयमाल देखि देव बरिसहिं सुमन ।
सकुचे सकल भुआल जनु बिलोकि रबि कुमुदगन ॥

१ पुर अरु ब्योम बाजने बाजे ।
खल भए मलिन साधु सब राजे ॥
सुर किंनर नर नाग मुनीसा ।
जय जय जय कहि देहिं असीसा ॥

२ नाचहिं गावहिं बिबुध बधूटीं ।
बार बार कुसुमांजलि छूटीं ॥
जहँ तहँ बिप्र बेद धुनि करहीं ।
बंदी बिरिदावलि उच्चरहीं ॥

३ महि पाताल नाक जसु ब्यापा ।
राम बरी सिय भंजेउ चापा ॥
करहिं आरती पुर नर नारी ।
देहिं निछावरि बित्त बिसारी ॥

४ सोहति सीय राम कै जोरी ।
छबि सिंगारु मनहुँ एक ठोरी ॥
सखीं कहहिं प्रभु पद गहु सीता ।
करति न चरन परस अति भीता ॥

At this fair sight, her friends began singing,
and Sita placed the garland on Ram's chest.

Seeing the garland on the Raghu lord's breast,   264
the gods rained blossoms,
while the kings were as abashed
as a field of night lilies sighting the sun.

Music resounded through city and sky,   1
and the wicked grew glum while the holy beamed.
Gods, demigods, and men, serpents and sages
gave blessings, repeatedly crying "Victory!"
Heavenly women danced and sang,   2
showering flowers from cupped hands.
On all sides, Brahmans chanted the Veda
and royal bards intoned heroic lays.
Word spread through earth, netherworld, and sky: 3
"Ram has broken the bow and won Sita!"
Worshiping them with lamps, the cityfolk
gave lavish gifts, forgetting all constraints.
Sita and Ram were a radiant pair,   4
like grace and amorous beauty joined in one place.
Her friends said, "Sita, clasp your lord's feet,"
yet, greatly afraid, she did not touch them.

२६५ गौतम तिय गति सुरति करि नहिं परसति पग पानि ।
मन बिहसे रघुबंसमनि प्रीति अलौकिक जानि ॥

१ तब सिय देखि भूप अभिलाषे ।
कूर कपूत मूढ़ मन माखे ॥
उठि उठि पहिरि सनाह अभागे ।
जहँ तहँ गाल बजावन लागे ॥

२ लेहु छड़ाइ सीय कह कोऊ ।
धरि बाँधहु नृप बालक दोऊ ॥
तोरें धनुषु चाड़ नहिं सरई ।
जीवत हमहि कुअँरि को बरई ॥

३ जौं बिदेहु कछु करै सहाई ।
जीतहु समर सहित दोउ भाई ॥
साधु भूप बोले सुनि बानी ।
राजसमाजहि लाज लजानी ॥

४ बलु प्रतापु बीरता बड़ाई ।
नाक पिनाकहि संग सिधाई ॥
सोइ सूरता कि अब कहुँ पाई ।
असि बुधि तौ बिधि मुहँ मसि लाई ॥

२६६ देखहु रामहि नयन भरि तजि इरिषा मदु कोहु ।
लखन रोषु पावकु प्रबल जानि सलभ जनि होहु ॥

Recalling the release of Gautam's wife,   265
she held back from touching his feet.[73]
The jewel of the Raghus understood her unearthly love
and smiled to himself.

Seeing Sita there, some kings grew desirous.   1
Cruel, ill-bred fools, they were filled with rage.
Springing up, those unfortunates donned armor
and rushed about boasting brazenly.
Some said, "Let us carry off Sita   2
and capture and bind the two princelings.
Just breaking the bow will not suffice—
who dares wed the maid while we yet live?
And if King Videha offers them aid,   3
we'll best him in battle along with the brothers."
Hearing these words, good kings replied,
"Shame itself is shamed by this royal horde.
Your might, valor, virility, and fame   4
have all gone the way of the bow.
Now where did you get this heroism?
For such dull wit, Brahma has tarred your faces!

Behold Ram to your eyes' content,   266
abandoning jealousy, delusion, and anger.
Do not go forth, like a swarm of locusts,
into the flames of Lakshman's rage.

१ बैनतेय बलि जिमि चह कागू ।
   जिमि ससु चहै नाग अरि भागू ॥
   जिमि चह कुसल अकारन कोही ।
   सब संपदा चहै सिवद्रोही ॥

२ लोभी लोलुप कल कीरति चहई ।
   अकलंकता कि कामी लहई ॥
   हरि पद बिमुख परम गति चाहा ।
   तस तुम्हार लालचु नरनाहा ॥

३ कोलाहलु सुनि सीय सकानी ।
   सखीं लवाइ गईं जहँ रानी ॥
   रामु सुभायँ चले गुरु पाहीं ।
   सिय सनेहु बरनत मन माहीं ॥

४ रानिन्ह सहित सोच बस सीया ।
   अब धौं बिधिहि काह करनीया ॥
   भूप बचन सुनि इत उत तकहीं ।
   लखनु राम डर बोलि न सकहीं ॥

२६७ अरुन नयन भृकुटी कुटिल चितवत नृपन्ह सकोप ।
     मनहुँ मत्त गजगन निरखि सिंघकिसोरहि चोप ॥

१ खरभरु देखि बिकल पुर नारीं ।
   सब मिलि देहिं महीपन्ह गारीं ॥
   तेहिं अवसर सुनि सिवधनु भंगा ।
   आयउ भृगुकुल कमल पतंगा ॥

Like a crow craving Garuda's might,   1
or a rabbit demanding the lion's share,
like a choleric man hoping for contentment,
or an enemy of Shiva expecting prosperity,
or a stingy, greedy person wanting renown,   2
or a lustful one reaching for purity,
or a foe of the Lord's feet seeking salvation—
even so is your desire, lords of men!"
Hearing the uproar, Sita grew anxious   3
and her friends brought her to the queen.
Ram calmly returned to his guru,
praising Sita's love in his heart.
The queens and Sita, overcome by doubt,   4
wondered, "What will fate do now?"
Hearing the kings' words and glaring about,
Lakshman could say nothing for fear of Ram.

With reddened eyes and arched brows,   267
he looked angrily at the kings,
like an eager young lion eyeing
a herd of rampaging elephants.

Seeing the uproar, the townswomen were upset   1
and began hurling insults at the kings.
Just then, having heard the breaking of Shiva's bow,
the sun to the lotuses of Bhrigu's line arrived.[74]

२ देखि महीप सकल सकुचाने ।
बाज झपट जनु लवा लुकाने ॥
गौरि सरीर भूति भल भ्राजा ।
भाल बिसाल त्रिपुंड बिराजा ॥

३ सीस जटा ससिबदनु सुहावा ।
रिस बस कछुक अरुन होइ आवा ॥
भृकुटी कुटिल नयन रिस राते ।
सहजहुँ चितवत मनहुँ रिसाते ॥

४ बृषभ कंध उर बाहु बिसाला ।
चारु जनेउ माल मृगछाला ॥
कटि मुनिबसन तून दुइ बाँधें ।
धनु सर कर कुठारु कल काँधें ॥

२६८ सांत बेषु करनी कठिन बरनि न जाइ सरूप ।
धरि मुनितनु जनु बीर रसु आयउ जहँ सब भूप ॥

१ देखत भृगुपति बेषु कराला ।
उठे सकल भय बिकल भुआला ॥
पितु समेत कहि कहि निज नामा ।
लगे करन सब दंड प्रनामा ॥

२ जेहि सुभायँ चितवहिं हितु जानी ।
सो जानइ जनु आइ खुटानी ॥
जनक बहोरि आइ सिरु नावा ।
सीय बोलाइ प्रनामु करावा ॥

At sight of him all the kings cringed   2
like quails taking cover from a swooping hawk.
His fair body was adorned with sacred ash
and his broad brow shone with Shiva's three lines.
He wore matted locks, and his handsome face   3
was half flushed from overpowering rage.
With bent brows and eyes red with wrath,
even his ordinary glance looked angry.
Bull-shouldered, with great chest and arms,   4
he wore a sacred thread, garland, and deerskin,
and a bark-cloth waistband securing two quivers.
He held bow and arrows and had a hatchet on his shoulder.

In saintly dress, yet known for dreadful deeds—   268
this figure challenges description,
as if poetry's martial mood took on a sage's body
and came to the concourse of kings.

Seeing the fearsome garb of the Bhrigu lord,   1
the kings arose, stricken with terror.
Naming their sires and themselves,
they all fell prostrate before him.
If he routinely glanced, even benignly,   2
at someone, that man thought, "I am done for!"
Then Janak came and bowed his head
and, calling Sita, made her pay her respects.

३   आसिष दीन्हि सखीं हरषानीं ।
निज समाज लै गईं सयानीं ॥
बिस्वामित्रु मिले पुनि आई ।
पद सरोज मेले दोउ भाई ॥

४   रामु लखनु दसरथ के ढोटा ।
दीन्हि असीस देखि भल जोटा ॥
रामहि चितइ रहे थकि लोचन ।
रूप अपार मार मद मोचन ॥

२६९   बहुरि बिलोकि बिदेह सन कहहु काह अति भीर ।
पूँछत जानि अजान जिमि ब्यापेउ कोपु सरीर ॥

१   समाचार कहि जनक सुनाए ।
जेहि कारन महीप सब आए ॥
सुनत बचन फिरि अनत निहारे ।
देखे चापखंड महि डारे ॥

२   अति रिस बोले बचन कठोरा ।
कहु जड़ जनक धनुष कै तोरा ॥
बेगि देखाउ मूढ़ न त आजू ।
उलटउँ महि जहँ लहि तव राजू ॥

३   अति डरु उतरु देत नृपु नाहीं ।
कुटिल भूप हरषे मन माहीं ॥
सुर मुनि नाग नगर नर नारी ।
सोचहिं सकल त्रास उर भारी ॥

The sage blessed her, and her relieved companions 3
brought her back to the women's company.
Vishvamitra then came to meet him
and had the brothers bow at his holy feet,
saying, "Ram and Lakshman, Dasarath's sons." 4
Seeing that lovely pair, he gave his blessing,
but his gaze stayed fixed on Ram,
whose boundless beauty relieved Kama of pride.

Then he turned to King Videha and said, 269
"Tell me, why this multitude?"—
asking, though he knew, as if he knew not,
his body boiling with rage.

Janak fully recounted the reason 1
for the coming of all those kings.
At this, the Bhrigu turned his gaze
and saw the bow's pieces lying on the earth.
In great wrath he uttered harsh words: 2
"Speak, Janak, you fool! Who broke this bow?
Show him to me at once, dunce, or this very day
I will turn your whole realm upside down!"
The terrified ruler gave no reply 3
and devious kings were inwardly pleased,
but gods, sages, serpents, and townspeople
were all anxious and filled with great dread.

४ मन पछिताति सीय महतारी ।
बिधि अब सँवरी बात बिगारी ॥
भृगुपति कर सुभाउ सुनि सीता ।
अरध निमेष कलप सम बीता ॥

२७० सभय बिलोके लोग सब जानि जानकी भीरु ।
हृदयँ न हरषु बिषादु कछु बोले श्रीरघुबीरु ॥

१ नाथ संभुधनु भंजनिहारा ।
होइहि केउ एक दास तुम्हारा ॥
आयसु काह कहिअ किन मोही ।
सुनि रिसाइ बोले मुनि कोही ॥

२ सेवकु सो जो करै सेवकाई ।
अरि करनी करि करिअ लराई ॥
सुनहु राम जेहिं सिवधनु तोरा ।
सहसबाहु सम सो रिपु मोरा ॥

३ सो बिलगाउ बिहाइ समाजा ।
न त मारे जैहहिं सब राजा ॥
सुनि मुनि बचन लखन मुसुकाने ।
बोले परसुधरहि अपमाने ॥

४ बहु धनुहीं तोरीं लरिकाई ।
कबहुँ न असि रिस कीन्हि गोसाईं ॥
एहि धनु पर ममता केहि हेतू ।
सुनि रिसाइ कह भृगुकुलकेतू ॥

Sita's mother lamented to herself,   4
"Everything was set, and now fate has ruined it!"
Having heard of the Bhrigu's temper, Sita
suffered each half-instant like an aeon.

Seeing everyone in terror   270
and understanding Janaki's anguish,
the Raghu hero spoke, his heart free
of both joy and sorrow.

"Lord, the breaker of Shambhu's bow   1
must surely be one of your own servants.
So why not give me your command?"
Hearing this, the angry sage flared up again.
"A servant is one who serves,   2
but an enemy's act warrants a battle!
Hear me, Ram: whoever broke Shiva's bow
is no less an enemy to me than Sahasbahu.[75]
Let him be singled out in this assembly,   3
or else all these kings will be slaughtered."
Hearing the sage's talk, Lakshman smiled
and spoke insultingly to the axe-wielder.
"In our youth, we broke a lot of little bows,   4
master, yet you never got so upset.
Why the fondness for this one?"
At this, the banner of the Bhrigus spoke in rage,

२७१ रे नृप बालक काल बस बोलत तोहि न सँभार ।
धनुही सम तिपुरारि धनु बिदित सकल संसार ॥

१ लखन कहा हँसि हमरें जाना ।
सुनहु देव सब धनुष समाना ॥
का छति लाभु जून धनु तोरें ।
देखा राम नयन के भोरें ॥

२ छुअत टूट रघुपतिहु न दोसू ।
मुनि बिनु काज करिअ कत रोसू ॥
बोले चितइ परसु की ओरा ।
रे सठ सुनेहि सुभाउ न मोरा ॥

३ बालकु बोलि बधउँ नहिं तोही ।
केवल मुनि जड़ जानहि मोही ॥
बाल ब्रह्मचारी अति कोही ।
बिस्व बिदित छत्रियकुल द्रोही ॥

४ भुज बल भूमि भूप बिनु कीन्ही ।
बिपुल बार महिदेवन्ह दीन्ही ॥
सहसबाहु भुज छेदनिहारा ।
परसु बिलोकु महीपकुमारा ॥

२७२ मातु पितहि जनि सोचबस करसि महीसकिसोर ।
गर्भन्ह के अर्भक दलन परसु मोर अति घोर ॥

"Royal brat! Under the spell of doom 271
you prattle without self-control.
Is any bow like that of the foe of the three cities,[76]
famed throughout the world?"

Lakshman said, laughing, "To my mind, 1
your holiness, all bows are equal.
What harm or gain if an old one breaks?
Seeing it, Ram mistook it for new
and it broke at a touch—no fault of the Raghu. 2
Why are you upset, sage, for no reason?"
Eyeing his axe, the ascetic spoke,
"Knave! Have you not heard of my nature?
Because I call you a child, I do not kill you, 3
fool, though you regard me as a mere sage.
A lifelong celibate and exceedingly irascible,
I am famed worldwide as the foe of royal lines.
By my arms' might, I emptied the earth of kings 4
and gave it, numerous times, to the Brahmans.
This axe that hacked off the thousand limbs
of Sahasbahu—take a look at it, princeling!

Do not cause your mother and father 272
to panic, son of a king.
My awesome axe annihilates
even the fetus in the womb."

१   बिहसि लखनु बोले मृदु बानी ।
अहो मुनीसु महा भटमानी ॥
पुनि पुनि मोहि देखाव कुठारू ।
चहत उड़ावन फूँकि पहारू ॥

२   इहाँ कुम्हड़बतिया कोउ नाहीं ।
जे तरजनी देखि मरि जाहीं ॥
देखि कुठारु सरासन बाना ।
मैं कछु कहा सहित अभिमाना ॥

३   भृगुसुत समुझि जनेउ बिलोकी ।
जो कछु कहहु सहउँ रिस रोकी ॥
सुर महिसुर हरिजन अरु गाई ।
हमरें कुल इन्ह पर न सुराई ॥

४   बधें पापु अपकीरति हारें ।
मारतहूँ पा परिअ तुम्हारें ॥
कोटि कुलिस सम बचनु तुम्हारा ।
ब्यर्थ धरहु धनु बान कुठारा ॥

२७३   जो बिलोकि अनुचित कहेउँ छमहु महामुनि धीर ।
सुनि सरोष भृगुबंसमनि बोले गिरा गभीर ॥

१   कौसिक सुनहु मंद यहु बालकु ।
कुटिल कालबस निज कुल घालकु ॥
भानु बंस राकेस कलंकू ।
निपट निरंकुस अबुध असंकू ॥

With a chuckle Lakshman coolly replied,   1
"Oh ho! The big sage fancies himself a hero.
You keep showing me your hatchet,
hoping thus to blow away a mountain.
But I am not some little unripe gourd   2
that will wilt at the wave of a forefinger.
Observing your axe, arrows, and bow,
I spoke a bit haughtily.
But knowing you for a Bhrigu, seeing your sacred thread,   3
I suffer whatever you say, suppressing my anger.
Deities, Brahmans, Hari's folk, and cows,
in our clan, can never be targets of virility.
To slay them is sin, to be beaten by them, shameful,   4
and even if you strike me I will fall at your feet.
Your speech is potent as a million thunderbolts
and you needlessly bear bow, arrows, and axe.[77]

So if, seeing them, I spoke improperly,   273
pardon me, great and forbearing sage!"
Hearing this, the jewel of the Bhrigu clan
thundered in furious rage—

"Listen Kaushik, this child is a fool,   1
perverse, doomed, destructive of his kin,
a stain on the moon of the solar clan,
utterly unchecked, ignorant, and brazen.

२   काल कवलु होइहि छन माहीं ।
      कहउँ पुकारि खोरि मोहि नाहीं ॥
      तुम्ह हटकहु जौं चहहु उबारा ।
      कहि प्रतापु बलु रोषु हमारा ॥

३   लखन कहेउ मुनि सुजसु तुम्हारा ।
      तुम्हहि अछत को बरनै पारा ॥
      अपने मुँह तुम्ह आपनि करनी ।
      बार अनेक भाँति बहु बरनी ॥

४   नहिं संतोषु त पुनि कछु कहहू ।
      जनि रिस रोकि दुसह दुख सहहू ॥
      बीरब्रती तुम्ह धीर अछोभा ।
      गारी देत न पावहु सोभा ॥

२७४   सूर समर करनी करहिं कहि न जनावहिं आपु ।
      बिद्यमान रन पाइ रिपु कायर कथहिं प्रतापु ॥

१   तुम्ह तौ कालु हाँक जनु लावा ।
      बार बार मोहि लागि बोलावा ॥
      सुनत लखन के बचन कठोरा ।
      परसु सुधारि धरेउ कर घोरा ॥

२   अब जनि देइ दोसु मोहि लोगू ।
      कटुबादी बालकु बधजोगू ॥
      बाल बिलोकि बहुत मैं बाँचा ।
      अब यहु मरनिहार भा साँचा ॥

He will be a morsel for death momentarily,   2
and I loudly declare: it will be no fault of mine!
Censure him if you wish him spared,
and tell him of my glory, power, and wrath."
Lakshman said, "Sage, regarding your fame,   3
with you present, who else could speak?
You yourself mouth your own exploits
repeatedly and every which way.
But if you are not content, say a bit more.   4
Do not bear insufferable pain by stifling rage.
Vowed to valor, patient, and imperturbable,
you gain no luster by hurling abuse.

A warrior does his work in war   274
and does not advertise himself.
Faced with a foe in battle,
only a coward brags of his might.

You keep bellowing for death, it seems,   1
summoning him, time and again, for me."
Hearing Lakshman's stinging words
the sage took his terrible axe in hand.
"Now let no one blame me.   2
This foul-mouthed child is fit to be killed.
Seeing his youth, I spared him plenty,
but now he is really about to die!"

३ कौसिक कहा छमिअ अपराधू ।
बाल दोष गुन गनहिं न साधू ॥
खर कुठार मैं अकरुन कोही ।
आगें अपराधी गुरुद्रोही ॥

४ उतर देत छोड़उँ बिनु मारें ।
केवल कौसिक सील तुम्हारें ॥
न त एहि काटि कुठार कठोरें ।
गुरहि उरिन होतेउँ श्रम थोरें ॥

२७५ गाधिसूनु कह हृदयँ हँसि मुनिहि हरिअरइ सूझ ।
अयमय खाँड़ न ऊखमय अजहुँ न बूझ अबूझ ॥

१ कहेउ लखन मुनि सीलु तुम्हारा ।
को नहिं जान बिदित संसारा ॥
माता पितहि उरिन भए नीकें ।
गुर रिनु रहा सोचु बड़ जी कें ॥

२ सो जनु हमरेहि माथे काढ़ा ।
दिन चलि गए ब्याज बड़ बाढ़ा ॥
अब आनिअ ब्यवहरिआ बोली ।
तुरत देउँ मैं थैली खोली ॥

३ सुनि कटु बचन कुठार सुधारा ।
हाय हाय सब सभा पुकारा ॥
भृगुबर परसु देखावहु मोही ।
बिप्र बिचारि बचउँ नृपद्रोही ॥

Kaushik said, "Pardon his offense,   3
for the holy do not count a child's merits and flaws."
But the other said, "My axe is keen, I am merciless and
     angry,
and before me is a guru-defying sinner.
He talks back, and I have spared him death,   4
Kaushik, only because of your virtues.
Otherwise, slashing him with this awful axe,
I would easily acquit my debt to my teacher."

Vishvamitra smiled and said to himself,   275
"The sage seems completely oblivious.
This ingot is iron, not congealed sugar-syrup,
and still the simpleton does not see!"[78]

Lakshman said, "Sage, your sterling qualities   1
are world famous. Who does not know of them?
Nicely clear of debt to mother and father,[79]
you still owe your guru, and it really irks you.
All right, suppose I take that on my head—   2
it has been a while and the interest has compounded,
so now, call an accountant
and I will promptly open my purse and pay up."
At this searing speech, the sage readied his axe,   3
while the whole assembly raised cries of woe.
Lakshman said, "Bhrigu lord, you brandish your axe
     before me,
but considering you are a Brahman, I spare you, foe of
     kings.

४ मिले न कबहुँ सुभट रन गाढ़े।
द्विज देवता घरहि के बाढ़े॥
अनुचित कहि सब लोग पुकारे।
रघुपति सयनहिं लखनु नेवारे॥

२७६ लखन उतर आहुति सरिस भृगुबर कोपु कृसानु।
बढ़त देखि जल सम बचन बोले रघुकुलभानु॥

१ नाथ करहु बालक पर छोहू।
सूध दूधमुख करिअ न कोहू॥
जौं पै प्रभु प्रभाउ कछु जाना।
तौ किं बराबरि करत अयाना॥

२ जौं लरिका कछु अचगरि करहीं।
गुर पितु मातु मोद मन भरहीं॥
करिअ कृपा सिसु सेवक जानी।
तुम्ह सम सील धीर मुनि ग्यानी॥

३ राम बचन सुनि कछुक जुड़ाने।
कहि कछु लखनु बहुरि मुसुकाने॥
हँसत देखि नख सिख रिस ब्यापी।
राम तोर भ्राता बड़ पापी॥

४ गौर सरीर स्याम मन माहीं।
कालकूटमुख पयमुख नाहीं॥
सहज टेढ़ अनुहरइ न तोही।
नीचु मीचु सम देख न मोही॥

186

You have never faced a war-hardened hero,   4
twice-born lord, and are mighty only at home."
"Most objectionable!" everyone shouted,
and the Raghu lord checked Lakshman with a sign.

Lakshman's rejoinders were like oblations of oil   276
in the fire of that Bhrigu's wrath.
Seeing it flare up, the sun of the Raghu race
spoke words like cooling water.

"Lord, have pity on this child,   1
guileless and barely weaned.[80] Do not be angry with him.
If he knew anything of your lordship's might
would the foolish child assert equality with you?
When a little boy makes mischief,   2
teacher and parents are filled with delight.
Knowing he is child and servant, show mercy,
for you are a just, virtuous, patient, and wise sage."
When he heard Ram's words he cooled a little,   3
but Lakshman said something else and grinned.
Seeing that smile, he was filled with fury.
"Ram, your brother is a mighty sinner!
His body is fair but his heart is black   4
and his mouth holds venom,[81] not mother's milk.
Innately perverse, he does not act like you,
and is too base to recognize me as death!"

२७७ लखन कहेउ हँसि सुनहु मुनि क्रोधु पाप कर मूल ।
जेहि बस जन अनुचित करहिं चरहिं बिस्व
प्रतिकूल ॥

१ मैं तुम्हार अनुचर मुनिराया ।
परिहरि कोपु करिअ अब दाया ॥
टूट चाप नहिं जुरिहि रिसाने ।
बैठिअ होइहिं पाय पिराने ॥

२ जौं अति प्रिय तौ करिअ उपाई ।
जोरिअ कोउ बड़ गुनी बोलाई ॥
बोलत लखनहिं जनकु डेराहीं ।
मष्ट करहु अनुचित भल नाहीं ॥

३ थर थर काँपहिं पुर नर नारी ।
छोट कुमार खोट बड़ भारी ॥
भृगुपति सुनि सुनि निरभय बानी ।
रिस तन जरइ होइ बल हानी ॥

४ बोले रामहि देइ निहोरा ।
बचउँ बिचारि बंधु लघु तोरा ॥
मनु मलीन तनु सुंदर कैसें ।
बिष रस भरा कनक घटु जैसें ॥

२७८ सुनि लछिमन बिहसे बहुरि नयन तरेरे राम ।
गुर समीप गवने सकुचि परिहरि बानी बाम ॥

Lakshman laughed and said, "Listen, sage. 277
Anger is the very root of sin.
In its grip, people commit wrongs
and act in opposition to the world.

I am but your servant, lord of sages, 1
so now, abandon anger and show mercy.
The broken bow will not be fixed by rage.
And do sit down—your feet must ache!
If you are so fond of that bow, I have an idea: 2
call a clever craftsman and get it patched."
Lakshman's talk terrified Janak, who said,
"Be still! Unseemly speech is not good."
The townsfolk all shuddered and declared, 3
"The junior prince is much too impious!"
Hearing all that audacious talk, the Bhrigu
felt his body burning, his strength waning.
Entreatingly, he said to Ram, 4
"I spare him because he is your little brother.
His mind is foul though his body is fair,
like a gold pot filled with poisonous brew."

Hearing this, Lakshman laughed again, 278
but Ram shot him a sharp glance
and he went sheepishly to the guru,
forgoing his defiant talk.

१ अति बिनीत मृदु सीतल बानी ।
बोले रामु जोरि जुग पानी ॥
सुनहु नाथ तुम्ह सहज सुजाना ।
बालक बचनु करिअ नहिं काना ॥

२ बररै बालकु एकु सुभाऊ ।
इन्हहि न संत बिदूषहिं काऊ ॥
तेहिं नाहीं कछु काज बिगारा ।
अपराधी मैं नाथ तुम्हारा ॥

३ कृपा कोपु बधु बँधब गोसाईं ।
मो पर करिअ दास की नाईं ॥
कहिअ बेगि जेहि बिधि रिस जाई ।
मुनिनायक सोइ करौं उपाई ॥

४ कह मुनि राम जाइ रिस कैसें ।
अजहुँ अनुज तव चितव अनैसें ॥
एहि कें कंठ कुठारु न दीन्हा ।
तौ मैं काह कोपु करि कीन्हा ॥

२७९ गर्भ स्रवहिं अवनिप रवनि सुनि कुठार गति घोर ।
परसु अछत देखउँ जिअत बैरी भूपकिसोर ॥

१ बहइ न हाथु दहइ रिस छाती ।
भा कुठारु कुंठित नृपघाती ॥
भयउ बाम बिधि फिरेउ सुभाऊ ।
मोरे हृदयँ कृपा कसि काऊ ॥

With great deference, in a sweet, calm voice,   1
and with hands joined in supplication, Ram spoke.
"Master, you who are innately wise
should not give an ear to a child's speech.
Children and wasps are alike in nature   2
and godly folk never tease them.[82]
Then, too, he has done no harm.
It is I, sir, who am your culprit.
Mercy, wrath, death, or bondage, master,   3
deliver to me, as to a slave.
Say at once how your ire may be appeased,
lord of sages, and I will act accordingly."
The sage said, "Ram, how can my rage depart?   4
Even now, your little brother smirks at me.
If I have not set my blade on that neck of his,
of what potency is my anger?

The pregnant wives of kings miscarry,   279
just hearing the awful saga of my axe.
But even while I bear that blade, I behold
the hateful princeling yet alive.

My hand stays, but my breast burns with rage,   1
as if this king-killing blade has gone blunt!
Fate has turned on me and altered my nature,
or how else would mercy ever enter my heart?

२   आजु दया दुखु दुसह सहावा ।
    सुनि सौमित्रि बिहसि सिरु नावा ॥
    बाउ कृपा मूरति अनुकूला ।
    बोलत बचन झरत जनु फूला ॥
३   जौं पै कृपाँ जरिहिं मुनि गाता ।
    क्रोध भएँ तनु राख बिधाता ॥
    देखु जनक हठि बालकु एहू ।
    कीन्ह चहत जड़ जमपुर गेहू ॥
४   बेगि करहु किन आँखिन्ह ओटा ।
    देखत छोट खोट नृप ढोटा ॥
    बिहसे लखनु कहा मन माहीं ।
    मूदें आँखि कतहुँ कोउ नाहीं ॥

२८० परसुरामु तब राम प्रति बोले उर अति क्रोधु ।
    संभु सरासनु तोरि सठ करसि हमार प्रबोधु ॥

१   बंधु कहइ कटु संमत तोरें ।
    तू छल बिनय करसि कर जोरें ॥
    करु परितोषु मोर संग्रामा ।
    नाहिं त छाड़ कहाउब रामा ॥
२   छलु तजि करहि समरु सिवद्रोही ।
    बंधु सहित न त मारउँ तोही ॥
    भृगुपति बकहिं कुठार उठाएँ ।
    मन मुसुकाहिं रामु सिर नाएँ ॥

Today, compassion makes me bear this misery." 2
At this, Sumitra's son smiled and bowed his head:
"This breeze of mercy well suits your demeanor
and turns your words into a rain of blossoms.
But, sage, if kindness makes your body burn, 3
God save it should you actually get angry!"
"Look here, Janak," said Parashuram, "this idiot boy
    insists
on taking up residence in Yama's* realm.
Get him out of my sight, and quick! 4
Though he looks young, this prince is wicked."
Lakshman chuckled to himself,
"Just shut your eyes and no one will be there."

Then Parashuram turned to Ram and spoke, 280
his heart consumed with rage:
"You shattered Shambhu's bow, you scoundrel,
and now you would instruct me?

You collude in your brother's rude talk 1
even as you feign reverence.
Either give me satisfaction in combat,
or give up calling yourself 'Ram.'
Foe of Shiva! Enough of your wiles. Fight me 2
or I will kill you along with your brother."
Ranting like this, the Bhrigu raised his axe.
Ram smiled to himself, lowered his head,

—————

* The god of death.

३   गुनह लखन कर हम पर रोषू ।
कतहुँ सुधाइहु ते बड़ दोषू ॥
टेढ़ जानि सब बंदइ काहू ।
बक्र चंद्रमहि ग्रसइ न राहू ॥

४   राम कहेउ रिस तजिअ मुनीसा ।
कर कुठारु आगें यह सीसा ॥
जेहिं रिस जाइ करिअ सोइ स्वामी ।
मोहि जानिअ आपन अनुगामी ॥

२८१   प्रभुहि सेवकहि समरु कस तजहु बिप्रबर रोसु ।
बेषु बिलोकें कहेसि कछु बालककहू नहिं दोसु ॥

१   देखि कुठार बान धनु धारी ।
भै लरिकहि रिस बीरु बिचारी ॥
नामु जान पै तुम्हहि न चीन्हा ।
बंस सुभायँ उतरु तेहिं दीन्हा ॥

२   जौं तुम्ह औतेहु मुनि की नाईं ।
पद रज सिर सिसु धरत गोसाईं ॥
छमहु चूक अनजानत केरी ।
चहिअ बिप्र उर कृपा घनेरी ॥

३   हमहि तुम्हहि सरिबरि कसि नाथा ।
कहहु न कहाँ चरन कहँ माथा ॥
राम मात्र लघु नाम हमारा ।
परसु सहित बड़ नाम तोहारा ॥

194

and mused, "Lakshman is at fault, yet the sage is angry   3
    at me.
Sometimes, being straightforward is a real flaw.
One known to be crooked is praised by all
and the curved moon eludes Rahu's maw."[83]
But outwardly, Ram said, "Calm your rage, king of sages.   4
The axe is in your hand, my head before you.
Do whatever will appease your anger, master,
considering me your devout follower.

How can there be combat between lord and servant?   281
Abandon anger, best of Brahmans.
When he saw your martial attire, this child babbled a bit,
but he, too, is not at fault.

Seeing you bearing axe, arrows, and bow   1
the boy grew vexed, thinking you a warrior.
Even learning your name, he did not know you
and talked back in the manner of our clan.
If you came as a holy recluse, master, this lad   2
would daub the dust of your feet on his head.
Forgive the error made in ignorance,
for a Brahman's heart should be full of kindness.
Can there be equality, my lord, between us and you?   3
Where, tell, is the foot, and where the forehead?
Mine is but the modest name 'Ram,'
while your grand one comes with an 'axe.'

४ देव एकु गुनु धनुष हमारें ।
नव गुन परम पुनीत तुम्हारें ॥
सब प्रकार हम तुम्ह सन हारे ।
छमहु बिप्र अपराध हमारे ॥

२८२ बार बार मुनि बिप्रबर कहा राम सन राम ।
बोले भृगुपति सरुष हसि तहूँ बंधु सम बाम ॥

१ निपटहिं द्विज करि जानहि मोही ।
मैं जस बिप्र सुनावउँ तोही ॥
चाप सुवा सर आहुति जानू ।
कोपु मोर अति घोर कृसानू ॥

२ समिधि सेन चतुरंग सुहाई ।
महा महीप भए पसु आई ॥
मैं एहिं परसु काटि बलि दीन्हे ।
समर जग्य जप कोटिन्ह कीन्हे ॥

३ मोर प्रभाउ बिदित नहिं तोरें ।
बोलसि निदरि बिप्र के भोरें ॥
भंजेउ चापु दापु बड़ बाढ़ा ।
अहमिति मनहुँ जीति जगु ठाढ़ा ॥

४ राम कहा मुनि कहहु बिचारी ।
रिस अति बढ़ि लघु चूक हमारी ॥
छुअतहिं टूट पिनाक पुराना ।
मैं केहि हेतु करौं अभिमाना ॥

196

I carry but a one-stringed bow, divine one,   4
whereas you bear nine most holy attributes.[84]
We are bested by you in every way,
Brahman seer, so pardon our offense."

Time and again, one Ram hailed the other   282
as "sage" and "noble Brahman."
With an angry snort, the Bhrigu exclaimed,
"You are as perverse as your brother!

You think me but a Brahman?   1
I shall tell you what sort of Brahman I am:
know my bow to be a ladle, my arrows, oblations,
and my wrath, a roaring sacred fire.
Armies of four divisions are fuel sticks   2
and mighty kings come as cattle.
Slaughtering them with this axe, I offer them
with a myriad mantras of martial sacrifice.
You do not know my power, and so   3
insult me, mistaking me for a Brahman.
By breaking the bow, your pride has swelled
and you think you stand astride the world."
Ram said, "Sage, please reflect on this—   4
your ire is immense and my offense trifling.
The antique bow broke at a mere touch.
Why, then, should I show any arrogance?

२८३ जौं हम निदरहिं बिप्र बदि सत्य सुनहु भृगुनाथ ।
तौ अस को जग सुभटु जेहि भय बस नावहिं माथ ॥

१ देव दनुज भूपति भट नाना ।
समबल अधिक होउ बलवाना ॥
जौं रन हमहि पचारै कोऊ ।
लरहिं सुखेन कालु किन होऊ ॥

२ छत्रिय तनु धरि समर सकाना ।
कुल कलंकु तेहिं पावँर आना ॥
कहउँ सुभाउ न कुलहि प्रसंसी ।
कालहु डरहिं न रन रघुबंसी ॥

३ बिप्रबंस कै असि प्रभुताई ।
अभय होइ जो तुम्हहि डेराई ॥
सुनि मृदु गूढ़ बचन रघुपति के ।
उघरे पटल परसुधर मति के ॥

४ राम रमापति कर धनु लेहू ।
खैंचहु मिटै मोर संदेहू ॥
देत चापु आपुहिं चलि गयऊ ।
परसुराम मन बिसमय भयऊ ॥

२८४ जाना राम प्रभाउ तब पुलक प्रफुल्लित गात ।
जोरि पानि बोले बचन हृदयँ न प्रेमु अमात ॥

If I have given offense by calling you a Brahman—   283
hear me well, Bhrigu lord!—
before what other warrior in this world
would I bow my head, awestruck?

Gods, demons, kings, and hordes of heroes,   1
either equal or superior to me in strength—
if anyone challenges me in battle,
I will gladly fight, though he be Death himself.
A man of Kshatriya birth who hesitates in war   2
is contemptible and defames his lineage.
I say sincerely and not to praise my clan,
Death himself does not scare a Raghu in battle.
Yet such is the sovereignty of the Brahman line   3
that one who fears you becomes fearless."[85]
Hearing Ram's sweet and enigmatic words,
the axe-wielder's understanding was unveiled,
and he said, "Ram, take this bow of Lakshmi's lord[86]   4
and draw it to erase my doubt."
Held out, the bow went to him of itself
and Parashuram was wonderstruck.

Then at last he understood Ram's majesty,   284
and his body shivered with joy.
Hands joined in adoration, he spoke,
his heart unable to contain his love.

१   जय रघुबंस बनज बन भानू।
     गहन दनुज कुल दहन कृसानू॥
     जय सुर बिप्र धेनु हितकारी।
     जय मद मोह कोह भ्रम हारी॥

२   बिनय सील करुना गुन सागर।
     जयति बचन रचना अति नागर॥
     सेवक सुखद सुभग सब अंगा।
     जय सरीर छबि कोटि अनंगा॥

३   करौं काह मुख एक प्रसंसा।
     जय महेस मन मानस हंसा॥
     अनुचित बहुत कहेउँ अग्याता।
     छमहु छमामंदिर दोउ भ्राता॥

४   कहि जय जय जय रघुकुलकेतू।
     भृगुपति गए बनहि तप हेतू॥
     अपभयँ कुटिल महीप डेराने।
     जहँ तहँ कायर गवँहिं पराने॥

२८५   देवन्ह दीन्हीं दुंदुभीं प्रभु पर बरषहिं फूल।
       हरषे पुर नर नारि सब मिटी मोहमय सूल॥

"Hail, sun to the lotus lake of the Raghu line,[87]   1
and fire, scorching the thicket of demons!
Hail, benefactor of gods, Brahmans, and cows,
remover of pride, infatuation, anger, delusion—hail!
Ocean of humility, mercy, and all virtues,   2
hail, ingenious creator of the works of speech!
Comforter of your servants, lovely in every limb,
embodiment of the beauty of a billion bodiless ones.*
With but one tongue, what praise can I offer?   3
Hail, *haṃsa* on the holy lake of Shiva's heart!
In ignorance, I uttered many unseemly words.
You brothers, twin temples of mercy—forgive me!"
Ever glorifying the ensign of the Raghu clan,   4
the Bhrigu lord left for the forest, set on asceticism.
The wicked kings, fearing imagined retribution,
fled here and there, showing their cowardice.

The celestials sounded kettledrums   285
and rained flowers on the Lord
as the men and women of the city rejoiced,
freed of their unfounded fears.

---

* Kama.

201

The Marriage of Sita and Ram

१ अति गहगहे बाजने बाजे ।
सबहिं मनोहर मंगल साजे ॥
जूथ जूथ मिलि सुमुखि सुनयनीं ।
करहिं गान कल कोकिलबयनीं ॥

२ सुखु बिदेह कर बरनि न जाई ।
जन्मदरिद्र मनहुँ निधि पाई ॥
बिगत त्रास भइ सीय सुखारी ।
जनु बिधु उदयँ चकोरकुमारी ॥

३ जनक कीन्ह कौसिकहि प्रनामा ।
प्रभु प्रसाद धनु भंजेउ रामा ॥
मोहि कृतकृत्य कीन्ह दुहुँ भाई ।
अब जो उचित सो कहिअ गोसाई ॥

४ कह मुनि सुनु नरनाथ प्रबीना ।
रहा बिबाहु चाप आधीना ॥
टूटतहीं धनु भयउ बिबाहू ।
सुर नर नाग बिदित सब काहू ॥

२८६ तदपि जाइ तुम्ह करहु अब जथा बंस ब्यवहारु ।
बूझि बिप्र कुलबृद्ध गुर बेद बिदित आचारु ॥

१ दूत अवधपुर पठवहु जाई ।
आनहिं नृप दसरथहि बोलाई ॥
मुदित राउ कहि भलेहिं कृपाला ।
पठए दूत बोलि तेहि काला ॥

204

A joyous chorus of instruments resounded   1
and everyone began auspicious preparations.
Throngs of attractive, lovely-eyed women
gave sweet voice to beautiful songs.
King Videha felt indescribable joy,   2
like a lifelong pauper who finds treasure.
Free of fear, Sita became as glad
as a young *cakor* hen at moonrise.
Janak paid homage to Sage Kaushik, saying,   3
"By your grace, lord, Ram has broken the bow.
The two brothers have fully satisfied me,
so now say, master, what should rightly happen."
The sage declared, "Indeed, wise ruler of men,   4
matrimony was conditional on the bow.
At its mere breaking, the marriage occurred,
as all celestial and human beings know.

Even so, you should now proceed   286
according to the customs of your clan,
asking Brahmans, elders, and teachers
about the rites prescribed in the Veda.

Send emissaries to Avadh city   1
and invite King Dasarath to come."
Joyfully, the king replied, "Very well, gracious one."
At once, he summoned messengers and dispatched them,

२ बहुरि महाजन सकल बोलाए ।
आइ सबन्हि सादर सिर नाए ॥
हाट बाट मंदिर सुरबासा ।
नगरु सँवारहु चारिहुँ पासा ॥

३ हरषि चले निज निज गृह आए ।
पुनि परिचारक बोलि पठाए ॥
रचहु बिचित्र बितान बनाई ।
सिर धरि बचन चले सचु पाई ॥

४ पठए बोलि गुनी तिन्ह नाना ।
जे बितान बिधि कुसल सुजाना ॥
बिधिहि बंदि तिन्ह कीन्ह अरंभा ।
बिरचे कनक कदलि के खंभा ॥

२८७ हरित मनिन्ह के पत्र फल पदुमराग के फूल ।
रचना देखि बिचित्र अति मनु बिरंचि कर भूल ॥

१ बेनु हरित मनिमय सब कीन्हे ।
सरल सपरब परहिं नहिं चीन्हे ॥
कनक कलित अहिबेलि बनाई ।
लखि नहिं परइ सपरन सुहाई ॥

२ तेहि के रचि पचि बंध बनाए ।
बिच बिच मुकुता दाम सुहाए ॥
मानिक मरकत कुलिस पिरोजा ।
चीरि कोरि पचि रचे सरोजा ॥

then called the leading townsmen together, 2
and they came before him, bowing reverently.
"Markets, streets, homes, and temples—
let every corner of the city be adorned."
Each one happily hurried home, 3
and then he summoned his retainers, saying,
"Have a marvelous pavilion erected."
Honoring his command, they went joyfully
and summoned a legion of craftsmen 4
superbly skilled in canopy construction.
Worshiping Brahma, they began to work,
fashioning plantain-tree pillars of pure gold

with leaves and fruits of emerald 287
and flowers formed of rubies.
Beholding this astonishing artifice,
even the world-creator was lost in wonder.[1]

They made bamboo stalks wholly of emerald, 1
smooth and jointed, indistinguishable from the real,
and crafted a beautiful betel vine, all of gold,
and with lovely leaves, that fooled the eye.
Of this, they artfully braided a chain 2
set here and there with fringes of pearls.
Ruby, emerald, diamond, and turquoise
they sliced and inlaid to fashion lotuses.

३ किए भृंग बहुरंग बिहंगा ।
गुंजहिं कूजहिं पवन प्रसंगा ॥
सुर प्रतिमा खंभन गढ़ि काढ़ीं ।
मंगल द्रब्य लिएँ सब ठाढ़ीं ॥

४ चौकें भाँति अनेक पुराईं ।
सिंधुर मनिमय सहज सुहाईं ॥

२८८ सौरभ पल्लव सुभग सुठि किए नीलमनि कोरि ।
हेम बौर मरकत घवरि लसत पाटमय डोरि ॥

१ रचे रुचिर बर बंदनिवारे ।
मनहुँ मनोभवँ फंद सँवारे ॥
मंगल कलस अनेक बनाए ।
ध्वज पताक पट चमर सुहाए ॥

२ दीप मनोहर मनिमय नाना ।
जाइ न बरनि बिचित्र बिताना ॥
जेहिं मंडप दुलहिनि बैदेही ।
सो बरनै असि मति कबि केही ॥

३ दूलहु रामु रूप गुन सागर ।
सो बितानु तिहुँ लोक उजागर ॥
जनक भवन कै सोभा जैसी ।
गृह गृह प्रति पुर देखिअ तैसी ॥

४ जेहिं तेरहुति तेहि समय निहारी ।
तेहि लघु लगहिं भुवन दस चारी ॥

They made bees and multicolored birds 3
that hummed and cooed in the breeze.
On the pillars, they carved likenesses of gods,
standing with auspicious gifts in hand.
They drew diverse sacred squares 4
filled-in with gorgeous giant pearls.

They crafted young mango leaves 288
from hollowed-out sapphires,
with gold flowers set in emerald sprays,
shimmering on silken cords.

They wove wondrous festoons of flowers, 1
like snares set by the mind-born god.
They fashioned countless ceremonial vessels,
beautiful banners, flags, curtains, and fly whisks,[2]
and innumerable gem-studded lamps. 2
That marvelous pavilion, beyond description,
to which Vaidehi would come as bride—
what poet has the skill to describe it?
And where Ram, sea of beauty and merit, would be 3
     groom—
that marriage tent illumines the three worlds.
The same splendor found in Janak's palace
was seen in every home in the city.
To one beholding Tirahut* town at that time, 4
all fourteen spheres would seem meager,

----

* Videha, Janak's city.

जो संपदा नीच गृह सोहा ।
सो बिलोकि सुरनायक मोहा ॥

२८९ बसइ नगर जेहिं लच्छि करि कपट नारि बर बेषु ।
तेहि पुर कै सोभा कहत सकुचहिं सारद सेषु ॥

१ पहुँचे दूत राम पुर पावन ।
हरषे नगर बिलोकि सुहावन ॥
भूप द्वार तिन्ह खबरि जनाई ।
दसरथ नृप सुनि लिए बोलाई ॥

२ करि प्रनामु तिन्ह पाती दीन्ही ।
मुदित महीप आपु उठि लीन्ही ॥
बारि बिलोचन बाँचत पाती ।
पुलक गात आई भरि छाती ॥

३ रामु लखनु उर कर बर चीठी ।
रहि गए कहत न खाटी मीठी ॥
पुनि धरि धीर पत्रिका बाँची ।
हरषी सभा बात सुनि साँची ॥

४ खेलत रहे तहाँ सुधि पाई ।
आए भरतु सहित हित भाई ॥
पूछत अति सनेहँ सकुचाई ।
तात कहाँ तें पाती आई ॥

and the wealth gracing even lowly homes
would dazzle the king of the gods.

That city wherein Lakshmi[3] lives, in the artifice   289
of a lovely woman's guise—
even Sharada and thousand-tongued Shesh
shrink from speaking of its splendor.

The messengers reached Ram's blessed city   1
and beheld its beauty with delight.
They announced themselves at the palace gate
and King Dasarath heard and sent for them.
Offering salutations, they presented a letter   2
and the king himself happily rose to receive it.
As he read it, tears filled his eyes,
his body shivered, and his chest swelled.
With Ram and Lakshman in his heart, letter in hand,   3
he sat there, unable to utter a word.
Then, composing himself, he read out the letter
and the assembly rejoiced at its true import.[4]
Receiving news while he was at play,   4
Bharat came with his brother and friends.
With hesitation born of great love, he asked,
"Father, from where has this letter come?

२९०   कुसल प्रानप्रिय बंधु दोउ अहहिं कहहु केहिं देस ।
सुनि सनेह साने बचन बाची बहुरि नरेस ॥

१   सुनि पाती पुलके दोउ भ्राता ।
अधिक सनेहु समात न गाता ॥
प्रीति पुनीत भरत कै देखी ।
सकल सभाँ सुखु लहेउ बिसेषी ॥

२   तब नृप दूत निकट बैठारे ।
मधुर मनोहर बचन उचारे ॥
भैआ कहहु कुसल दोउ बारे ।
तुम्ह नीकें निज नयन निहारे ॥

३   स्यामल गौर धरें धनु भाथा ।
बय किसोर कौसिक मुनि साथा ॥
पहिचानहु तुम्ह कहहु सुभाऊ ।
प्रेम बिबस पुनि पुनि कह राऊ ॥

४   जा दिन तें मुनि गए लवाई ।
तब तें आजु साँचि सुधि पाई ॥
कहहु बिदेह कवन बिधि जाने ।
सुनि प्रिय बचन दूत मुसुकाने ॥

२९१   सुनहु महीपति मुकुट मनि तुम्ह सम धन्य न कोउ ।
रामु लखनु जिन्ह के तनय बिस्व बिभूषन दोउ ॥

Tell me whether my two beloved brothers are well, 290
and in what land."
At these affectionate words, the king
read out the letter once more.

Hearing the letter, both brothers were thrilled 1
and could not contain their immense love,
and to see Bharat's pure affection
gave the whole court special satisfaction.
The king had the messengers sit nearby 2
and addressed them with charming sweetness.
"Brothers! Tell me, are the two lads well?
You saw them with your own eyes, did you not?—
dark and fair, bearing bow and quiver, 3
tender youths, accompanying Sage Kaushik?
If you have knowledge of them, tell me at once."
So the king asked again and again, overcome by love.
"Since the day the sage took them away, 4
I have received reliable news only today.
Tell me, too, how King Videha came to know them."
At these loving words, the emissaries smiled.

"Hear us, crown jewel of kings: 291
there is no one as fortunate as you,
who have for sons Ram and Lakshman,
the twin ornaments of this earth.

१ पूछन जोगु न तनय तुम्हारे ।
पुरुषसिंघ तिहु पुर उजिआरे ॥
जिन्ह के जस प्रताप कें आगे ।
ससि मलीन रबि सीतल लागे ॥

२ तिन्ह कहँ कहिअ नाथ किमि चीन्हे ।
देखिअ रबि कि दीप कर लीन्हे ॥
सीय स्वयंबर भूप अनेका ।
समिटे सुभट एक तें एका ॥

३ संभु सरासनु काहुँ न टारा ।
हारे सकल बीर बरिआरा ॥
तीनि लोक महँ जे भटमानी ।
सभ कै सकति संभु धनु भानी ॥

४ सकइ उठाइ सरासुर मेरू ।
सोउ हियँ हारि गयउ करि फेरू ॥
जेहिं कौतुक सिवसैलु उठावा ।
सोउ तेहि सभाँ पराभउ पावा ॥

२९२ तहाँ राम रघुबंसमनि सुनिअ महा महिपाल ।
भंजेउ चाप प्रयास बिनु जिमि गज पंकज नाल ॥

१ सुनि सरोष भृगुनायकु आए ।
बहुत भाँति तिन्ह आँखि देखाए ॥
देखि राम बलु निज धनु दीन्हा ।
करि बहु बिनय गवनु बन कीन्हा ॥

214

There is no need to ask about your sons,   1
lions among men, who illumine the three worlds
and before whose glory and renown
the moon seems tainted, the sun tepid.
You ask, lord, how they were recognized,   2
but does one lift a lamp to see the sun?
At Sita's bridegroom-choice, countless kings
gathered, each of surpassing valor,
yet none could budge the bow of Shambhu.   3
All those mighty heroes failed,
the proudest warriors in the three worlds!
Shambhu's bow sapped all their strength.
Banasur, the arrow-demon who could lift Mount Meru,   4
merely circled that bow and left, crestfallen.
And even he who had playfully hefted Shiva's summit*
found defeat in that arena as well.

But there—hear us well, earth-guarding king!—   292
the jewel of the house of Raghu
broke that bow as effortlessly
as an elephant snaps a lotus stalk.

When the Bhrigu lord heard, he came in a rage   1
and threatened him in all sorts of ways.
But glimpsing Ram's power, he gave him his own bow
and, in great humility, left for the forest.

* Ravan.

२   राजन रामु अतुलबल जैसें ।
तेज निधान लखनु पुनि तैसें ॥
कंपहिं भूप बिलोकत जाकें ।
जिमि गज हरि किसोर के ताकें ॥

३   देव देखि तव बालक दोऊ ।
अब न आँखि तर आवत कोऊ ॥
दूत बचन रचना प्रिय लागी ।
प्रेम प्रताप बीर रस पागी ॥

४   सभा समेत राउ अनुरागे ।
दूतन्ह देन निछावरि लागे ॥
कहि अनीति ते मूदहिं काना ।
धरमु बिचारि सबहिं सुखु माना ॥

२९३   तब उठि भूप बसिष्ट कहुँ दीन्हि पत्रिका जाइ ।
कथा सुनाई गुरहि सब सादर दूत बोलाइ ॥

१   सुनि बोले गुर अति सुखु पाई ।
पुन्य पुरुष कहुँ महि सुख छाई ॥
जिमि सरिता सागर महुँ जाहीं ।
जद्यपि ताहि कामना नाहीं ॥

२   तिमि सुख संपति बिनहिं बोलाएँ ।
धरमसील पहिं जाहिं सुभाएँ ॥
तुम्ह गुर बिप्र धेनु सुर सेबी ।
तसि पुनीत कौसल्या देबी ॥

And Your Majesty, just as Ram is matchless in might,   2
so is Lakshman a storehouse of fiery will,
at whose glance the other kings quaked
like elephants under the gaze of a young lion.
Divine king, having beheld your two boys,   3
no one else seems to us worth seeing!"
The messengers' account was pleasing to all,
imbued with the emotions of love, glory, and valor.[5]
The king and his court were captivated   4
and he began to offer them gifts,
but protesting impropriety, they covered their ears,
delighting all by their adherence to dharma.[6]

The king arose and hurried to Vasishtha   293
and gave him the letter,
and then respectfully asked the messengers
to tell his guru the full tale.

Overjoyed by what he heard, the guru said,   1
"Earth abounds in joy for men of merit.
Just as rivers flow into the sea
though it has no craving for them,
so happiness and prosperity, unbidden,   2
come naturally to those of great virtue.
You serve guru, Brahmans, cows, and gods,
and so does good Queen Kausalya.

३ सुकृती तुम्ह समान जग माहीं ।
भयउ न है कोउ होनेउ नाहीं ॥
तुम्ह ते अधिक पुन्य बड़ काकें ।
राजन राम सरिस सुत जाकें ॥

४ बीर बिनीत धरम ब्रत धारी ।
गुन सागर बर बालक चारी ॥
तुम्ह कहुँ सर्ब काल कल्याना ।
सजहु बरात बजाइ निसाना ॥

२९४ चलहु बेगि सुनि गुर बचन भलेहिं नाथ सिरु नाइ ।
भूपति गवने भवन तब दूतन्ह बासु देवाइ ॥

१ राजा सबु रनिवास बोलाई ।
जनक पत्रिका बाचि सुनाई ॥
सुनि संदेसु सकल हरषानीं ।
अपर कथा सब भूप बरखानीं ॥

२ प्रेम प्रफुल्लित राजहिं रानी ।
मनहुँ सिखिनि सुनि बारिद बानी ॥
मुदित असीस देहिं गुर नारीं ।
अति आनंद मगन महतारीं ॥

३ लेहिं परस्पर अति प्रिय पाती ।
हृदयँ लगाइ जुड़ावहिं छाती ॥
राम लखन कै कीरति करनी ।
बारहिं बार भूपबर बरनी ॥

In pious works, no one in this world   3
was, is, or will ever be your compeer.
Who could surpass you in merit,
Your Majesty, who have a son like Ram?
Heroic, humble, adhering to dharma—   4
your four fine boys are oceans of virtue.
And for you, all times are propitious,[7]
so prepare the wedding procession with fanfare

and with haste!" At his guru's command,   294
he bowed and said, "Very good, master."
Then the king had the emissaries accommodated
and went to his palace.

He summoned all the royal women   1
and read out to them Janak's letter.
They rejoiced to hear the message
and the king recounted the full story.
The queens were as excited with love   2
as peahens hearing the rumble of rainclouds.[8]
Joyfully, the elder women[9] offered blessings,
and the three mothers were elated.
They passed the precious letter around,   3
pressing it to their hearts to calm them,
while the glorious deeds of Ram and Lakshman
were recounted time and again by the king.

४ मुनि प्रसादु कहि द्वार सिधाए ।
रानिन्ह तब महिदेव बोलाए ॥
दिए दान आनंद समेता ।
चले बिप्रबर आसिष देता ॥

२९५ जाचक लिए हँकारि दीन्हि निछावरि कोटि बिधि ।
चिरु जीवहुँ सुत चारि चक्रबर्ति दसरत्थ के ॥

१ कहत चले पहिरें पट नाना ।
हरषि हने गहगहे निसाना ॥
समाचार सब लोगन्ह पाए ।
लागे घर घर होन बधाए ॥

२ भुवन चारिदस भरा उछाहू ।
जनकसुता रघुबीर बिआहू ॥
सुनि सुभ कथा लोग अनुरागे ।
मग गृह गलीं सँवारन लागे ॥

३ जद्यपि अवध सदैव सुहावनि ।
राम पुरी मंगलमय पावनि ॥
तदपि प्रीति कै रीति सुहाई१ ।
मंगल रचना रची बनाई ॥

४ ध्वज पताक पट चामर चारू ।
छावा परम बिचित्र बजारू ॥
कनक कलस तोरन मनि जाला ।
हरद दूब दधि अच्छत माला ॥

"It is the sage's grace!" he said as he departed,   4
while the queens summoned the gods of earth
to joyously offer them gifts.
Bestowing blessings, those learned Brahmans left.

Then beggars were sent for   295
and given countless kinds of alms.
Cheering, "Long live the four sons
of world-conquering Dasarath!"

they went off, draped in abundant rich clothes,   1
as great kettledrums were joyously sounded.
The news reached everyone
and every home broke out in celebration.
Excitement filled the fourteen worlds: 2
"Janak's daughter will wed the Raghu hero!"
People were elated to hear the good news
and began decorating streets, houses, and lanes.
Although Avadh is ever beautiful,   3
for it is Ram's own city, blessed and pure,
yet by the charming customs of love[10]
it was redone in auspicious adornment.
Banners, pennants, draperies, and fans   4
formed a wondrous canopy over the markets.
With gold vessels, gateways, fringes of gems,
turmeric, sacred grass, curd, rice, and garlands,

२९६ मंगलमय निज निज भवन लोगन्ह रचे बनाइ ।
बीथीं सींचीं चतुरसम चौकें चारु पुराइ ॥

१ जहँ तहँ जूथ जूथ मिलि भामिनि ।
सजि नव सप्त सकल दुति दामिनि ॥
बिधुबदनीं मृग सावक लोचनि ।
निज सरूप रति मानु बिमोचनि ॥

२ गावहिं मंगल मंजुल बानीं ।
सुनि कल रव कलकंठि लजानीं ॥
भूप भवन किमि जाइ बखाना ।
बिस्व बिमोहन रचेउ बिताना ॥

३ मंगल द्रब्य मनोहर नाना ।
राजत बाजत बिपुल निसाना ॥
कतहुँ बिरिद बंदी उच्चरहीं ।
कतहुँ बेद धुनि भूसुर करहीं ॥

४ गावहिं सुंदरि मंगल गीता ।
लै लै नामु रामु अरु सीता ॥
बहुत उछाहु भवनु अति थोरा ।
मानहुँ उमगि चला चहु ओरा ॥

२९७ सोभा दसरथ भवन कइ को कबि बरनै पार ।
जहाँ सकल सुर सीस मनि राम लीन्ह अवतार ॥

the townspeople sanctified and adorned 296
their homes, while the streets
were sprinkled with four fragrances
and marked with sacred squares.[11]

Everywhere, groups of women assembled, 1
gorgeously adorned[12] and gleaming like lightning,
with moon-like faces, fawn-like eyes,
and beauty to embarrass the love god's consort.
They gave sweet voice to songs of blessing, 2
whose tones put cuckoos to shame.
And how to describe the king's own dwelling,
where a world-dazzling canopy was constructed?
Countless sacred substances shone there 3
and massive kettledrums resounded.
Here, bards intoned heroic lays,
while there, Brahmans chanted the Vedas.
Beautiful women sang auspicious songs 4
with the refrain of Ram and Sita's names.
The palace was too small for the excitement
that seemed to overflow it on every side.

What poet's account can do justice to the splendor 297
of Dasarath's home,
where Ram, the diadem of all deities,
took birth as avatar?

१ भूप भरत पुनि लिए बोलाई ।
हय गय स्यंदन साजहु जाई ॥
चलहु बेगि रघुबीर बराता ।
सुनत पुलक पूरे दोउ भ्राता ॥

२ भरत सकल साहनी बोलाए ।
आयसु दीन्ह मुदित उठि धाए ॥
रचि रुचि जीन तुरग तिन्ह साजे ।
बरन बरन बर बाजि बिराजे ॥

३ सुभग सकल सुठि चंचल करनी ।
अय इव जरत धरत पग धरनी ॥
नाना जाति न जाहिं बखाने ।
निदरि पवनु जनु चहत उड़ाने ॥

४ तिन्ह सब छयल भए असवारा ।
भरत सरिस बय राजकुमारा ॥
सब सुंदर सब भूषनधारी ।
कर सर चाप तून कटि भारी ॥

२९८ छरे छबीले छयल सब सूर सुजान नबीन ।
जुग पदचर असवार प्रति जे असिकला प्रबीन ॥

१ बाँधें बिरद बीर रन गाढ़े ।
निकसि भए पुर बाहेर ठाढ़े ॥
फेरहिं चतुर तुरग गति नाना ।
हरषहिं सुनि सुनि पनव निसाना ॥

Then the king summoned Bharat, saying,   1
"Decorate horses, elephants, and chariots
and quickly go forth with Ram's wedding party."
Hearing this, the two brothers[13] were thrilled.
Bharat called all the stablemen   2
and gave orders. They joyfully ran to their tasks,
outfitting horses with splendid saddles—
resplendent horses of many hues,
all lovely and spirited, stepping as lightly   3
on earth as if it were red-hot iron.
Of breeds too numerous to describe,
they seemed eager to fly, challenging the wind.
Astride them all were smartly dressed youths,   4
elegant princes of Bharat's own age,
all handsome and richly adorned,
with bows and arrows, and quivers strapped to their
    waists.

All were dashing, hand-picked heroes,   298
youthful yet experienced,
and with each horseman, a pair of foot soldiers
adept at swordplay.

Arrayed as warriors bent on battle,   1
they came and stood outside the city.
Leading their horses in skilled maneuvers,
they reveled in the tumult of drums.[14]

२ रथ सारथिन्ह बिचित्र बनाए ।
ध्वज पताक मनि भूषन लाए ॥
चवँर चारु किंकिनि धुनि करहीं ।
भानु जान सोभा अपहरहीं ॥

३ साँवँकरन अगनित हय होते ।
ते तिन्ह रथन्ह सारथिन्ह जोते ॥
सुंदर सकल अलंकृत सोहे ।
जिन्हहि बिलोकत मुनि मन मोहे ॥

४ जे जल चलहिं थलहि की नाईं ।
टाप न बूड़ बेग अधिकाईं ॥
अस्त्र सस्त्र सबु साजु बनाई ।
रथी सारथिन्ह लिए बोलाई ॥

२९९ चढ़ि चढ़ि रथ बाहेर नगर लागी जुरन बरात ।
होत सगुन सुंदर सबहि जो जेहि कारज जात ॥

१ कलित करिबरन्हि परीं अँबारीं ।
कहि न जाहिं जेहि भाँति सँवारीं ॥
चले मत्त गज घंट बिराजी ।
मनहुँ सुभग सावन घन राजी ॥

२ बाहन अपर अनेक बिधाना ।
सिबिका सुभग सुखासन जाना ॥
तिन्ह चढ़ि चले बिप्रबर बृंदा ।
जनु तनु धरें सकल श्रुति छंदा ॥

Charioteers marvelously adorned their cars 2
with banners, pennants, jeweled ornaments,
fine fly whisks, and chiming bells,
till they stole the splendor of the sun's vehicle.
Countless were the sacred, black-eared stallions 3
that the drivers yoked to those chariots,
all with such beauty and adornment
that they stunned even sages' minds,
and who raced over water as if it were earth, 4
their hooves not sinking, such was their speed.
Heavily armed, richly ornamented warriors
were summoned by the drivers

to mount those chariots, and the procession 299
assembled outside the city.
All saw fair omens, favoring the task
for which they were going forth.

On great elephants were canopied litters 1
adorned with indescribable splendor;
those bulls in rut swayed along, bells ringing,
like lines of rumbling monsoon clouds.
In many other kinds of conveyance— 2
fine palanquins, sedan chairs, chariots—
rode companies of learned Brahmans,
like all the Vedic verses incarnate.

३   मागध सूत बंदि गुनगायक ।
चले जान चढ़ि जो जेहि लायक ॥
बेसर ऊँट बृषभ बहु जाती ।
चले बस्तु भरि अगनित भाँती ॥

४   कोटिन्ह काँवरि चले कहारा ।
बिबिध बस्तु को बरनै पारा ॥
चले सकल सेवक समुदाई ।
निज निज साजु समाजु बनाई ॥

३००   सब कें उर निर्भर हरषु पूरित पुलक सरीर ।
कबहिं देखिबे नयन भरि रामु लखनु दोउ बीर ॥

१   गरजहिं गज घंटा धुनि घोरा ।
रथ रव बाजि हिंस चहु ओरा ॥
निदरि घनहि घुर्म्मरहिं निसाना ।
निज पराइ कछु सुनिअ न काना ॥

२   महा भीर भूपति के द्वारें ।
रज होइ जाइ पषान पबारें ॥
चढ़ी अटारिन्ह देखहिं नारीं ।
लिएँ आरती मंगल थारीं ॥

३   गावहिं गीत मनोहर नाना ।
अति आनंदु न जाइ बखाना ॥
तब सुमंत्र दुइ स्यंदन साजी ।
जोते रबि हय निंदक बाजी ॥

Bards, genealogists, and royal praise-singers   3
went mounted on vehicles suited to their rank.
Diverse breeds of donkeys, camels, and bullocks
lumbered along, loaded with countless goods.
Myriads of bearers[15] moved forward,   4
shouldering goods too diverse to describe,
and many masses of servants walked along
in splendidly uniformed companies.

Their hearts all overflowed with joy   300
and their bodies shivered in expectation.
"When will we feast our eyes
on those two heroes, Ram and Lakshman?"

Elephants trumpeted, their great bells clanging,   1
amid chariot din and neighing of horse on every side
and throbbing drums that put thunder to shame,
till none could hear himself or another!
So dense was the throng at the royal gate   2
that a stone tossed in would be crushed to dust.
Women clambered to upper floors to watch,
bearing lamps on lovely offering-trays
and singing countless charming songs   3
with rapture that words cannot describe.
Then Sumantra[16] prepared two chariots
yoked with horses to humble the sun's,

४ दोउ रथ रुचिर भूप पहिं आने ।
नहिं सारद पहिं जाहिं बखाने ॥
राज समाजु एक रथ साजा ।
दूसर तेज पुंज अति भ्राजा ॥

३०१ तेहिं रथ रुचिर बसिष्ठ कहुँ हरषि चढ़ाइ नरेसु ।
आपु चढ़ेउ स्यंदन सुमिरि हर गुर गौरि गनेसु ॥

१ सहित बसिष्ठ सोह नृप कैसें ।
सुर गुर संग पुरंदर जैसें ॥
करि कुल रीति बेद बिधि राऊ ।
देखि सबहि सब भाँति बनाऊ ॥

२ सुमिरि रामु गुर आयसु पाई ।
चले महीपति संख बजाई ॥
हरषे बिबुध बिलोकि बराता ।
बरषहिं सुमन सुमंगल दाता ॥

३ भयउ कोलाहल हय गय गाजे ।
ब्योम बरात बाजने बाजे ॥
सुर नर नारि सुमंगल गाईं ।
सरस राग बाजहिं सहनाईं ॥

४ घंट घंटि धुनि बरनि न जाहीं ।
सरव करहिं पाइक फहराहीं ॥
करहिं बिदूषक कौतुक नाना ।
हास कुसल कल गान सुजाना ॥

and brought them to the king—two cars   4
too beautiful for even Sharada to tell.
One vehicle was regally outfitted,
the other was a mass of fiery splendor.

On that glorious chariot, the lord of men   301
happily seated Sage Vasishtha,
then mounted the other himself,
invoking Shiva, guru, Gauri, and Ganesh.

Accompanied by Vasishtha, the king seemed   1
like Indra beside the guru of the gods.
He performed his lineage and Vedic rites
and, seeing that all were fully arrayed,
invoked Ram, and with his guru's leave,   2
the lord of earth blew a conch shell and set forth.
The gods rejoiced to see the procession
and rained down blossoms in blessing.
There was a great tumult of horses, elephants,   3
and instruments, in the sky and in the wedding party.
Divine and human women sang in blessing
while oboes warbled lovely melodies
and the clamor of bells beggared description.   4
Flag-waving marchers displayed acrobatics,[17]
and jesters performed numerous hijinks
with adept humor and charming song.

३०२ तुरग नचावहिं कुअँर बर अकनि मृदंग निसान ।
नागर नट चितवहिं चकित डगहिं न ताल बँधान ॥

१ बनइ न बरनत बनी बराता ।
होहिं सगुन सुंदर सुभदाता ॥
चारा चाषु बाम दिसि लेई ।
मनहुँ सकल मंगल कहि देई ॥

२ दाहिन काग सुखेत सुहावा ।
नकुल दरसु सब काहूँ पावा ॥
सानुकूल बह त्रिबिध बयारी ।
सघट सबाल आव बर नारी ॥

३ लोवा फिरि फिरि दरसु देखावा ।
सुरभी सनमुख सिसुहि पिआवा ॥
मृगमाला फिरि दाहिनि आई ।
मंगल गन जनु दीन्हि देखाई ॥

४ छेमकरी कह छेम बिसेषी ।
स्यामा बाम सुतरु पर देखी ॥
सनमुख आयउ दधि अरु मीना ।
कर पुस्तक दुइ बिप्र प्रबीना ॥

३०३ मंगलमय कल्यानमय अभिमत फल दातार ।
जनु सब साचे होन हित भए सगुन एक बार ॥

Young noblemen made their horses prance 302
to the sound of the many drums,
leaving expert dancers aghast to see
how they never missed the beat.

This wedding procession, indescribably grand, 1
met with lovely and auspicious omens.
To the left, a bluebird[18] bore a tuft of grass
as if announcing all good auguries.
To the right stood a crow in a fertile field 2
and everyone sighted a mongoose.
A cool, fragrant breeze fanned their faces[19]
as a handsome woman approached, bearing water and
    a babe.
A fox turned again and again to show itself, 3
while, just ahead, a cow nursed her calf.
A line of deer moved toward the right
as if to display an array of good omens.
A white-crowned hawk gave a gladdening cry,[20] 4
and, to the left, a blackbird appeared on a tree.
In front came a bearer of fish and curds,
and a pair of learned Brahmans, books in hand.

Abounding in auspiciousness and blessing, 303
yielding every desired fruit,
all fair portents appeared at once,
as if to reaffirm their own truth.

१ मंगल सगुन सुगम सब ताकें ।
सगुन ब्रह्म सुंदर सुत जाकें ॥
राम सरिस बरु दुलहिनि सीता ।
समधी दसरथु जनकु पुनीता ॥

२ सुनि अस ब्याहु सगुन सब नाचे ।
अब कीन्हे बिरंचि हम साँचे ॥
एहि बिधि कीन्ह बरात पयाना ।
हय गय गाजहिं हने निसाना ॥

३ आवत जानि भानुकुल केतू ।
सरितन्हि जनक बँधाए सेतू ॥
बीच बीच बर बास बनाए ।
सुरपुर सरिस संपदा छाए ॥

४ असन सयन बर बसन सुहाए ।
पावहिं सब निज निज मन भाए ॥
नित नूतन सुख लखि अनुकूले ।
सकल बरातिन्ह मंदिर भूले ॥

३०४ आवत जानि बरात बर सुनि गहगहे निसान ।
सजि गज रथ पदचर तुरग लेन चले अगवान ॥

१ कनक कलस भरि कोपर थारा ।
भाजन ललित अनेक प्रकारा ॥
भरे सुधा सम सब पकवाने ।
नाना भाँति न जाहिं बखाने ॥

All attributes of auspiciousness come easily to him   1
whose lovely son is the Absolute with attributes.[21]
With a bridegroom like Ram, a bride like Sita,
and noble fathers-in-law like Dasarath and Janak—
at word of such a wedding, all fair omens dance   2
proclaiming, "Now the creator has proven us true!"
And so the marriage party set forth
amid the thunder of horses, elephants, and great drums.
Knowing the solar monarch was coming,   3
Janak had built bridges over the rivers
and fine accommodations along the way,
outfitted to rival the gods' own city,
with superb food, bedding, and garments   4
to please each and every one in the party.
Beholding these endlessly new delights,
the marchers all forgot their own homes.

Learning of the procession's approach   304
and hearing the rumble of its drums,
elephants, cars, footmen, and horses, finely adorned,
went out to receive it.

Brimming gold pots, trays, and platters   1
and lovely vessels of every variety,
filled with fried treats fine as nectar,
of more kinds than can be told,

२ फल अनेक बर बस्तु सुहाई ।
हरषि भेंट हित भूप पठाई ॥
भूषन बसन महामनि नाना ।
खग मृग हय गय बहु बिधि जाना ॥

३ मंगल सगुन सुगंध सुहाए ।
बहुत भाँति महिपाल पठाए ॥
दधि चिउरा उपहार अपारा ।
भरि भरि काँवरि चले कहारा ॥

४ अगवानन्ह जब दीखि बराता ।
उर आनंदु पुलक भर गाता ॥
देखि बनाव सहित अगवाना ।
मुदित बरातिन्ह हने निसाना ॥

३०५ हरषि परसपर मिलन हित कछुक चले बगमेल ।
जनु आनंद समुद्र दुइ मिलत बिहाइ सुबेल ॥

१ बरषि सुमन सुर सुंदरि गावहिं ।
मुदित देव दुंदुभीं बजावहिं ॥
बस्तु सकल राखीं नृप आगें ।
बिनय कीन्हि तिन्ह अति अनुरागें ॥

२ प्रेम समेत रायँ सबु लीन्हा ।
भै बकसीस जाचकन्हि दीन्हा ॥
करि पूजा मान्यता बड़ाई ।
जनवासे कहुँ चले लवाई ॥

and fruits of all sorts, and superb goods—   2
the joyful king sent these as welcoming gifts.
Jewelry, garments, heaps of precious gems,
birds, deer, horses, elephants, all kinds of conveyances,
auspicious substances, and lovely perfumes   3
of many kinds were sent by that earth-protector.
Curds, crisped rice, and countless other guest-gifts
crammed bundles hanging from bearers' poles.
When these greeters sighted the procession   4
their hearts leapt and they trembled with joy,
and seeing the reception party's array
the happy marchers beat their kettledrums.

Overcome with the joy of meeting,   305
some from each party surged forward
to merge like two oceans of bliss
abandoning their shorelines.

Showering blossoms, celestial women sang   1
and the joyful gods beat sonorous drums.
Placing all their offerings before the king,
the greeters honored him with fervent love.
The monarch affectionately accepted it all   2
and distributed the bounty to supplicants.
Then, with greeting rites and lavish praise,
the party was brought to its lodgings.

३   बसन बिचित्र पाँवड़े परहीं ।
देखि धनदु धन मदु परिहरहीं ॥
अति सुंदर दीन्हेउ जनवासा ।
जहँ सब कहुँ सब भाँति सुपासा ॥

४   जानी सियँ बरात पुर आई ।
कछु निज महिमा प्रगटि जनाई ॥
हृदयँ सुमिरि सब सिद्धि बोलाईं ।
भूप पहुनई करन पठाईं ॥

३०६   सिधि सब सिय आयसु अकनि गईं जहाँ जनवास ।
लिएँ संपदा सकल सुख सुरपुर भोग बिलास ॥

१   निज निज बास बिलोकि बराती ।
सुर सुख सकल सुलभ सब भाँती ॥
बिभव भेद कछु कोउ न जाना ।
सकल जनक कर करहिं बखाना ॥

२   सिय महिमा रघुनायक जानी ।
हरषे हृदयँ हेतु पहिचानी ॥
पितु आगमनु सुनत दोउ भाई ।
हृदयँ न अति आनंदु अमाई ॥

३   सकुचन्ह कहि न सकत गुरु पाहीं ।
पितु दरसन लालचु मन माहीं ॥
बिस्वामित्र बिनय बड़ि देखी ।
उपजा उर संतोषु बिसेषी ॥

The ground was spread with multicolored cloths, 3
sight of which made the god of riches shed his pride.
Surpassingly beautiful were the guest quarters,
where all were provided with every comfort.
Knowing the wedding party had come to town, 4
Sita showed a little of her own majesty.
Inwardly summoning all the occult powers,[22]
she sent them to entertain Avadh's king.

Heeding Sita's command, all those powers 306
went to the wedding party's abode,
bearing every luxury and comfort
and the pleasures of Indra's paradise.

When they beheld their quarters, the guests 1
found every divine delight at hand.
None knew the secret behind this splendor
and all praised King Janak's largesse.
But the Raghu lord perceived Sita's power 2
and rejoiced at heart, recognizing her love.
The two brothers heard of their father's arrival
and could not contain their hearts' joy.
Though too shy to say it to the guru, 3
inwardly they longed to see their father.
Perceiving their great deference, Vishvamitra
experienced profound satisfaction.

४ हरषि बंधु दोउ हृदयँ लगाए ।
पुलक अंग अंबक जल छाए ॥
चले जहाँ दसरथु जनवासे ।
मनहुँ सरोबर तकेउ पिआसे ॥

३०७ भूप बिलोके जबहिं मुनि आवत सुतन्ह समेत ।
उठे हरषि सुखसिंधु महुँ चले थाह सी लेत ॥

१ मुनिहि दंडवत कीन्ह महीसा ।
बार बार पद रज धरि सीसा ॥
कौसिक राउ लिए उर लाई ।
कहि असीस पूछी कुसलाई ॥

२ पुनि दंडवत करत दोउ भाई ।
देखि नृपति उर सुखु न समाई ॥
सुत हियँ लाइ दुसह दुख मेटे ।
मृतक सरीर प्रान जनु भेंटे ॥

३ पुनि बसिष्ठ पद सिर तिन्ह नाए ।
प्रेम मुदित मुनिबर उर लाए ॥
बिप्र बृंद बंदे दुहुँ भाई ।
मनभावती असीसें पाईं ॥

४ भरत सहानुज कीन्ह प्रनामा ।
लिए उठाइ लाइ उर रामा ॥
हरषे लखन देखि दोउ भ्राता ।
मिले प्रेम परिपूरित गाता ॥

He drew both brothers to his breast   4
and shivered with joy, tears blurring his eyes.
They set out for Dasarath's lodgings,
like a lake that has sighted a thirsting man.[23]

When the king saw the sage   307
approaching with his sons,
he rose in delight and came forward
like one feeling for a foothold in a sea of joy.

The lord of earth fell prostrate before the sage,   1
repeatedly taking the dust of his feet on his head.
Kaushik drew up the king, embraced him,
and gave a blessing, inquiring of his welfare.
Then the brothers made their prostration,   2
and at the sight, the king's heart overflowed with joy.
Hugging his sons, he erased his anguish
like a corpse receiving the breath of life.
Then the boys bowed at Vasishtha's feet   3
and the great sage embraced them with delight.
Both brothers saluted the assembly of Brahmans
and obtained their encouraging blessings.
Bharat paid homage with his younger brother,   4
and Ram lifted both into his embrace.
Lakshman looked joyfully at both brothers
and took them in his loving arms.

३०८ पुरजन परिजन जातिजन जाचक मंत्री मीत ।
मिले जथाबिधि सबहि प्रभु परम कृपाल बिनीत ॥

१ रामहि देखि बरात जुड़ानी ।
प्रीति कि रीति न जाति बखानी ॥
नृप समीप सोहहिं सुत चारी ।
जनु धन धरमादिक तनुधारी ॥

२ सुतन्ह समेत दसरथहि देखी ।
मुदित नगर नर नारि बिसेषी ॥
सुमन बरिसि सुर हनहिं निसाना ।
नाकनटीं नाचहिं करि गाना ॥

३ सतानंद अरु बिप्र सचिव गन ।
मागध सूत बिदुष बंदीजन ॥
सहित बरात राउ सनमाना ।
आयसु मागि फिरे अगवाना ॥

४ प्रथम बरात लगन तें आई ।
तातें पुर प्रमोदु अधिकाई ॥
ब्रह्मानंदु लोग सब लहहीं ।
बढ़हुँ दिवस निसि बिधि सन कहहीं ॥

३०९ रामु सीय सोभा अवधि सुकृत अवधि दोउ राज ।
जहँ तहँ पुरजन कहहिं अस मिलि नर नारि समाज ॥

Townspeople, clan and caste members,   308
dependents, courtiers, and friends—
the Lord, most merciful and modest,
appropriately greeted one and all.

The sight of Ram comforted the wedding party,[24]   1
and their expressions of love elude description.
With the lord of men, his four sons shone
as if all the aims of life had taken form.[25]
Seeing Dasarath together with his sons   2
gave the townsmen and women rare delight.
The gods rained flowers and beat their drums
while celestial courtesans danced and sang.
Sage Shatanand, Brahmans, royal ministers,   3
bards, singers, scholars, and panegyrists
paid homage to the king and his party.
Then, with his leave, the greeters returned.
The party's arrival, well before the wedding date,   4
caused great rejoicing in the city,[26]
and everyone, savoring divine bliss,
begged God to lengthen days and nights.

"Ram and Sita are the epitome of beauty,   309
the two kings, the epitome of merit!"
So the townspeople, men and women,
said among themselves wherever they met.

१ जनक सुकृत मूरति बैदेही ।
दसरथ सुकृत रामु धरें देही ॥
इन्ह सम काहुँ न सिव अवराधे ।
काहुँ न इन्ह समान फल लाधे ॥

२ इन्ह सम कोउ न भयउ जग माहीं ।
है नहिं कतहूँ होनेउ नाहीं ॥
हम सब सकल सुकृत कै रासी ।
भए जग जनमि जनकपुर बासी ॥

३ जिन्ह जानकी राम छबि देखी ।
को सुकृती हम सरिस बिसेषी ॥
पुनि देखब रघुबीर बिआहू ।
लेब भली बिधि लोचन लाहू ॥

४ कहहिं परसपर कोकिलबयनीं ।
एहि बिआहँ बड़ लाभु सुनयनीं ॥
बड़ें भाग बिधि बात बनाई ।
नयन अतिथि होइहहिं दोउ भाई ॥

३१० बारहिं बार सनेह बस जनक बोलाउब सीय ।
लेन आइहहिं बंधु दोउ कोटि काम कमनीय ॥

१ बिबिध भाँति होइहि पहुनाई ।
प्रिय न काहि अस सासुर माई ॥
तब तब राम लखनहि निहारी ।
होइहहिं सब पुर लोग सुखारी ॥

244

"Janak's merit has taken shape as Vaidehi   1
and Dasarath's is embodied in Ram.
None has worshiped Shiva like these two
nor obtained such fruit as they.
There has been no one like them in this world,   2
nor is there now, nor will there ever be!
And we all, too, must have amassed much merit
to take earthly birth as dwellers in Janakpur
and to have seen the beauty of Janaki and Ram.   3
What pious soul can compare with us?
And soon we will watch the Raghu hero's wedding
and reap the full reward of having eyes!"
Sweet-voiced women said to one another,   4
"My dear, this wedding is such good fortune!
What luck that fate has arranged
for these two brothers to linger before our eyes.[27]

Time and again, compelled by his love,   310
King Janak will surely send for Sita,
and the two brothers, comely as a billion Kamas,
will come to fetch her back.

They will receive abundant hospitality,   1
and, dears, who wouldn't love such in-laws?
Then, each time, gazing at Ram and Lakshman
how we townsfolk will all rejoice!

२ सखि जस राम लखन कर जोटा ।
तैसेइ भूप संग दुइ ढोटा ॥
स्याम गौर सब अंग सुहाए ।
ते सब कहहिं देखि जे आए ॥

३ कहा एक मैं आजु निहारे ।
जनु बिरंचि निज हाथ सँवारे ॥
भरतु रामही की अनुहारी ।
सहसा लखि न सकहिं नर नारी ॥

४ लखनु सत्रुसूदनु एकरूपा ।
नख सिख ते सब अंग अनूपा ॥
मन भावहिं मुख बरनि न जाहीं ।
उपमा कहुँ त्रिभुवन कोउ नाहीं ॥

५ उपमा न कोउ कह दास तुलसी
कतहुँ कबि कोबिद कहैं ।
बल बिनय बिद्या सील सोभा
सिंधु इन्ह से एइ अहैं ॥
पुर नारि सकल पसारि अंचल
बिधिहि बचन सुनावहीं ।
ब्याहिअहुँ चारिउ भाइ एहिं पुर
हम सुमंगल गावहीं ॥

३११ कहहिं परस्पर नारि बारि बिलोचन पुलक तन ।
सखि सबु करब पुरारि पुन्य पयोनिधि भूप दोउ ॥

And friend, just as Ram and Lakshman are a pair, 2
a matching set of lads came with the king,
dark and fair too, pleasing in every limb.
So say all who have seen them."
Another said, "Yes, I saw them today, 3
and they seem like the creator's own handiwork.
Bharat looks so exactly like Ram
that at a glance none could distinguish them.
And Lakshman's double is Shatrughna, 4
as matchlessly fair from head to foot.
More charming than speech can describe,
none in all three worlds compares with them."

They have no compeer anywhere— 5
so says servant Tulsi, echoing poets and savants.
Seas of strength, humility, wisdom, virtue, and beauty,
they resemble but themselves.
Holding out their sari borders,[28] all the townswomen
entreated the maker of fate:
"May all four brothers marry in this very city,
and may we sing at their nuptials!"

With tear-filled eyes and trembling limbs, 311
the women said to one another,
"Friend, Lord Shiva will arrange all this,
for the two kings are oceans of merit."

१ एहि बिधि सकल मनोरथ करहीं ।
आनँद उमगि उमगि उर भरहीं ॥
जे नृप सीय स्वयंबर आए ।
देखि बंधु सब तिन्ह सुख पाए ॥

२ कहत राम जसु बिसद बिसाला ।
निज निज भवन गए महिपाला ॥
गए बीति कछु दिन एहि भाँती ।
प्रमुदित पुरजन सकल बराती ॥

३ मंगल मूल लगन दिनु आवा ।
हिम रितु अगहनु मासु सुहावा ॥
ग्रह तिथि नखतु जोगु बर बारू ।
लगन सोधि बिधि कीन्ह बिचारू ॥

४ पठै दीन्हि नारद सन सोई ।
गनी जनक के गनकन्ह जोई ॥
सुनी सकल लोगन्ह यह बाता ।
कहहिं जोतिषी आहिं बिधाता ॥

३१२ धेनुधूरि बेला बिमल सकल सुमंगल मूल ।
बिप्रन्ह कहेउ बिदेह सन जानि सगुन अनुकूल ॥

१ उपरोहितहि कहेउ नरनाहा ।
अब बिलंब कर कारनु काहा ॥
सतानंद तब सचिव बोलाए ।
मंगल सकल साजि सब ल्याए ॥

In this way, they all made their wishes,   1
bliss welling up to fill their hearts.
Kings who had come for Sita's bridegroom rite
rejoiced, too, at seeing all the brothers.
Proclaiming Ram's pure fame and grandeur,   2
those earth-protectors left for their homes.
Thus some days passed, to the delight
of the townspeople and the whole wedding party.
Then came the appointed day, root of blessing,   3
in the pleasant winter month of Agahan,[29]
when planets, asterisms, and conjunctions were ideal,
as carefully calculated by the creator,
who sent word of it through Sage Narad.   4
Janak's astrologers had reckoned the same,
and when the people heard this, they declared,
"Our astrologers are like Brahma himself!"

It was the sacred hour of late afternoon,[30]   312
source of all well-being.
Perceiving favorable omens,
the Brahmans informed King Videha.

The lord of men told his family priest,   1
"Now, why delay any longer?"
Then Shatanand summoned the ministers
who brought all auspicious materials.

२ संख निसान पनव बहु बाजे ।
मंगल कलस सगुन सुभ साजे ॥
सुभग सुआसिनि गावहिं गीता ।
करहिं बेद धुनि बिप्र पुनीता ॥

३ लेन चले सादर एहि भाँती ।
गए जहाँ जनवास बराती ॥
कोसलपति कर देखि समाजू ।
अति लघु लाग तिन्हहि सुरराजू ॥

४ भयउ समउ अब धारिअ पाऊ ।
यह सुनि परा निसानहिं घाऊ ॥
गुरहि पूछि करि कुल बिधि राजा ।
चले संग मुनि साधु समाजा ॥

३१३ भाग्य बिभव अवधेस कर देखि देव ब्रह्मादि ।
लगे सराहन सहस मुख जानि जनम निज बादि ॥

१ सुरन्ह सुमंगल अवसरु जाना ।
बरषहिं सुमन बजाइ निसाना ॥
सिव ब्रह्मादिक बिबुध बरूथा ।
चढ़े बिमानन्हि नाना जूथा ॥

२ प्रेम पुलक तन हृदयँ उछाहू ।
चले बिलोकन राम बिआहू ॥
देखि जनकपुरु सुर अनुरागे ।
निज निज लोक सबहिं लघु लागे ॥

Conchs sounded, and drums big and small,   2
as sacred vessels and substances were arrayed.
Lovely married women began to sing
and pious Brahmans intoned the Veda.
Thus they all went reverently to bring   3
the bridegroom's party from their lodgings.
Beholding the entourage of Kosala's king,
Indra's glory seemed trifling to them.
They said, "Now it is time to proceed,"   4
and at once, mighty drums were sounded.
Consulting his guru, the king performed the clan rites
and went forth with a host of sages and sadhus.

Seeing the splendor and fortune of the lord of Avadh,   313
Brahma and the other gods
praised him with a thousand voices,
reckoning their own status as worthless.

The gods, knowing the blessed hour had come,   1
showered blossoms and sounded deep drums.
Shiva, Brahma, and the divine hosts
boarded an array of celestial vehicles.
Their bodies flushed with love, hearts eager,   2
they set out to witness the wedding of Ram.
Sighting Janakpur, the gods were infatuated
and all felt their own realms to be paltry.

३ चितवहिं चकित बिचित्र बिताना ।
रचना सकल अलौकिक नाना ॥
नगर नारि नर रूप निधाना ।
सुघर सुधरम सुसील सुजाना ॥

४ तिन्हहि देखि सब सुर सुरनारीं ।
भए नखत जनु बिधु उजिआरीं ॥
बिधिहि भयउ आचरजु बिसेषी ।
निज करनी कछु कतहुँ न देखी ॥

३१४ सिवँ समुझाए देव सब जनि आचरज भुलाहु ।
हृदयँ बिचारहु धीर धरि सिय रघुबीर बिआहु ॥

१ जिन्ह कर नामु लेत जग माहीं ।
सकल अमंगल मूल नसाहीं ॥
करतल होहिं पदारथ चारी ।
तेइ सिय रामु कहेउ कामारी ॥

२ एहि बिधि संभु सुरन्ह समुझावा ।
पुनि आगें बर बसह चलावा ॥
देवन्ह देखे दसरथु जाता ।
महामोद मन पुलकित गाता ॥

३ साधु समाज संग महिदेवा ।
जनु तनु धरें करहिं सुख सेवा ॥
सोहत साथ सुभग सुत चारी ।
जनु अपबरग सकल तनुधारी ॥

252

They gazed in awe at the wondrous pavilion   3
with its unearthly adornments,
and at the wealth and beauty of the townspeople—
all elegant, pious, polite, and learned.
Seeing them, the gods and their women   4
faded like stars when the moon waxes bright.
Brahma was especially abashed,
for nowhere did he spy his own handiwork.

Shiva admonished all the gods,   314
"Do not be lost in wonder. Calm yourselves
and ponder within: it is the wedding
of Sita and the Raghu champion,

by the utterance of whose name   1
all impurities are severed at the root
and the four aims fall into one's palm—
that very Sita-Ram."[31] So Kama's foe declared,
and having thus instructed the celestials,   2
Shambhu urged his great bull forward.
Then the deities saw Dasarath proceeding,
his body flushed with supreme delight,
together with throngs of sadhus and priests,   3
as if pure joy had taken form in his service.
With him shone his four handsome sons,
as though embodying all ultimate good,[32]

४ मरकत कनक बरन बर जोरी ।
देखि सुरन्ह भै प्रीति न थोरी ॥
पुनि रामहि बिलोकि हियँ हरषे ।
नृपहि सराहि सुमन तिन्ह बरषे ॥

३१५ राम रूपु नख सिख सुभग बारहिं बार निहारि ।
पुलक गात लोचन सजल उमा समेत पुरारि ॥

१ केकि कंठ दुति स्यामल अंगा ।
तड़ित बिनिंदक बसन सुरंगा ॥
ब्याह बिभूषन बिबिध बनाए ।
मंगल सब सब भाँति सुहाए ॥

२ सरद बिमल बिधु बदनु सुहावन ।
नयन नवल राजीव लजावन ॥
सकल अलौकिक सुंदरताई ।
कहि न जाइ मनहीं मन भाई ॥

३ बंधु मनोहर सोहहिं संगा ।
जात नचावत चपल तुरंगा ॥
राजकुअँर बर बाजि देखावहिं ।
बंस प्रसंसक बिरिद सुनावहिं ॥

४ जेहि तुरंग पर रामु बिराजे ।
गति बिलोकि खगनायकु लाजे ॥
कहि न जाइ सब भाँति सुहावा ।
बाजि बेषु जनु काम बनावा ॥

two pairs, each of emerald and golden hue.   4
Seeing them, the gods were smitten with love.
Then they looked at Ram with happy hearts,
praising the king and raining down blossoms.

Gazing time and again at Ram's form   315
and at the beauty of his every limb,
Uma and her lord shivered in ecstasy
and their eyes filled with tears.

His dark limbs radiant as a peacock's throat,   1
in yellow garb that outshone lightning,
and richly adorned with wedding jewelry,
utterly auspicious and lovely,
with face bright as the autumn moon   2
and eyes that embarrass day's new lotuses—
his beauty, utterly transcendent
and unutterable, delights the innermost heart.[33]
His handsome brothers accompanied him,   3
artfully maneuvering their spirited horses.
The princes showed off their fine mounts
as the royal bards chanted heroic lays.
The horse on which Ram was mounted   4
showed swiftness to shame the king of birds*
and a beauty entirely beyond description,
as though Kama had taken equine form.

---

* Garuda, Vishnu's mount.

५　जनु बाजि बेषु बनाइ मनसिजु
राम हित अति सोहई ।
आपनें बय बल रूप गुन गति
सकल भुवन बिमोहई ॥
जगमगत जीनु जराव जोति
सुमोति मनि मानिक लगे ।
किंकिनि ललाम लगामु ललित
बिलोकि सुर नर मुनि ठगे ॥

३१६　प्रभु मनसहिं लयलीन मनु चलत बाजि छबि पाव ।
भूषित उड़गन तड़ित घनु जनु बर बरहि नचाव ॥

१　जेहिं बर बाजि रामु असवारा ।
तेहि सारदउ न बरनै पारा ॥
संकरु राम रूप अनुरागे ।
नयन पंचदस अति प्रिय लागे ॥
२　हरि हित सहित रामु जब जोहे ।
रमा समेत रमापति मोहे ॥
निरखि राम छबि बिधि हरषाने ।
आठइ नयन जानि पछिताने ॥
३　सुर सेनप उर बहुत उछाहू ।
बिधि ते डेवढ़ लोचन लाहू ॥
रामहि चितव सुरेस सुजाना ।
गौतम श्रापु परम हित माना ॥

As if the mind-born one had taken, for Ram's sake,   5
the guise of a glorious stallion,
his youth, strength, beauty, excellence,
and swift gait captivated all the worlds.
His jeweled saddle, set with fine pearls,
diamonds, and rubies, shimmered with light,
and the sight of his exquisitely belled bridle
robbed gods, men, and sages of their wits.

Guided by the Lord's inner prompting, the horse   316
moved gracefully, as though
a rain cloud wreathed in stars and lightning
was making a fine peacock dance.

That horse on which Ram was riding   1
beggared Sharada's powers of description.
Shankar was captivated by Ram's beauty
and well pleased to possess fifteen eyes.[34]
When Hari gazed with affection at Ram   2
both he and his consort were entranced.[35]
Seeing Ram's grace, Brahma grew happy,
though he regretted having but eight eyes,
and Skanda, the gods' general, was elated,   3
since in sight's abundance he bested Brahma by half.[36]
Looking at Ram, Indra sagely reflected
on the great good fortune of Gautam's curse.[37]

४ देव सकल सुरपतिहि सिहाहीं ।
आजु पुरंदर सम कोउ नाहीं ॥
मुदित देवगन रामहि देखी ।
नृपसमाज दुहुँ हरषु बिसेषी ॥

५ अति हरषु राजसमाज दुहु दिसि
दुंदुभीं बाजहिं घनी ।
बरषहिं सुमन सुर हरषि कहि
जय जयति जय रघुकुलमनी ॥
एहि भाँति जानि बरात आवत
बाजने बहु बाजहीं ।
रानी सुआसिनि बोलि परिछनि
हेतु मंगल साजहीं ॥

३१७ सजि आरती अनेक बिधि मंगल सकल सँवारि ।
चलीं मुदित परिछनि करन गजगामिनि बर नारि ॥

१ बिधुबदनीं सब सब मृगलोचनि ।
सब निज तन छबि रति मदु मोचनि ॥
पहिरें बरन बरन बर चीरा ।
सकल बिभूषन सजें सरीरा ॥

२ सकल सुमंगल अंग बनाएँ ।
करहिं गान कलकंठि लजाएँ ॥

All the celestials were in envy of their king,   4
and said, "None is as lucky as Indra today!"
The assembled gods gazed happily at Ram,
and incomparable joy suffused both royal parties.

On each side, the royal cohorts rejoiced,   5
as great kettledrums thundered
and the happy gods threw flowers, shouting
"Victory to the jewel of the Raghus!"
Knowing the procession was approaching,
musicians sounded diverse instruments
and the queen summoned married women
to prepare the welcoming ceremony.[38]

Adorning the worship tray   317
with all sorts of pure and auspicious things,
those shapely women happily went
to perform the greeting rite.

All of them were fair-faced, all doe-eyed,   1
all of a comeliness to shame Kama's consort,
dressed in gorgeous fabrics of many hues,
and all adorned, head to toe, with jewelry.
Thus made auspicious in every limb,   2
they sang in voices to disgrace a cuckoo.

कंकन किंकिनि नूपुर बाजहिं ।
चालि बिलोकि काम गज लाजहिं ॥

३ बाजहिं बाजने बिबिध प्रकारा ।
नभ अरु नगर सुमंगलचारा ॥
सची सारदा रमा भवानी ।
जे सुरतिय सुचि सहज सयानी ॥

४ कपट नारि बर बेष बनाई ।
मिलीं सकल रनिवासहिं जाई ॥
करहिं गान कल मंगल बानीं ।
हरष बिबस सब काहुँ न जानीं ॥

५ को जान केहि आनंद बस सब
ब्रह्मु बर परिछन चली ।
कल गान मधुर निसान बरषहिं
सुमन सुर सोभा भली ॥
आनंदकंदु बिलोकि दूलहु
सकल हियँ हरषित भई ।
अंभोज अंबक अंबु उमगि
सुअंग पुलकावलि छई ॥

३१८ जो सुखु भा सिय मातु मन देखि राम बर बेषु ।
सो न सकहिं कहि कलप सत सहस सारदा सेषु ॥

With tinkling bangles, anklets, and waist bells,
their swaying gait put Love's elephant to shame.[39]
Countless musical instruments sounded   3
as sky and city echoed with benedictions.
Shachi, Sharada, Lakshmi, Bhavani,[40]
and other divine consorts, pure and wise,
disguising themselves as beautiful women   4
went to join those of the inner palace,
singing auspicious songs in sweet voices.
Distracted by joy, no one noticed them.

But who noticed anyone? Overcome with joy,   5
all went to welcome God as bridegroom.
Lilting songs and soft, deep drums, a rain
of heavenly flowers—what immense beauty!
Beholding that bridegroom, the very source of bliss,
all the women's hearts rejoiced,
their lotus eyes brimmed with tears,
and their lovely limbs trembled in ecstasy.

The heartfelt joy of Sita's mother,   318
seeing Ram in bridegroom's guise,
could not be told in a hundred aeons
by a thousand Sharadas and serpent kings.

१ नयन नीरु हटि मंगल जानी ।
परिछनि करहिं मुदित मन रानी ॥
बेद बिहित अरु कुल आचारू ।
कीन्ह भली बिधि सब ब्यवहारू ॥

२ पंच सबद धुनि मंगल गाना ।
पट पाँवड़े परहिं बिधि नाना ॥
करि आरती अरघु तिन्ह दीन्हा ।
राम गमनु मंडप तब कीन्हा ॥

३ दसरथु सहित समाज बिराजे ।
बिभव बिलोकि लोकपति लाजे ॥
समयँ समयँ सुर बरषहिं फूला ।
सांति पढ़हिं महिसुर अनुकूला ॥

४ नभ अरु नगर कोलाहल होई ।
आपनि पर कछु सुनइ न कोई ॥
एहि बिधि रामु मंडपहिं आए ।
अरघु देइ आसन बैठाए ॥

५ बैठारि आसन आरती करि
निरखि बरु सुखु पावहीं ।
मनि बसन भूषन भूरि वारहिं
नारि मंगल गावहीं ॥
ब्रह्मादि सुरबर बिप्र बेष
बनाइ कौतुक देखहीं ।

Checking her tears at this blessed juncture,   1
the queen joyously performed the lamp greeting,
with Vedic injunctions and family customs
all fully and correctly observed.
Fivefold instruments and chants sounded, amid songs of   2
    blessing
as variegated carpets were spread in welcome.
Greeted with sacred lamp and guest libation,[41]
Ram entered the marriage pavilion.
So glorious was Dasarath and his entourage   3
that the sight put to shame the world guardians.
As the celestials repeatedly rained blossoms,
Brahmans recited a peace-giving benediction.
Such tumult filled the sky and city   4
that none could hear himself or another.
And so Ram entered the marriage pavilion,
was welcomed with sacred water, and was seated.

Seated on a fine couch, greeted with lamps—   5
the sight of that bridegroom gave delight
to the women, singing in blessing,
who offered him heaps of gems, clothes, and jewelry.
Taking form as Brahmans, Brahma
and the great gods witnessed the spectacle

263

अवलोकि रघुकुल कमल रबि छबि
सुफल जीवन लेखहीं ॥

३१९   नाऊ बारी भाट नट राम निछावरि पाइ ।
मुदित असीसहिं नाइ सिर हरषु न हृदयँ समाइ ॥

१   मिले जनकु दसरथु अति प्रीतीं ।
करि बैदिक लौकिक सब रीतीं ॥
मिलत महा दोउ राज बिराजे ।
उपमा खोजि खोजि कबि लाजे ॥

२   लही न कतहुँ हारि हियँ मानी ।
इन्ह सम एइ उपमा उर आनी ॥
सामध देखि देव अनुरागे ।
सुमन बरषि जसु गावन लागे ॥

३   जगु बिरंचि उपजावा जब तें ।
देखे सुने ब्याह बहु तब तें ॥
सकल भाँति सम साजु समाजू ।
सम समधी देखे हम आजू ॥

४   देव गिरा सुनि सुंदर साँची ।
प्रीति अलौकिक दुहु दिसि माची ॥
देत पाँवड़े अरघु सुहाए ।
सादर जनकु मंडपहिं ल्याए ॥

and, seeing the beauty of that sun of the Raghu-lotuses,
reckoned their lives fulfilled.

Barbers, artisans, bards, and entertainers   319
received Ram's guest-gift[42]
and gave their blessings, heads bowed
and hearts overflowing with happiness.

Meeting with much affection, Janak and Dasarath   1
performed all Vedic and customary rites.
The encounter of these two great kings
makes embarrassed poets scramble for a simile
and, finding none, admit defeat, musing,   2
"Their likeness is only to themselves!"[43]
The sight of the two fathers[44] entranced the gods,
who rained blossoms and sang their praises.
"Ever since Brahma brought forth the world,   3
we have seen and heard of weddings galore,
but two clans so fully comparable in splendor
and with patriarchs so equal, we behold only today."
Hearing the gods' infallible testimony,   4
an unearthly love arose in both parties.
Crossing splendid carpets, giving the guest libation,
Janak reverently brought Dasarath into the pavilion.

५   मंडपु बिलोकि बिचित्र रचनाँ
रुचिरताँ मुनि मन हरे ।
निज पानि जनक सुजान सब कहुँ
आनि सिंघासन धरे ॥
कुल इष्ट सरिस बसिष्ठ पूजे
बिनय करि आसिष लही ।
कौसिकहि पूजत परम प्रीति
कि रीति तौ न परै कही ॥

३२०   बामदेव आदिक रिषय पूजे मुदित महीस ।
दिए दिब्य आसन सबहि सब सन लही असीस ॥

१   बहुरि कीन्हि कोसलपति पूजा ।
जानि ईस सम भाउ न दूजा ॥
कीन्हि जोरि कर बिनय बड़ाई ।
कहि निज भाग्य बिभव बहुताई ॥

२   पूजे भूपति सकल बराती ।
समधी सम सादर सब भाँती ॥
आसन उचित दिए सब काहू ।
कहौं काह मुख एक उछाहू ॥

३   सकल बरात जनक सनमानी ।
दान मान बिनती बर बानी ॥
बिधि हरि हरु दिसिपति दिनराऊ ।
जे जानहिं रघुबीर प्रभाऊ ॥

Seeing the pavilion's marvelous design and beauty,   5
even sages were captivated.
With his own hands, wise King Janak
set out splendid seats for all the guests.
Humbly saluting Vasishtha like his own clan-deity,
he received his blessing,
and the gracious love with which
he venerated Vishvamitra beggars description.

Joyfully paying homage to Vamadeva[45]   320
and the host of sages, the lord of men
offered them all sanctified seats
and received their blessings.

Then he venerated the king of Kosala,   1
reckoning him fully equal to Shiva.
Hands joined in supplication, he praised him,
citing his own glorious good fortune.
The king honored each of the entourage   2
with the same respect given to Ram's father,
and offered each one a suitable seat
with an ardor my one tongue cannot express.
Janak paid homage to the whole party   3
with gifts and eloquently humble praise.
Brahma, Hari, Hara, the world guardians, and sun—
gods who grasp the Raghu hero's true glory[46]—

४   कपट बिप्र बर बेष बनाएँ ।
     कौतुक देखहिं अति सचु पाएँ ॥
     पूजे जनक देव सम जानें ।
     दिए सुआसन बिनु पहिचानें ॥

५   पहिचान को केहि जान सबहि
     अपान सुधि भोरी भई ।
     आनंद कंदु बिलोकि दूलहु
     उभय दिसि आनँदमई ॥
     सुर लखे राम सुजान पूजे
     मानसिक आसन दए ।
     अवलोकि सीलु सुभाउ प्रभु को
     बिबुध मन प्रमुदित भए ॥

३२१ रामचंद्र मुख चंद्र छबि लोचन चारु चकोर ।
     करत पान सादर सकल प्रेमु प्रमोदु न थोर ॥

१   समउ बिलोकि बसिष्ठ बोलाए ।
     सादर सतानंदु सुनि आए ॥
     बेगि कुआँरि अब आनहु जाई ।
     चले मुदित मुनि आयसु पाई ॥
२   रानी सुनि उपरोहित बानी ।
     प्रमुदित सखिन्ह समेत सयानी ॥

268

took on the disguise of noble Brahmans   4
for the bliss of beholding the grand spectacle.
Janak honored them, considering them divine,
and, without recognizing them, gave them fine seats.

But who could recognize anyone,   5
when everyone lost even self-awareness?
At the sight of the groom who is the root of bliss,
bliss pervaded both parties.
But all-knowing Ram marked the immortals,
and mentally worshiped and seated them,
and perceiving the Lord's innate magnanimity,
the gods rejoiced in their hearts.

Ram's face was a radiant moon, and the eyes of all,   321
lovely *cakor* birds.
Reverently sipping its beams, they imbibed
love's exultation to the full.

Marking the moment, Vasishtha called   1
for Shatanand, who respectfully appeared.
"Go quickly now and bring the princess!"
With this sacred charge, he happily left.
At the family priest's message, the queen   2
and her companions rejoiced.

बिप्र बधू कुल बृद्ध बोलाईं ।
करि कुल रीति सुमंगल गाईं ॥

३ नारि बेष जे सुर बर बामा ।
सकल सुभायँ सुंदरी स्यामा ॥
तिन्हहि देखि सुखु पावहिं नारीं ।
बिनु पहिचानि प्रानहु ते प्यारीं ॥

४ बार बार सनमानहिं रानी ।
उमा रमा सारद सम जानी ॥
सीय सँवारि समाजु बनाई ।
मुदित मंडपहिं चलीं लवाई ॥

५ चलि ल्याइ सीतहि सखीं सादर
सजि सुमंगल भामिनीं ।
नवसप्त साजें सुंदरीं सब
मत्त कुंजर गामिनीं ॥
कल गान सुनि मुनि ध्यान त्यागहिं
काम कोकिल लाजहीं ।
मंजीर नूपुर कलित कंकन
ताल गति बर बाजहीं ॥

३२२ सोहति बनिता बृंद महुँ सहज सुहावनि सीय ।
छबि ललना गन मध्य जनु सुषमा तिय कमनीय ॥

270

She bade Brahman wives and women elders of the clan
perform family rites with songs of blessing.
The goddesses who had taken human form   3
were all naturally youthful and comely.
Seeing them, the women felt delight
and deep intimacy, yet without knowing them.
The queen greatly honored them   4
as equal to Uma, Lakshmi, and Sharada.
Assembling around Sita and adorning her,
the women joyfully escorted her to the pavilion.

Auspiciously adorned, Sita was reverently brought   5
by friends and lovely matrons
graced with the sixteen kinds of ornament
and swaying with the gait of elephants.
Their sweet song drew sages from meditation
and shamed the love god's cuckoos,
as the pleasing sound of their anklets, bracelets,
and bells followed its rhythm.

Glowing within that concourse of women,   322
Sita with her inborn loveliness
seemed like supreme feminine allure,
set amid a bevy of beauties.

१ सिय सुंदरता बरनि न जाई ।
लघु मति बहुत मनोहरताई ॥
आवत दीखि बरातिन्ह सीता ।
रूप रासि सब भाँति पुनीता ॥

२ सबहि मनहिं मन किए प्रनामा ।
देखि राम भए पूरनकामा ॥
हरषे दसरथ सुतन्ह समेता ।
कहि न जाइ उर आनँदु जेता ॥

३ सुर प्रनामु करि बरिसहिं फूला ।
मुनि असीस धुनि मंगल मूला ॥
गान निसान कोलाहलु भारी ।
प्रेम प्रमोद मगन नर नारी ॥

४ एहि बिधि सीय मंडपहिं आई ।
प्रमुदित सांति पढ़हिं मुनिराई ॥
तेहि अवसर कर बिधि ब्यवहारू ।
दुहुँ कुलगुर सब कीन्ह अचारू ॥

५ आचारु करि गुर गौरि गनपति
मुदित बिप्र पुजावहीं ।
सुर प्रगटि पूजा लेहिं देहिं
असीस अति सुखु पावहीं ॥

Sita's beauty cannot be described,   1
for my wit is as slight as her charm is vast.
The groom's party saw Sita approaching,
the epitome of loveliness and purity.
All paid homage to her inwardly   2
and, looking at Ram, felt their wishes fulfilled.[47]
Dasarath rejoiced along with his sons,
feeling heartfelt bliss that words cannot tell.
The celestials saluted with a shower of petals   3
and the sages chanted their sanctifying blessings.
Amid a tumult of song and drumbeat
all men and women were lost in love's rapture.
So Sita entered the pavilion   4
and the delighted sages began the chant of peace.
All obligatory Vedic and customary rites
were carried out by the two family priests.

The gurus performed the rites   5
as Brahmans joyously invoked Gauri and Ganesh,
and the gods, appearing to receive offerings
and bestow blessings, felt utter joy.

273

मधुपर्क मंगल द्रब्य जो जेहि
समय मुनि मन महुँ चहैं ।
भरे कनक कोपर कलस सो तब
लिएहिं परिचारक रहैं ॥

६   कुल रीति प्रीति समेत रबि कहि
देत सबु सादर कियो ।
एहि भाँति देव पुजाइ सीतहि
सुभग सिंघासनु दियो ॥
सिय राम अवलोकनि परसपर
प्रेमु काहुँ न लखि परै ।
मन बुद्धि बर बानी अगोचर
प्रगट कबि कैसें करै ॥

३२३   होम समय तनु धरि अनलु अति सुख आहुति लेहिं ।
बिप्र बेष धरि बेद सब कहि बिबाह बिधि देहिं ॥

१   जनक पाटमहिषी जग जानी ।
सीय मातु किमि जाइ बखानी ॥
सुजसु सुकृत सुख सुंदरताई ।
सब समेटि बिधि रची बनाई ॥

२   समउ जानि मुनिबरन्ह बोलाईं ।
सुनत सुआसिनि सादर ल्याईं ॥
जनक बाम दिसि सोह सुनयना ।
हिमगिरि संग बनी जनु मयना ॥

Whatever sacred substances were needed,[48]
whenever the sages thought of them,
were instantly brought in brimming gold pots
and platters by attentive servants.
The lineage rites were done with reverence,   6
lovingly directed by the sun god himself,[49]
and having propitiated the gods, they placed Sita
on a magnificent lion-seat.
The loving look exchanged by Sita and Ram
was beyond anyone's ability to comprehend,
eluding heart, intellect, or even the fairest speech—
how can any poet reveal it?

At the time of the fire offering, Agni took form   323
to gladly receive the oblation,
and all the Vedas, in Brahman guise,
guided every stage of the nuptials.

Janak's queen consort, of world renown,   1
and mother of Sita—how to magnify her?
For in her, fame, merit, bliss, and beauty
had all been artfully combined by the creator.
At the auspicious moment, the sages sent for her   2
and she was brought by reverent matrons.[50]
Seated at Janak's left, Sunayana shone
like Maina alongside King Himalaya.

३ कनक कलस मनि कोपर रूरे ।
सुचि सुगंध मंगल जल पूरे ॥
निज कर मुदित रायँ अरु रानी ।
धरे राम के आगें आनी ॥

४ पढ़हिं बेद मुनि मंगल बानी ।
गगन सुमन झरि अवसरु जानी ॥
बरु बिलोकि दंपति अनुरागे ।
पाय पुनीत पखारन लागे ॥

५ लागे पखारन पाय पंकज
प्रेम तन पुलकावली ।
नभ नगर गान निसान जय
धुनि उमगि जनु चहुँ दिसि चली ॥
जे पद सरोज मनोज अरि उर
सर सदैव बिराजहीं ।
जे सकृत सुमिरत बिमलता मन
सकल कलि मल भाजहीं ॥

६ जे परसि मुनिबनिता लही गति
रही जो पातकमई ।
मकरंदु जिन्ह को संभु सिर
सुचिता अवधि सुर बरनई ॥
करि मधुप मन मुनि जोगिजन जे
सेइ अभिमत गति लहैं ।

Taking a gold pitcher and gem-studded basin   3
filled with pure water, fragrant and holy,
in their own hands, the king and queen
joyfully came and set them before Ram.
As sages sonorously chanted the Veda,   4
heaven, aware of the moment, showered blossoms.
Gazing at the groom, the enraptured couple
began to wash his holy feet.[51]

They began washing his feet, pure as lotuses,   5
their limbs shivering with love,
as sky and city overflowed on all sides
with song, drumming, and cries of "Victory!"
Those lotus feet that forever shine
on Shiva's heart-lake, that are passion's nemesis,
and whose mere recall instantly cleanses the mind
and dispels the dark age's taints,
at whose touch the sage's wife found salvation,   6
though suffused by sin,
and whose nectar, borne on Shambhu's brow,
is hailed by the gods as the apex of purity,[52]
and which the heart-bees of sages and yogis
worship to attain their desired states—

ते पद परखारत भाग्यभाजनु
जनकु जय जय सब कहैं ॥

७ बर कुअँरि करतल जोरि साखोचारु
दोउ कुलगुर करैं ।
भयो पानिगहनु बिलोकि बिधि
सुर मनुज मुनि आनँद भरैं ॥
सुखमूल दूलहु देखि दंपति
पुलक तन हुलस्यो हियो ।
करि लोक बेद बिधानु कन्यादानु
नृपभूषन कियो ॥

८ हिमवंत जिमि गिरिजा महेसहि
हरिहि श्री सागर दई ।
तिमि जनक रामहि सिय समरपी
बिस्व कल कीरति नई ॥
क्यों करै बिनय बिदेहु कियो
बिदेहु मूरति साँवरीं ।
करि होमु बिधिवत गाँठि जोरी
होन लागीं भावँरीं ॥

३२४ जय धुनि बंदी बेद धुनि मंगल गान निसान ।
सुनि हरषहिं बरषहिं बिबुध सुरतरु सुमन सुजान ॥

१ कुअँरु कुअँरि कल भावँरि देहीं ।
नयन लाभु सब सादर लेहीं ॥

278

those feet were bathed by the supremely blessed Janak
to the acclamation of all.
Joining bride and groom's hands,   7
the two family priests recited their lineages,
as gods, humans, and sages, witnessing
this sacred union,[53] were filled with bliss.
Seeing that bridegroom, source of delight,
the royal pair trembled with heartfelt joy,
and that jewel of kings, obeying Vedic
and worldly custom, gave his daughter away.
As Himalaya gave his girl-child to Shiva   8
and as the ocean offered Shri to Hari,
so did Janak present Sita to Ram,
earning new and glorious fame in all the world.
How could Videha praise him? The form
of that dark youth had stolen away his wits.[54]
After prescribed oblations, with garments tied,
the pair began circling the fire altar.[55]

Hearing the din of victory cries, Vedic chants,   324
blessing songs, and drums,
the knowing gods rejoiced and rained down flowers
from the tree of heaven.[56]

As the youth and maiden circled gracefully,   1
reverent onlookers gained their eyes' reward.

जाइ न बरनि मनोहर जोरी ।
जो उपमा कछु कहौं सो थोरी ॥

२ राम सीय सुंदर प्रतिछाहीं ।
जगमगात मनि खंभन माहीं ॥
मनहुँ मदन रति धरि बहु रूपा ।
देखत राम बिआहु अनूपा ॥

३ दरस लालसा सकुच न थोरी ।
प्रगटत दुरत बहोरि बहोरी ॥
भए मगन सब देखनिहारे ।
जनक समान अपान बिसारे ॥

४ प्रमुदित मुनिन्ह भाँवरीं फेरीं ।
नेगसहित सब रीति निबेरीं ॥
राम सीय सिर सेंदुर देहीं ।
सोभा कहि न जाति बिधि केहीं ॥

५ अरुन पराग जलजु भरि नीकें ।
ससिहि भूष अहि लोभ अमी कें ॥
बहुरि बसिष्ठ दीन्हि अनुसासन ।
बरु दुलहिनि बैठे एक आसन ॥

६ बैठे बरासन रामु जानकि
मुदित मन दसरथु भए ।
तनु पुलक पुनि पुनि देखि अपनें
सुकृत सुरतरु फल नए ॥

That captivating pair cannot be described,
for any simile one might speak would fall short.
Ram and Sita's lovely reflections   2
shimmered in the gem-cut columns,
as if Love and his mate had taken myriad forms
to witness the matchless marriage of Ram,
but feeling shy, though craving that sight,   3
appeared and disappeared time and again.
All the spectators were so enthralled
that, like Janak, they forgot themselves.
The sages joyfully guided the circumambulation,   4
and the completion of gifting and other rites.
Then Ram placed vermilion on Sita's forehead
in a gesture beautiful beyond description,
as if a cobra filled a lotus-cup with ruddy pollen   5
and adorned the moon, desiring its nectar.[57]
Then sage Vasishtha gave the order
that bride and groom be seated on one couch.

With Ram and Janaki together on a splendid seat,   6
Dasarath's heart rejoiced
and his limbs thrilled again and again
to see this new fruit on the tree of his merit.

भरि भुवन रहा उछाहु राम
बिबाहु भा सबहीं कहा ।
केहि भाँति बरनि सिरात रसना
एक यहु मंगलु महा ॥

७ तब जनक पाइ बसिष्ठ आयसु
ब्याह साज सँवारि कै ।
मांडवी श्रुतकीरति उरमिला
कुअँरि लईं हँकारि कै ॥
कुसकेतु कन्या प्रथम जो गुन
सील सुख सोभामई ।
सब रीति प्रीति समेत करि सो
ब्याहि नृप भरतहि दई ॥

८ जानकी लघु भगिनी सकल
सुंदरि सिरोमनि जानि कै ।
सो तनय दीन्ही ब्याहि लखनहि
सकल बिधि सनमानि कै ॥
जेहि नामु श्रुतकीरति सुलोचनि
सुमुखि सब गुन आगरी ।
सो दई रिपुसूदनहि भूपति
रूप सील उजागरी ॥

९ अनुरूप बर दुलहिनि परस्पर
लखि सकुच हियँ हरषहीं ।
सब मुदित सुंदरता सराहहिं
सुमन सुर गन बरषहीं ॥

Exultation pervaded the worlds
as all beings exclaimed, "Ram has been wed!"
But how can a single tongue complete the account
of this great act of blessing?
Then Janak, with Vasishtha's permission,   7
had the ritual materials readied
and called for princesses Mandvi, Shrutakirti,
and Urmila to be brought in.[58]
Kushadhvaj's elder daughter, a paragon
of virtue, joy, and loveliness,
was lovingly bestowed on Bharat
by the king with full rites of marriage.
Knowing Janaki's younger sister to be   8
a crown jewel of beauties, the king
gave this daughter in marriage,
with greatest reverence, to Lakshman.
She who bore the name "Renowned,"[59] with fair eyes
and features, abode of virtue,
aglow with beauty and goodness, was given
by the king to Shatrughna, slayer of foes.
Seeing one another as brides and grooms,   9
so suitably paired, they felt shy delight,
as everyone else exulted over their beauty
and the divine hosts dispensed blossoms.

सुंदरीं सुंदर बरन्ह सह सब
एक मंडप राजहीं ।
जनु जीव उर चारिउ अवस्था
बिभुन सहित बिराजहीं ॥

३२५ मुदित अवधपति सकल सुत बधुन्ह समेत निहारि ।
जनु पाए महिपाल मनि क्रियन्ह सहित फल चारि ॥

१ जसि रघुबीर ब्याह बिधि बरनी ।
सकल कुअँर ब्याहे तेहिं करनी ॥
कहि न जाइ कछु दाइज भूरी ।
रहा कनक मनि मंडपु पूरी ॥

२ कंबल बसन बिचित्र पटोरे ।
भाँति भाँति बहु मोल न थोरे ॥
गज रथ तुरग दास अरु दासी ।
धेनु अलंकृत कामदुहा सी ॥

३ बस्तु अनेक करिअ किमि लेखा ।
कहि न जाइ जानहिं जिन्ह देखा ॥
लोकपाल अवलोकि सिहाने ।
लीन्ह अवधपति सबु सुखु माने ॥

४ दीन्ह जाचकन्हि जो जेहि भावा ।
उबरा सो जनवासेहिं आवा ॥
तब कर जोरि जनकु मृदु बानी ।
बोले सब बरात सनमानी ॥

Beneath a single wedding canopy,
these handsome couples appeared as glorious
as the four states of awareness, with their lords,
shining in the hearts of all beings.⁶⁰

Seeing all his sons and their wives,   325
the lord of Avadh felt as joyful as if he,
jewel among rulers, had gained life's four goals
and the good deeds that win them.⁶¹

Just like the Raghu hero's nuptials, as recounted,   1
were the weddings of the other princes.
The vast dowry can scarcely be described—
the pavilion was filled with gold and gems,
blankets, garments, and multicolored silks   2
of all sorts and immensely costly,
elephants, chariots, horses, male and female servants,
and cattle adorned like the heavenly cow—
goods uncountable and beyond accounting   3
or telling, for only one who has seen can know.
Even the world guardians grew envious at the sight.
The lord of Avadh accepted it all with pleasure.
He gave supplicants⁶² whatever they desired,   4
and what remained was sent to the groom's camp.
Then Janak, with palms joined and in a sweet voice,
respectfully addressed the bridegrooms' party.

५ सनमानि सकल बरात आदर
दान बिनय बड़ाइ कै ।
प्रमुदित महामुनि बृंद बंदे
पूजि प्रेम लड़ाइ कै ॥
सिरु नाइ देव मनाइ सब सन
कहत कर संपुट किएँ ।
सुर साधु चाहत भाउ सिंधु कि
तोष जल अंजलि दिएँ ॥

६ कर जोरि जनकु बहोरि
बंधु समेत कोसलराय सों ।
बोले मनोहर बयन सानि
सनेह सील सुभाय सों ॥
संबंध राजन रावरें हम
बड़े अब सब बिधि भए ।
एहि राज साज समेत सेवक
जानिबे बिनु गथ लए ॥

७ ए दारिका परिचारिका करि
पालिबीं करुना नई ।
अपराधु छमिबो बोलि पठए
बहुत हौं ढीट्यो कई ॥
पुनि भानुकुलभूषन सकल
सनमान निधि समधी किए ।
कहि जाति नहिं बिनती परस्पर
प्रेम परिपूरन हिए ॥

He honored all the guests with reverence, 5
gifts, humility, and praise,
then with blissful adoration, saluted
and worshiped the host of great sages.
Head bowed and with cupped palms,
he saluted the gods and declared to all,
"Gods and saintly people crave only love.
Is the sea sated by a handful of water?"[63]
Then Janak and his brother, hands joined 6
in supplication, addressed Kosala's king
in gentle voices, with words imbued
with affection, propriety, and virtue.
"Through this alliance with Your Majesty
we are magnified in every way,
so consider this land and its assets, with us
as servants, willingly gifted to you.
Making these daughters your maidservants, 7
foster them with ever-renewed mercy,
and pardon the sin of our great presumption
in summoning you here!"
Then the jewel of the solar line paid
his paternal counterpart fully equal honor,
and their reciprocal humility
and heartfelt love cannot be expressed.

८ बृंदारका गन सुमन बरिसहिं
राउ जनवासेहि चले ।
दुंदुभी जय धुनि बेद धुनि नभ
नगर कौतूहल भले ॥
तब सखीं मंगल गान करत
मुनीस आयसु पाइ कै ।
दूलह दुलहिनिन्ह सहित सुंदरि
चलीं कोहबर ल्याइ कै ॥

३२६ पुनि पुनि रामहि चितव सिय सकुचति मनु सकुचै न ।
हरत मनोहर मीन छबि प्रेम पिआसे नैन ॥

१ स्याम सरीरु सुभायँ सुहावन ।
सोभा कोटि मनोज लजावन ॥
जावक जुत पद कमल सुहाए ।
मुनि मन मधुप रहत जिन्ह छाए ॥
२ पीत पुनीत मनोहर धोती ।
हरति बाल रबि दामिनि जोती ॥
कल किंकिनि कटि सूत्र मनोहर ।
बाहु बिसाल बिभूषन सुंदर ॥
३ पीत जनेउ महाछबि देई ।
कर मुद्रिका चोरि चितु लेई ॥
सोहत ब्याह साज सब साजे ।
उर आयत उरभूषन राजे ॥

As the celestial host showered blossoms,   8
the king repaired to his party's quarters
amid a tumult of kettledrums, exultant shouts,
and Vedic chants in sky and city.
The princesses' friends, auspiciously singing,
sought permission of the great sage,
and then those beauties brought the newlyweds
to the inner nuptial chamber.⁶⁴

Time and again, Sita glanced shyly at Ram,   326
though her heart was anything but shy,
and her eyes, athirst with love,
stole the charm of a pair of sporting fish.

His dark form so naturally pleasing,   1
with beauty to embarrass a billion Loves
and red-stained feet, lovely as lotuses
above which hover bees of sages' hearts.
His yellow lower garment, so pure and charming,   2
steals the glow of sunrise and lightning.
He wears an alluring belt and waistband
and his great arms are splendidly adorned.
A yellow sacred thread enhances his beauty   3
and his signet ring snatches away one's very wits.
He is so handsome in all his wedding finery,
his broad chest shining with pendants.

४ पिअर उपरना काखासोती ।
दुहुँ आँचरन्हि लगे मनि मोती ॥
नयन कमल कल कुंडल काना ।
बदनु सकल सौंदर्ज निधाना ॥

५ सुंदर भृकुटि मनोहर नासा ।
भाल तिलकु रुचिरता निवासा ॥
सोहत मौरु मनोहर माथे ।
मंगलमय मुकुता मनि गाथे ॥

६ गाथे महामनि मौर मंजुल
अंग सब चित चोरहीं ।
पुर नारि सुर सुंदरीं बरहिं
बिलोकि सब तिन तोरहीं ॥
मनि बसन भूषन वारि आरति
करहिं मंगल गावहीं ।
सुर सुमन बरिसहिं सूत मागध
बंदि सुजसु सुनावहीं ॥

७ कोहबरहिं आने कुअँर कुअँरि
सुआसिनिन्ह सुख पाइ कै ।
अति प्रीति लौकिक रीति लागीं
करन मंगल गाइ कै ॥
लहकौरि गौरि सिखाव रामहि
सीय सन सारद कहैं ।

His upper wrap,[65] likewise yellow,   4
has borders woven with gems and pearls.
Lotus eyes and lovely earrings adorn
a countenance that contains all beauty,
with fine eyebrows, charming nose,   5
and forehead mark that embodies allure.
And shining above it, a bridegroom's crown
braided with pearls and gemstones.

His wedding crown braided with great jewels,   6
and all his limbs distractingly lovely—
beholding this bridegroom, townswomen
and heavenly beauties break blades of grass[66]
and adore him with offerings of gems, clothes,
ornaments, and songs of blessing,
as the gods scatter flowers and royal bards
and minstrels recite celebratory lays.
With delight, married women took the youths   7
and maidens into the nuptial room
and, singing wedding songs, began customary rites
with the greatest affection.
Gauri guided Ram, and Sharada, Sita, in putting
sweets into one another's mouths.[67]

रनिवासु हास बिलास रस बस
जन्म को फलु सब लहैं ॥

८ निज पानि मनि महुँ देखिअति
मूरति सुरूपनिधान की ।
चालति न भुजबल्ली बिलोकनि
बिरह भय बस जानकी ॥
कौतुक बिनोद प्रमोदु प्रेमु
न जाइ कहि जानहिं अलीं ।
बर कुअँरि सुंदर सकल सखीं
लवाइ जनवासेहि चलीं ॥

९ तेहि समय सुनिअ असीस जहँ तहँ
नगर नभ आनँदु महा ।
चिरु जिअहुँ जोरीं चारु चार्यो
मुदित मन सबहीं कहा ॥
जोगींद्र सिद्ध मुनीस देव
बिलोकि प्रभु दुंदुभि हनी ।
चले हरषि बरषि प्रसून निज निज लोक
जय जय जय भनी ॥

३२७ सहित बधूटिन्ह कुअँर सब तब आए पितु पास ।
सोभा मंगल मोद भरि उमगेउ जनु जनवास ॥

१ पुनि जेवनार भई बहु भाँती ।
पठए जनक बोलाइ बराती ॥

The women's quarters rang with playful laughter
as they all enjoyed their birth's reward.
As she gazed at the treasury of beauty   8
reflected in the gemstone of her ring,
Janaki, dreading separation from this sight,
kept her eyes and supple arm immobile.
All the merriment and loving fun cannot be described,[68]
but her dear friends knew it.
Then those companions brought the brides
and grooms back to the guest quarters.
At that time, only blissful benediction was heard   9
throughout city and firmament
as everyone joyously wished long life
to the four handsome couples.
Great yogis, adepts, seers, and gods gazed
at the Lord and sounded their drums,
as, showering him with petals and shouting "Victory!"
they left for their respective realms.

Then all the sons came before their father   327
together with their new brides,
and beauty, blessedness, and delight
seemed to overflow the wedding camp.

A great banquet was soon prepared   1
and Janak summoned the wedding guests.

परत पाँवड़े बसन अनूपा ।
सुतन्ह समेत गवन कियो भूपा ॥

२ सादर सब के पाय पखारे ।
जथाजोगु पीढ़न्ह बैठारे ॥
धोए जनक अवधपति चरना ।
सीलु सनेहु जाइ नहिं बरना ॥

३ बहुरि राम पद पंकज धोए ।
जे हर हृदय कमल महुँ गोए ॥
तीनिउ भाइ राम सम जानी ।
धोए चरन जनक निज पानी ॥

४ आसन उचित सबहि नृप दीन्हे ।
बोलि सूपकारी सब लीन्हे ॥
सादर लगे परन पनवारे ।
कनक कील मनि पान सँवारे ॥

३२८ सूपोदन सुरभी सरपि सुंदर स्वादु पुनीत ।
छन महुँ सब कें परुसि गे चतुर सुआर बिनीत ॥

१ पंच कवल करि जेवन लागे ।
गारि गान सुनि अति अनुरागे ॥
भाँति अनेक परे पकवाने ।
सुधा सरिस नहिं जाहिं बखाने ॥

२ परुसन लगे सुआर सुजाना ।
बिंजन बिबिध नाम को जाना ॥

294

Over a path strewn with the finest fabrics
the king and his sons proceeded there.
With great respect, the feet of all were washed   2
and they were suitably seated on low stools.
Janak himself cleansed the feet of Avadh's king
with humility and affection beyond words.
Then he bathed Ram's beautiful feet   3
that lie hidden in the lotus of Shiva's heart.
And knowing all three brothers to be like Ram,
with his own hands, Janak washed their feet.
The king gave everyone a proper seat   4
and then called for the cooks and servers.
Respectfully, they laid out leaf-plates
wrought of gems, fastened with pins of gold.

Fragrant dal, rice, and clarified butter—   328
pleasing to the eye, pure, and delicious—
were swiftly served to everyone
by skilled and gracious cooks.

After the fivefold rite,[69] the feast began   1
as they listened with delight to ribald songs.[70]
Countless fried savories were served,
nectar-like and indescribable.
Then those clever cooks began dispensing   2
dishes so diverse, who even knows their names?

चारि भाँति भोजन बिधि गाई ।
एक एक बिधि बरनि न जाई ॥

३ छरस रुचिर बिंजन बहु जाती ।
एक एक रस अगनित भाँती ॥
जेवँत देहिं मधुर धुनि गारी ।
लै लै नाम पुरुष अरु नारी ॥

४ समय सुहावनि गारि बिराजा ।
हँसत राउ सुनि सहित समाजा ॥
एहि बिधि सबहीं भोजनु कीन्हा ।
आदर सहित आचमनु दीन्हा ॥

३२९ देइ पान पूजे जनक दसरथु सहित समाज ।
जनवासेहि गवने मुदित सकल भूप सिरताज ॥

१ नित नूतन मंगल पुर माहीं ।
निमिष सरिस दिन जामिनि जाहीं ॥
बड़े भोर भूपतिमनि जागे ।
जाचक गुन गन गावन लागे ॥

२ देखि कुअँर बर बधुन्ह समेता ।
किमि कहि जात मोदु मन जेता ॥
प्रातक्रिया करि गे गुरु पाहीं ।
महाप्रमोदु प्रेमु मन माहीं ॥

३ करि प्रनामु पूजा कर जोरी ।
बोले गिरा अमिअँ जनु बोरी ॥

296

Of the four kinds of food noted by authorities,[71]
there were too many of each to ever describe,
and so many fine dishes of the six flavors   3
that the varieties of each were countless.
The diners were treated to sweet songs of abuse
naming men and women of the family.
These risqué songs well suited the occasion,   4
and king and company listened with mirth.
In this way, all partook of the feast
and were politely offered rinsing water.[72]

Presenting fragrant quids of spiced betel,   329
Janak saluted Dasarath and his cohorts,
and that crown jewel of kings, well pleased,
repaired to the guest quarters.

With ever-new celebrations in the city,   1
day and night passed like the blink of an eye.
Well before sunrise, the king of kings awoke
as bards began intoning his virtues.
Seeing the princes with their lovely brides,   2
his heart's delight surpassed expression.
After the morning rites, he went to his guru
with immense joy and affection in his heart.
He saluted him with reverence, and spoke   3
in a voice that seemed steeped in nectar.

तुम्हरी कृपाँ सुनहु मुनिराजा ।
भयउँ आजु मैं पूरन काजा ॥
४ अब सब बिप्र बोलाइ गोसाई ।
देहु धेनु सब भाँति बनाई ॥
सुनि गुर करि महिपाल बड़ाई ।
पुनि पठए मुनिबृंद बोलाई ॥

३३० बामदेउ अरु देवरिषि बालमीकि जाबालि ।
आए मुनिबर निकर तब कौसिकादि तपसालि ॥

१ दंड प्रनाम सबहि नृप कीन्हे ।
पूजि सप्रेम बरासन दीन्हे ॥
चारि लच्छ बर धेनु मगाईं ।
काम सुरभि सम सील सुहाईं ॥
२ सब बिधि सकल अलंकृत कीन्हीं ।
मुदित महिप महिदेवन्ह दीन्हीं ॥
करत बिनय बहु बिधि नरनाहू ।
लहेउँ आजु जग जीवन लाहू ॥
३ पाइ असीस महीसु अनंदा ।
लिए बोलि पुनि जाचक बृंदा ॥
कनक बसन मनि हय गय स्यंदन ।
दिए बूझि रुचि रबिकुलनंदन ॥
४ चले पढ़त गावत गुन गाथा ।
जय जय जय दिनकर कुल नाथा ॥

"By your grace, king of seers,
all my wishes are fulfilled today.
Now, lord, summon all the Brahmans   4
and give them cattle, richly adorned."
Praising that earth-protector, his teacher
sent for the company of sages.

Then Vamadeva and the divine seer Narad,   330
Valmiki and Jabali—
a host of sages assembled, with Vishvamitra
and other masterly ascetics.

The king prostrated before them all,   1
lovingly worshiped them, and offered them fine seats.
He ordered four hundred thousand cattle,
gentle and lovely as heaven's wishing cow,
and fully outfitting them,[73] the earth's guardian   2
gladly presented them to the earth's gods.
The lord of men said with utter humility,
"Today I reap the reward of worldly birth."
Receiving their blessing, the delighted king   3
called for all his dependents and distributed
gold, clothes, gems, horses, elephants, chariots,
the benevolent sun-king asking each one's liking.
They left singing a litany of his praise—   4
"Victory to the lord of the solar lineage!"

एहि बिधि राम बिआह उछाहू ।
सकइ न बरनि सहस मुख जाहू ॥

३३१ बार बार कौसिक चरन सीसु नाइ कह राउ ।
यह सबु सुखु मुनिराज तव कृपा कटाच्छ पसाउ ॥

१ जनक सनेहु सीलु करतूती ।
नृपु सब भाँति सराह बिभूती ॥
दिन उठि बिदा अवधपति मागा ।
राखहिं जनकु सहित अनुरागा ॥

२ नित नूतन आदरु अधिकाई ।
दिन प्रति सहस भाँति पहुनाई ॥
नित नव नगर अनंद उछाहू ।
दसरथ गवनु सोहाइ न काहू ॥

३ बहुत दिवस बीते एहि भाँती ।
जनु सनेह रजु बँधे बराती ॥
कौसिक सतानंद तब जाई ।
कहा बिदेह नृपहि समुझाई ॥

४ अब दसरथ कहँ आयसु देहू ।
जद्यपि छाड़ि न सकहु सनेहू ॥
भलेहिं नाथ कहि सचिव बोलाए ।
कहि जय जीव सीस तिन्ह नाए ॥

Such were the festivities of Ram's wedding,
which not even thousand-tongued Shesh can describe.

Bowing his head again and again   331
at Vishvamitra's feet, the king declared,
"All this joy, king of seers, is by the grace
of your kindly glance falling on us."

And of Janak's affection, virtue, comportment,   1
and majesty, the king voiced much praise.
Arising each morning, Avadh's lord asked leave
to go, yet Janak held him back out of love.
Amid ever new expressions of homage,   2
each day saw a thousand acts of hospitality
and new, joyous festivities in the city,
for no one could bear Dasarath departing.
In this way, many days passed,   3
as if the guests were bound by cords of love.
Then Vishvamitra and Shatanand went
to petition King Videha, saying,
"Now give Dasarath permission to go,   4
though your love cannot bear to release him."
Saying "Very well, lords," he summoned his ministers,
who saluted him with heads bowed.

३३२ अवधनाथु चाहत चलन भीतर करहु जनाउ ।
भए प्रेमबस सचिव सुनि बिप्र सभासद राउ ॥

१ पुरबासी सुनि चलिहि बराता ।
बूझत बिकल परस्पर बाता ॥
सत्य गवनु सुनि सब बिलखाने ।
मनहुँ साँझ सरसिज सकुचाने ॥

२ जहँ जहँ आवत बसे बराती ।
तहँ तहँ सिद्ध चला बहु भाँती ॥
बिबिध भाँति मेवा पकवाना ।
भोजन साजु न जाइ बखाना ॥

३ भरि भरि बसहँ अपार कहारा ।
पठईं जनक अनेक सुसारा ॥
तुरग लाख रथ सहस पचीसा ।
सकल सँवारे नख अरु सीसा ॥

४ मत्त सहस दस सिंधुर साजे ।
जिन्हहि देखि दिसिकुंजर लाजे ॥
कनक बसन मनि भरि भरि जाना ।
महिषीं धेनु बस्तु बिधि नाना ॥

३३३ दाइज अमित न सकिअ कहि दीन्ह बिदेहँ बहोरि ।
जो अवलोकत लोकपति लोक संपदा थोरि ॥

"The ruler of Avadh wishes to depart.   332
Inform the inner apartments."[74]
At this, advisers, priests, courtiers, and the king himself
were overcome by emotion.

The citizens heard of the guests' departure   1
and distractedly asked each other if it was true.
Hearing it was so, all grew disconsolate,
like lotuses folding up at dusk.
Wherever the party was to stay en route,[75]   2
abundant provisions were dispatched—
dried fruits and savories of all sorts
and ingredients too varied to recount,
borne by countless oxen and porters,   3
and fine bedding, too—all sent by Janak.
A hundred thousand horses and a quarter
as many chariots, all splendidly outfitted,
ten thousand decorated elephant bulls,   4
fit to shame those of the quadrants of space,
carts loaded with gold, gems, and clothing,
and bulls, cows, and all manner of goods—

once more, Videha bestowed   333
such an endless, indescribable dowry
that its sight made the riches
of heaven's rulers seem meager.

१ सबु समाजु एहि भाँति बनाई ।
जनक अवधपुर दीन्ह पठाई ॥
चलिहि बरात सुनत सब रानीं ।
बिकल मीनगन जनु लघु पानीं ॥

२ पुनि पुनि सीय गोद करि लेहीं ।
देइ असीस सिखावनु देहीं ॥
होएहु संतत पियहि पिआरी ।
चिरु अहिबात असीस हमारी ॥

३ सासु ससुर गुर सेवा करेहू ।
पति रुख लखि आयसु अनुसरेहू ॥
अति सनेह बस सखीं सयानी ।
नारि धरम सिखवहिं मृदु बानी ॥

४ सादर सकल कुअँरि समुझाई ।
रानिन्ह बार बार उर लाई ॥
बहुरि बहुरि भेटहिं महतारीं ।
कहहिं बिरंचि रचीं कत नारीं ॥

३३४ तेहि अवसर भाइन्ह सहित रामु भानु कुल केतु ।
चले जनक मंदिर मुदित बिदा करावन हेतु ॥

१ चारिउ भाइ सुभायँ सुहाए ।
नगर नारि नर देखन धाए ॥
कोउ कह चलन चहत हहिं आजू ।
कीन्ह बिदेह बिदा कर साजू ॥

And so, having assembled all this bounty,   1
King Janak dispatched it to Avadh city.
Hearing of the party's departure, all his queens
were distraught, like fish in a drying pond.
Embracing Sita again and again,   2
they blessed and instructed her.
"May you be ever dear to your husband
in long-lasting wedlock—this is our blessing.
Serve your in-laws and guru, and watching   3
your lord's countenance, carry out his commands."
With deep affection, her experienced friends
gently instructed her in woman's dharma.
Reverently teaching all their daughters,   4
the queens hugged them time and again.
Amid repeated embraces, their mothers cried,
"Oh, why did the creator make women?"

At that time, accompanied by his brothers,   334
Ram, ensign of the solar line,
went joyously to King Janak's abode
to initiate the leave-taking.[76]

All four brothers were so naturally handsome   1
that the city's women and men ran to see them.
One said, "They mean to leave today
and Videha has prepared the farewell.

२ लेहु नयन भरि रूप निहारी ।
प्रिय पाहुने भूप सुत चारी ॥
को जानै केहिं सुकृत सयानी ।
नयन अतिथि कीन्हे बिधि आनी ॥

३ मरनसीलु जिमि पाव पिऊषा ।
सुरतरु लहै जनम कर भूखा ॥
पाव नारकी हरिपदु जैसें ।
इन्ह कर दरसनु हम कहँ तैसें ॥

४ निरखि राम सोभा उर धरहू ।
निज मन फनि मूरति मनि करहू ॥
एहि बिधि सबहि नयन फलु देता ।
गए कुअँर सब राज निकेता ॥

३३५ रूप सिंधु सब बंधु लखि हरषि उठा रनिवासु ।
करहिं निछावरि आरती महा मुदित मन सासु ॥

१ देखि राम छबि अति अनुरागीं ।
प्रेमबिबस पुनि पुनि पद लागीं ॥
रही न लाज प्रीति उर छाई ।
सहज सनेहु बरनि किमि जाई ॥

२ भाइन्ह सहित उबटि अन्हवाए ।
छरस असन अति हेतु जेवाँए ॥
बोले रामु सुअवसरु जानी ।
सील सनेह सकुचमय बानी ॥

So feast your eyes on the beauty   2
of these four dear princely guests.
Who knows, friend, for what past merit of ours
God sent them to linger in our sight.
Like one at death's door gaining nectar,   3
or a born pauper the gods' wishing tree,
or a doomed sinner reaching Hari's haven—
such is the blessed sight of them for us all.
Gaze at Ram, set his beauty in your heart   4
and treasure it as a serpent does his gem."
And so, having gratified everyone's eyes,
the princes entered the king's abode.

Beholding all the brothers, seas of beauty,   335
the women arose with delight
and their ecstatic mothers-in-law greeted them
with gifts and blessed lamps.

At the sight of Ram's beauty, they were enamored   1
and, overpowered by love, they fell repeatedly at his feet,
shedding all propriety as endearment overtook their
     hearts.
But how can such pure affection be described?
They anointed him and his brothers, bathed them,   2
and lovingly fed them six kinds of cuisine.
Then Ram spoke, knowing it was time,
his voice imbued with virtue, love, and modesty.

३ राउ अवधपुर चहत सिधाए ।
बिदा होन हम इहाँ पठाए ॥
मातु मुदित मन आयसु देहू ।
बालक जानि करब नित नेहू ॥

४ सुनत बचन बिलखेउ रनिवासू ।
बोलि न सकहिं प्रेमबस सासू ॥
हृदयँ लगाइ कुआँरि सब लीन्ही ।
पतिन्ह सौंपि बिनती अति कीन्ही ॥

५ करि बिनय सिय रामहि समरपी
जोरि कर पुनि पुनि कहै ।
बलि जाउँ तात सुजान तुम्ह कहुँ
बिदित गति सब की अहै ॥
परिवार पुरजन मोहि राजहि
प्रानप्रिय सिय जानिबी ।
तुलसीस सीलु सनेहु लखि
निज किंकरी करि मानिबी ॥

३३६ तुम्ह परिपूरन काम जान सिरोमनि भावप्रिय ।
जन गुन गाहक राम दोष दलन करुनायतन ॥

१ अस कहि रही चरन गहि रानी ।
प्रेम पंक जनु गिरा समानी ॥

"The king wishes to set forth for Avadh   3
and has sent us here to bid farewell.
Mothers, give us your leave with glad hearts
and, considering us your children, cherish us always."
At these words, the royal women lamented   4
and the mothers were too overcome by love to speak.
They embraced all their daughters
and gave them to their husbands with humble petition.

Bestowing Sita on Ram, the queen entreated him   5
again and again with palms joined,
"Noble son! I avow that you comprehend
the inner state of one and all, and so
will know that Sita is dearer than life
to her family, townsfolk, father, and me.
Lord of Tulsi! Beholding her goodness and affection,
make her your maidservant.

Though all-sufficient and wisdom's crown,   336
yet, Ram, you are pleased by love
and mark the merits and destroy the sins of your devotees,
for you are mercy's home."

So the queen spoke, then lay at his feet,   1
her voice as if mired in love's quicksand.

सुनि सनेहसानी बर बानी ।
बहुबिधि राम सासु सनमानी ॥

२ राम बिदा मागत कर जोरी ।
कीन्ह प्रनामु बहोरि बहोरी ॥
पाइ असीस बहुरि सिरु नाई ।
भाइन्ह सहित चले रघुराई ॥

३ मंजु मधुर मूरति उर आनी ।
भईं सनेह सिथिल सब रानी ॥
पुनि धीरजु धरि कुअँरि हँकारीं ।
बार बार भेटहिं महतारीं ॥

४ पहुँचावहिं फिरि मिलहिं बहोरी ।
बढ़ी परस्पर प्रीति न थोरी ॥
पुनि पुनि मिलत सखिन्ह बिलगाई ।
बाल बच्छ जिमि धेनु लवाई ॥

३३७ प्रेमबिबस नर नारि सब सखिन्ह सहित रनिवासु ।
मानहुँ कीन्ह बिदेहपुर करुनाँ बिरहँ निवासु ॥

१ सुक सारिका जानकी ज्याए ।
कनक पिंजरन्हि राखि पढ़ाए ॥
ब्याकुल कहहिं कहाँ बैदेही ।
सुनि धीरजु परिहरइ न केही ॥

२ भए बिकल खग मृग एहि भाँती ।
मनुज दसा कैसें कहि जाती ॥

310

Having heard her noble and loving address,
Ram paid full homage to his mother-in-law.
With palms joined, Ram asked leave to depart,   2
saluting her again and again.
Receiving her blessing, bowing once more,
the Raghu lord left with his brothers.
Drawing his sweet and lovely form into their hearts,   3
the queens all grew faint with emotion.
Then, composing themselves and calling their daughters
the mothers embraced them repeatedly.
Sending them off only to clasp them once more,   4
their mutual love went on increasing
till their friends intervened in these embraces,
as if separating cows from newborn calves.

Like the queens and their companions,   337
all the townsmen and women were overcome by love,
for it was as though pathos and separation
had settled down in Videha's city.

Parrots and mynahs that Janaki had tended,   1
rearing and training them in golden cages,
now asked, distraught, "Where is Vaidehi?"
Who, hearing this, could remain composed?
If birds and beasts were thus afflicted,   2
how to describe the state of humankind?

बंधु समेत जनकु तब आए ।
प्रेम उमगि लोचन जल छाए ॥

३ सीय बिलोकि धीरता भागी ।
रहे कहावत परम बिरागी ॥
लीन्हि रायँ उर लाइ जानकी ।
मिटी महामरजाद ग्यान की ॥

४ समुझावत सब सचिव सयाने ।
कीन्ह बिचारु न अवसर जाने ॥
बारहिं बार सुता उर लाईं ।
सजि सुंदर पालकीं मगाईं ॥

३३८ प्रेमबिबस परिवारु सबु जानि सुलगन नरेस ।
कुअँरि चढ़ाईं पालकिन्ह सुमिरे सिद्धि गनेस ॥

१ बहुबिधि भूप सुता समुझाईं ।
नारिधरमु कुलरीति सिखाईं ॥
दासीं दास दिए बहुतेरे ।
सुचि सेवक जे प्रिय सिय केरे ॥

२ सीय चलत ब्याकुल पुरबासी ।
होहिं सगुन सुभ मंगल रासी ॥
भूसुर सचिव समेत समाजा ।
संग चले पहुँचावन राजा ॥

Then King Janak came with his brother,*
their eyes brimming with tears of love.
When he saw Sita, his composure fled,   3
famed though he was as most dispassionate.
The king clutched Janaki to his breast
and his wisdom's vast restraint was erased.
But admonished by his prudent ministers,   4
he reflected on the untimeliness of his grief.
Hugging his daughters again and again,
he called for richly decorated palanquins.

Seeing his whole clan undone by love,   338
and the auspicious moment at hand, the king
placed the princesses in their litters,
calling to mind Ganesh and his bride, Siddhi.[77]

He gave much instruction to his daughters   1
in woman's dharma and family customs,
and he gave many male and female servants
who were trusted retainers and dear to Sita.
As Sita set out, the citizens grew distraught   2
yet omens betokened great auspiciousness.
Along with Brahmans, ministers, and courtiers,
the king went forth to deliver the brides.

---

* Kushadhvaj, the father of two of the brides.

३ समय बिलोकि बाजने बाजे ।
रथ गज बाजि बरातिन्ह साजे ॥
दसरथ बिप्र बोलि सब लीन्हे ।
दान मान परिपूरन कीन्हे ॥

४ चरन सरोज धूरि धरि सीसा ।
मुदित महीपति पाइ असीसा ॥
सुमिरि गजाननु कीन्ह पयाना ।
मंगल मूल सगुन भए नाना ॥

३३९ सुर प्रसून बरषहिं हरषि करहिं अपछरा गान ।
चले अवधपति अवधपुर मुदित बजाइ निसान ॥

१ नृप करि बिनय महाजन फेरे ।
सादर सकल मागने टेरे ॥
भूषन बसन बाजि गज दीन्हे ।
प्रेम पोषि ठाढ़े सब कीन्हे ॥

२ बार बार बिरिदावलि भाषी ।
फिरे सकल रामहि उर राखी ॥
बहुरि बहुरि कोसलपति कहहीं ।
जनकु प्रेमबस फिरै न चहहीं ॥

३ पुनि कह भूपति बचन सुहाए ।
फिरिअ महीस दूरि बड़ि आए ॥
राउ बहोरि उतरि भए ठाढ़े ।
प्रेम प्रबाह बिलोचन बाढ़े ॥

Befitting the moment, instruments sounded   3
as the wedding party readied chariots, elephants, and
    horses.
Dasarath called for all the Brahmans
and sated them with gifts and reverence.
Placing the dust of their holy feet on his brow,   4
the delighted monarch gained their blessing.
Then he set out, calling to mind the elephant-faced god,
to the accompaniment of innumerable auspicious signs.

As the celestials happily showered blossoms   339
and as heavenly courtesans sang,
Avadh's lord left for Avadh city,
amid the joyful boom of kettledrums.

Reverently, the king sent back the leading townsmen,   1
then respectfully summoned all supplicants
to give them gems, clothes, horses, and elephants,
tenderly ensuring that all were well-provisioned.[78]
Singing his glory again and again,   2
and with Ram in their hearts, all returned.
Yet despite the Kosala king's constant entreaty,
Janak, overcome by love, did not wish to return.
Once more, the king gently addressed him,   3
"Your Majesty has come far. Please go back."
And then, getting down, Dasarath stood there
with tears of love flowing from his eyes.

४ तब बिदेह बोले कर जोरी ।
बचन सनेह सुधाँ जनु बोरी ॥
करौं कवन बिधि बिनय बनाई ।
महाराज मोहि दीन्हि बड़ाई ॥

३४० कोसलपति समधी सजन सनमाने सब भाँति ।
मिलनि परसपर बिनय अति प्रीति न हृदयँ समाति ॥

१ मुनि मंडलिहि जनक सिरु नावा ।
आसिरबादु सबहि सन पावा ॥
सादर पुनि भेंटे जामाता ।
रूप सील गुन निधि सब भ्राता ॥

२ जोरि पंकरुह पानि सुहाए ।
बोले बचन प्रेम जनु जाए ॥
राम करौं केहि भाँति प्रसंसा ।
मुनि महेस मन मानस हंसा ॥

३ करहिं जोग जोगी जेहि लागी ।
कोहु मोहु ममता मदु त्यागी ॥
ब्यापकु ब्रह्मु अलखु अबिनासी ।
चिदानंदु निरगुन गुनरासी ॥

४ मन समेत जेहि जान न बानी ।
तरकि न सकहिं सकल अनुमानी ॥
महिमा निगमु नेति कहि कहई ।
जो तिहुँ काल एकरस रहई ॥

Hands joined in reverence, Videha spoke   4
in words that seemed sunk in love's nectar.
"How may I make submission to you,
great king, who have so magnified me?"

The king of Kosala paid every respect   340
to his new kinsman by marriage
as they embraced with deep humility
and a love their hearts could not contain.

Janak bowed to the assembled sages   1
and received the blessings of them all.
Then he respectfully embraced his sons-in-law,
those brothers full of grace and goodness,
and with his lovely hands joined in homage   2
spoke words that seemed born of pure love.
"Ram, how may I praise you?
Holy *haṃsa* on the heart-lake of Shiva and sages,[79]
for whom yogis practice their discipline,   3
abandoning anger, delusion, passion, and selfishness,
all-pervading God, invisible and indestructible,
bliss-conscious and without attributes, but containing
    them all,
whom mind and speech cannot comprehend,   4
nor logicians with all their inferences,
whose majesty the Veda declares by saying 'not this'
and who endures, unchanging, in all times—

३४१ नयन बिषय मो कहुँ भयउ सो समस्त सुख मूल ।
सबइ लाभु जग जीव कहँ भएँ ईसु अनुकूल ॥

१ सबहि भाँति मोहि दीन्हि बड़ाई ।
निज जन जानि लीन्ह अपनाई ॥
होहिं सहस दस सारद सेषा ।
करहिं कलप कोटिक भरि लेखा ॥

२ मोर भाग्य राउर गुन गाथा ।
कहि न सिराहिं सुनहु रघुनाथा ॥
मैं कछु कहउँ एक बल मोरें ।
तुम्ह रीझहु सनेह सुठि थोरें ॥

३ बार बार मागउँ कर जोरें ।
मनु परिहरै चरन जनि भोरें ॥
सुनि बर बचन प्रेम जनु पोषे ।
पूरनकाम रामु परितोषे ॥

४ करि बर बिनय ससुर सनमाने ।
पितु कौसिक बसिष्ठ सम जाने ॥
बिनती बहुरि भरत सन कीन्ही ।
मिलि सप्रेमु पुनि आसिष दीन्ही ॥

३४२ मिले लखन रिपुसूदनहि दीन्हि असीस महीस ।
भए परसपर प्रेमबस फिरि फिरि नावहिं सीस ॥

that hidden source of all happiness   341
has become perceptible to my eyes,
for when God favors a soul in this world,
every advantage is obtained.

You have honored me in every way   1
by knowing and accepting me as your own.
Ten thousand Sharadas and serpent kings
reckoning, for a billion aeons, the account
of my good fortune and your graciousness,   2
could never exhaust it, Raghu lord!
What little I say rests on my conviction
that even an iota of love earns your pleasure.
Again and again, I entreat you: 3
let my heart not carelessly forsake your feet!"
Hearing this choice speech, nurtured by love,
Ram, the all-sufficient one, was well satisfied.
He graciously praised his father-in-law, considering him   4
equal to his father, Vishvamitra, and Vasishtha.
Then Janak humbly saluted Bharat,
embraced him with love, and blessed him.

Embracing Lakshman and Shatrughna,   342
the king gave them his blessing.
Overcome by mutual love,
they repeatedly bowed their heads to him.

१ बार बार करि बिनय बड़ाई ।
रघुपति चले संग सब भाई ॥
जनक गहे कौसिक पद जाई ।
चरन रेनु सिर नयनन्ह लाई ॥

२ सुनु मुनीस बर दरसन तोरें ।
अगमु न कछु प्रतीति मन मोरें ॥
जो सुखु सुजसु लोकपति चहहीं ।
करत मनोरथ सकुचत अहहीं ॥

३ सो सुखु सुजसु सुलभ मोहि स्वामी ।
सब सिधि तव दरसन अनुगामी ॥
कीन्हि बिनय पुनि पुनि सिरु नाई ।
फिरे महीसु आसिषा पाई ॥

४ चली बरात निसान बजाई ।
मुदित छोट बड़ सब समुदाई ॥
रामहि निरखि ग्राम नर नारी ।
पाइ नयन फलु होहिं सुखारी ॥

३४३ बीच बीच बर बास करि मग लोगन्ह सुख देत ।
अवध समीप पुनीत दिन पहुँची आइ जनेत ॥

१ हने निसान पनव बर बाजे ।
भेरि संख धुनि हय गय गाजे ॥
झाँझि बिरव डिंडिमीं सुहाई ।
सरस राग बाजहिं सहनाई ॥

320

And so, with much deference and praise,   1
the Raghu lord departed with his brothers.
Then Janak clasped the feet of Sage Kaushik,
placing their dust on his forehead and eyes,
and said, "Greatest of sages! By seeing you   2
nothing is unattainable—this is my conviction.
Such bliss and renown as the world guardians crave
yet dare not ask for,
that bliss, that renown, come readily to me, master,   3
for all attainments ensue from sight of you."
And so, with many bows and submissions
the king went back with the sage's blessings.
The procession departed with drums booming   4
to the delight of all assembled, great and lowly.
Beholding Ram, village men and women
rejoiced, gaining their eyes' reward.

Encamping at numerous splendid halts,   343
they gave joy to those along the way,
until, on an auspicious day,
the wedding procession approached Avadh.

Drums resounded, great and small,   1
and conchs, amid a tumult of horse and elephant,
as lovely cymbals, tambourines,[80]
and oboes played a melodious raga.

२ पुर जन आवत अकनि बराता ।
मुदित सकल पुलकावलि गाता ॥
निज निज सुंदर सदन सँवारे ।
हाट बाट चौहट पुर द्वारे ॥

३ गलीं सकल अरगजाँ सिंचाईं ।
जहँ तहँ चौकें चारु पुराईं ॥
बना बजारु न जाइ बखाना ।
तोरन केतु पताक बिताना ॥

४ सफल पूगफल कदलि रसाला ।
रोपे बकुल कदंब तमाला ॥
लगे सुभग तरु परसत धरनी ।
मनिमय आलबाल कल करनी ॥

३४४ बिबिध भाँति मंगल कलस गृह गृह रचे सँवारि ।
सुर ब्रह्मादि सिहाहिं सब रघुबर पुरी निहारि ॥

१ भूप भवनु तेहि अवसर सोहा ।
रचना देखि मदन मनु मोहा ॥
मंगल सगुन मनोहरताई ।
रिधि सिधि सुख संपदा सुहाई ॥

२ जनु उछाह सब सहज सुहाए ।
तनु धरि धरि दसरथ गृहँ छाए ॥
देखन हेतु राम बैदेही ।
कहहु लालसा होहि न केही ॥

322

When they heard the procession coming   2
all the townspeople trembled with delight
and began decorating their homes,
markets, streets, crossroads, and city gates.
All the lanes were sprinkled with perfumes[81]   3
and sacred squares were drawn everywhere.
The decoration of the markets can scarcely be described,
with gateways, banners, pennants, and awnings.
Betel, banana, and mango trees, all in full fruit,   4
were set up, with flowering trees—*bakul, kadamba,* and
    tamāl[82]—
their beautiful branches bending to the ground
around gem-studded planters, wondrously crafted.

Sacred vessels of many sorts, artfully adorned,   344
were placed in every home.
The sight of the Raghu lord's city
made Brahma and all the gods envious.

On that day, the king's abode was so resplendent   1
that its decoration bewitched Kama's heart.
Auspiciousness, fair omens, enchantment,
abundance and attainment, joy and wealth—
it was as if all innately good qualities   2
eagerly took form to grace Dasarath's home
in order to glimpse Ram and Vaidehi.
For, tell me, who does not yearn for this?

३ जूथ जूथ मिलि चलीं सुआसिनि ।
निज छबि निदरहिं मदन बिलासिनि ॥
सकल सुमंगल सजें आरती ।
गावहिं जनु बहु बेष भारती ॥

४ भूपति भवन कोलाहलु होई ।
जाइ न बरनि समउ सुखु सोई ॥
कौसल्यादि राम महतारीं ।
प्रेमबिबस तन दसा बिसारीं ॥

३४५ दिए दान बिप्रन्ह बिपुल पूजि गनेस पुरारि ।
प्रमुदित परम दरिद्र जनु पाइ पदारथ चारि ॥

१ मोद प्रमोद बिबस सब माता ।
चलहिं न चरन सिथिल भए गाता ॥
राम दरस हित अति अनुरागीं ।
परिछनि साजु सजन सब लागीं ॥

२ बिबिध बिधान बाजने बाजे ।
मंगल मुदित सुमित्राँ साजे ॥
हरद दूब दधि पल्लव फूला ।
पान पूगफल मंगल मूला ॥

३ अच्छत अंकुर लोचन लाजा ।
मंजुल मंजरि तुलसि बिराजा ॥
छुहे पुरट घट सहज सुहाए ।
मदन सकुन जनु नीड़ बनाए ॥

Bevies of married women went forth,   3
their beauty shaming the love lord's mistress,
all bearing trays arrayed for worship
and singing as if Bharati* herself had taken human forms.
There was commotion in the royal apartments   4
and indescribable joy in the occasion.
Kausalya and the other mothers of Ram,
distracted by love, lost bodily awareness.

They gave lavish gifts to Brahmans   345
and worshiped Ganesh and Shiva,
as ecstatic as utter paupers
who suddenly gain life's four rewards.

In their delirium of joy, the mothers   1
became weak-limbed and unable to walk.
Fervently longing to see Ram,
they began preparing for the lamp greeting.
As an array of instruments sounded,   2
Queen Sumitra assembled the sacred things—
turmeric, *dub* grass, curd, shoots, flowers,
betel leaves, and areca nuts, betokening auspiciousness,
unbroken rice, sprouts, yellow pigment, parched grain,   3
lovely sprigs of holy basil,[83]
waterpots of gold, beautifully painted,
like nests woven by the love god's weaver bird,

———

* An epithet of Sarasvati.

४ सगुन सुगंध न जाहिं बखानी ।
मंगल सकल सजहिं सब रानी ॥
रचीं आरतीं बहुत बिधाना ।
मुदित करहिं कल मंगल गाना ॥

३४६ कनक थार भरि मंगलन्हि कमल करन्हि लिएँ मात ।
चलीं मुदित परिछनि करन पुलक पल्लवित गात ॥

१ धूप धूम नभु मेचक भयऊ ।
सावन घन घमंडु जनु ठयऊ ॥
सुरतरु सुमन माल सुर बरषहिं ।
मनहुँ बलाक अवलि मनु करषहिं ॥

२ मंजुल मनिमय बंदनिवारे ।
मनहुँ पाकरिपु चाप सँवारे ॥
प्रगटहिं दुरहिं अटन्ह पर भामिनि ।
चारु चपल जनु दमकहिं दामिनि ॥

३ दुंदुभि धुनि घन गरजनि घोरा ।
जाचक चातक दादुर मोरा ॥
सुर सुगंध सुचि बरषहिं बारी ।
सुखी सकल ससि पुर नर नारी ॥

४ समउ जानि गुर आयसु दीन्हा ।
पुर प्रबेसु रघुकुलमनि कीन्हा ॥
सुमिरि संभु गिरिजा गनराजा ।
मुदित महीपति सहित समाजा ॥

326

and fragrances, too many to catalogue— 4
all were auspiciously arranged by the queens.
They adorned the festive ritual trays
and joyously sang songs of blessing.

Bearing in their lovely hands golden salvers 346
heaped with holy things, the mothers
went happily to perform the lamp ceremony,
their bodies flushed with emotion.

The smoke of incense darkened the skies 1
as if monsoon clouds had massed,
and the gods loosed strands of celestial blooms
like charming lines of flying cranes.
Ornamental arches wreathed with gems 2
resembled Indra's glorious celestial bow,*
and the coming and going of women on balconies
seemed like furtive flashes of lightning.
Kettledrums boomed like thunderclaps 3
as beggars called like *cātaks,* peacocks, and frogs,
and the celestials released fragrant showers
that gladdened the crop of the townspeople.
Knowing it was time, the guru gave the order 4
and the jewel of the Raghus entered the city,
invoking Shiva, the mountain's daughter, and Ganesh
and rejoicing with his royal entourage.

---

* The rainbow.

३४७ होहिं सगुन बरषहिं सुमन सुर दुंदुभीं बजाइ ।
बिबुध बधू नाचहिं मुदित मंजुल मंगल गाइ ॥

१ मागध सूत बंदि नट नागर ।
गावहिं जसु तिहु लोक उजागर ॥
जय धुनि बिमल बेद बर बानी ।
दस दिसि सुनिअ सुमंगल सानी ॥

२ बिपुल बाजने बाजन लागे ।
नभ सुर नगर लोग अनुरागे ॥
बने बराती बरनि न जाहीं ।
महा मुदित मन सुख न समाहीं ॥

३ पुरबासिन्ह तब राय जोहारे ।
देखत रामहि भए सुखारे ॥
करहिं निछावरि मनिगन चीरा ।
बारि बिलोचन पुलक सरीरा ॥

४ आरति करहिं मुदित पुर नारी ।
हरषहिं निरखि कुअँर बर चारी ॥
सिबिका सुभग ओहार उघारी ।
देखि दुलहिनिन्ह होहिं सुखारी ॥

३४८ एहि बिधि सबही देत सुखु आए राजदुआर ।
मुदित मातु परिछनि करहिं बधुन्ह समेत कुमार ॥

Amid favorable portents, the gods   347
rained down blossoms and beat their drums
while divine women danced with delight
to their own auspicious singing.

Minstrels, bards, genealogists, and entertainers   1
sang the glory of the light of the three worlds.
Victory cries and the pure sound of the Veda
filled all ten directions with auspiciousness.
As a host of instruments began to play,   2
gods above and townsfolk below were captivated.
The wedding party's finery surpassed description,
and their hearts were ecstatic with uncontainable joy.
The townspeople paid obeisance to the king   3
and, glimpsing Ram, were overcome with delight.
They proffered heaps of jewels and fabrics
with tear-filled eyes and trembling limbs.
The women joyously worshiped with lamps,   4
gazing happily at the four handsome princes.
Drawing back the rich drapes of the palanquins,
they saw the brides and were overjoyed.

And so, giving delight to all, the procession   348
approached the palace gate,
where the royal mothers performed the lamp-blessing
of the princes and their brides.

१ करहिं आरती बारहिं बारा ।
प्रेमु प्रमोदु कहै को पारा ॥
भूषन मनि पट नाना जाती ।
करहिं निछावरि अगनित भाँती ॥

२ बधुन्ह समेत देखि सुत चारी ।
परमानंद मगन महतारी ॥
पुनि पुनि सीय राम छबि देखी ।
मुदित सफल जग जीवन लेखी ॥

३ सखीं सीय मुख पुनि पुनि चाही ।
गान करहिं निज सुकृत सराही ॥
बरषहिं सुमन छनहिं छन देवा ।
नाचहिं गावहिं लावहिं सेवा ॥

४ देखि मनोहर चारिउ जोरीं ।
सारद उपमा सकल ढँढोरीं ॥
देत न बनहिं निपट लघु लागीं ।
एकटक रहीं रूप अनुरागीं ॥

३४९ निगम नीति कुल रीति करि अरघ पाँवड़े देत ।
बधुन्ह सहित सुत परिछि सब चलीं लवाइ निकेत ॥

१ चारि सिंघासन सहज सुहाए ।
जनु मनोज निज हाथ बनाए ॥
तिन्ह पर कुअँरि कुअँर बैठारे ।
सादर पाय पुनीत पखारे ॥

They did the greeting rite time and again—   1
who can describe their love and joy?—
with innumerable ornaments, gems, garments,
and countless other kinds of offerings.
Seeing their four sons with brides,   2
their mothers were plunged in sheer bliss.
Constantly gazing at Sita and Ram's beauty
they rejoiced and reckoned their lives fulfilled.
Their friends looked time and again at Sita's face,   3
praising past deeds that had earned this boon.
The gods incessantly rained blossoms,
danced and sang, and proffered adoration.
Seeing the four entrancing couples,   4
goddess Sharada searched the realm of similes,
yet finding them inadequate, could offer none
and just gazed unblinking, in love with their forms.

Performing Vedic and family rites,   349
pouring oblations and laying down rich cloths,
they blessed their sons and daughters-in-law
and brought them home.

Four lovely couches were arrayed there   1
as if made by the mind-born god's own hands.
On these, they seated the young couples
and reverently washed their holy feet.

२ धूप दीप नैबेद बेद बिधि ।
पूजे बर दुलहिनि मंगल निधि ॥
बारहिं बार आरती करहीं ।
ब्यजन चारु चामर सिर ढरहीं ॥

३ बस्तु अनेक निछावरि होहीं ।
भरीं प्रमोद मातु सब सोहीं ॥
पावा परम तत्व जनु जोगीं ।
अमृतु लहेउ जनु संतत रोगीं ॥

४ जनम रंक जनु पारस पावा ।
अंधहि लोचन लाभु सुहावा ॥
मूक बदन जनु सारद छाई ।
मानहुँ समर सूर जय पाई ॥

३५०क एहि सुख ते सत कोटि गुन पावहिं मातु अनंदु ।
भाइन्ह सहित बिआहि घर आए रघुकुलचंदु ॥

३५०ख लोक रीति जननीं करहिं बर दुलहिनि सकुचाहिं ।
मोदु बिनोदु बिलोकि बड़ रामु मनहिं मुसुकाहिं ॥

१ देव पितर पूजे बिधि नीकी ।
पूजीं सकल बासना जी की ॥
सबहि बंदि मागहिं बरदाना ।
भाइन्ह सहित राम कल्याना ॥

With incense, lights, and oblations, by Vedic rule,   2
they worshiped the pairs, treasuries of blessing,
repeatedly performing the lamp ritual
as fans and fly whisks waved over their heads.
Then countless goods were given away   3
by the mothers, as lovely in their joy
as a yogi who attains the supreme reality,
a chronic invalid who gains healing nectar,
or a lifelong pauper the alchemical stone,   4
a blind man the boon of healthy eyes,
a mute who is possessed by goddess Speech,
or a warrior who triumphs in battle—

a thousand million times such joy   350a
was the bliss those mothers gained
when, duly wed and with his brothers,
the moon of the Raghus came home.

Then the mothers indulged in folk customs,   350b
embarrassing the young couples.[84]
Watching all the merriment and festivity,
Lord Ram smiled to himself.

They gave due worship to ancestors and gods,   1
for their hearts' every longing was fulfilled,
and, paying obeisance to all, asked the boon
of the well-being of Ram and his brothers.

२ अंतरहित सुर आसिष देहीं ।
मुदित मातु अंचल भरि लेहीं ॥
भूपति बोलि बराती लीन्हे ।
जान बसन मनि भूषन दीन्हे ॥

३ आयसु पाइ राखि उर रामहि ।
मुदित गए सब निज निज धामहि ॥
पुर नर नारि सकल पहिराए ।
घर घर बाजन लगे बधाए ॥

४ जाचक जन जाचहिं जोइ जोई ।
प्रमुदित राउ देहिं सोइ सोई ॥
सेवक सकल बजनिआ नाना ।
पूरन किए दान सनमाना ॥

३५१ देहिं असीस जोहारि सब गावहिं गुन गन गाथ ।
तब गुर भूसुर सहित गृहँ गवनु कीन्ह नरनाथ ॥

१ जो बसिष्ट अनुसासन दीन्ही ।
लोक बेद बिधि सादर कीन्ही ॥
भूसुर भीर देखि सब रानी ।
सादर उठीं भाग्य बड़ जानी ॥

२ पाय पखारि सकल अन्हवाए ।
पूजि भली बिधि भूप जेवाँए ॥
आदर दान प्रेम परिपोषे ।
देत असीस चले मन तोषे ॥

Invisibly, the gods bestowed blessings   2
that the mothers gladly received, holding out their sari
    ends.
The king summoned the whole wedding party
and gave them carriages, clothes, and jewelry.
With his leave, and keeping Ram in their hearts,   3
they all returned happily to their homes.
The citizens, too, were abundantly outfitted,
and songs of celebration arose in every house.
Whatsoever humble suppliants asked for,   4
the delighted king dispensed to each and all.
His countless retainers and musicians
were sated with gifts and generous homage.

Reverently offering their blessings,   351
they all sang a litany of the king's virtues.
Then, accompanied by family priest and Brahmans,
the ruler of men returned home.

Whatever instructions Vasishtha gave   1
were piously fulfilled, following scripture and custom.
The queens saw the assembled Brahmans
and respectfully rose, knowing their good fortune.
They washed their feet and prepared their baths,   2
and the king, with all reverence, feasted them.
Nurtured by his homage, gifts, and love,
they left well pleased, bestowing blessings.

३ बहु बिधि कीन्हि गाधिसुत पूजा ।
नाथ मोहि सम धन्य न दूजा ॥
कीन्हि प्रसंसा भूपति भूरी ।
रानिन्ह सहित लीन्हि पग धूरी ॥

४ भीतर भवन दीन्ह बर बासू ।
मन जोगवत रह नृपु रनिवासू ॥
पूजे गुर पद कमल बहोरी ।
कीन्हि बिनय उर प्रीति न थोरी ॥

३५२ बधुन्ह समेत कुमार सब रानिन्ह सहित महीसु ।
पुनि पुनि बंदत गुर चरन देत असीस मुनीसु ॥

१ बिनय कीन्हि उर अति अनुरागें ।
सुत संपदा राखि सब आगें ॥
नेगु मागि मुनिनायक लीन्हा ।
आसिरबादु बहुत बिधि दीन्हा ॥

२ उर धरि रामहि सीय समेता ।
हरषि कीन्ह गुर गवनु निकेता ॥
बिप्रबधू सब भूप बोलाई ।
चैल चारु भूषन पहिराई ॥

३ बहुरि बोलाइ सुआसिनि लीन्हीं ।
रुचि बिचारि पहिरावनि दीन्हीं ॥
नेगी नेग जोग सब लेहीं ।
रुचि अनुरूप भूपमनि देहीं ॥

Then the king worshiped Gadhi's son,*   3
saying, "Master, no one is as fortunate as I."
The lord of earth paid him full homage,
and, with his queens, honored the dust of his feet.
He gave him fine quarters in the inner palace   4
where he and his women could serve him well.
Again, the king paid reverence to his own guru's feet,
making supplication with heartfelt love.

With his daughters-in-law, sons, and all his queens,   352
the lord of the world
bowed time and again at his teacher's feet,
and the lord of sages blessed him.

He venerated him with heartfelt devotion,   1
placing before him his sons and his wealth.
That best of sages asked only for his priest fee,
and showered the king with his blessings.
Placing Ram and Sita in his heart,   2
the guru went happily to his abode.
The king called for the Brahman wives
and adorned them with fine raiment and jewelry.
Then he summoned all the married women   3
and gave garments to each, discerning her liking.
The servants all received generous gifts,
as they wished, from that crown jewel of kings.

---

* Vishvamitra.

४ प्रिय पाहुने पूज्य जे जाने ।
भूपति भली भाँति सनमाने ॥
देव देखि रघुबीर बिबाहू ।
बरषि प्रसून प्रसंसि उछाहू ॥

३५३ चले निसान बजाइ सुर निज निज पुर सुख पाइ ।
कहत परसपर राम जसु प्रेम न हृदयँ समाइ ॥

१ सब बिधि सबहि समदि नरनाहू ।
रहा हृदयँ भरि पूरि उछाहू ॥
जहँ रनिवासु तहाँ पगु धारे ।
सहित बहूटिन्ह कुअँर निहारे ॥

२ लिए गोद करि मोद समेता ।
को कहि सकइ भयउ सुखु जेता ॥
बधू सप्रेम गोद बैठारीं ।
बार बार हियँ हरषि दुलारीं ॥

३ देखि समाजु मुदित रनिवासू ।
सब कें उर अनंद कियो बासू ॥
कहेउ भूप जिमि भयउ बिबाहू ।
सुनि सुनि हरषु होत सब काहू ॥

४ जनक राज गुन सीलु बड़ाई ।
प्रीति रीति संपदा सुहाई ॥
बहुबिधि भूप भाट जिमि बरनी ।
रानीं सब प्रमुदित सुनि करनी ॥

Those guests known to merit special reverence   4
were lavishly honored by earth's sovereign.
The gods, having witnessed the Raghu hero's wedding,
lauded the festivities and rained down blossoms.

Sounding deep drums, the deities departed,   353
well pleased, for their own realms,
recounting Ram's glory to one another,
their hearts overflowing with love.

Having fully satisfied all, the lord of men   1
savored deepest delight.
He proceeded to the women's apartments
and saw his sons with their brides.
As he blissfully embraced them,   2
who can tell the joy he knew?
Lovingly, he took his daughters-in-law
again and again into his tender embrace.
The sight of this meeting thrilled the royal women   3
and their hearts became abodes of bliss.
Then the king began to describe the wedding
as everyone listened with avid delight.[85]
Raja Janak's virtue and magnanimity,   4
loving ways and magnificent wealth,
the king recounted like a bard, in full detail,
and the queens rejoiced to hear of this.

३५४ सुतन्ह समेत नहाइ नृप बोलि बिप्र गुर ग्याती ।
भोजन कीन्ह अनेक बिधि घरी पंच गइ राति ॥

१ मंगलगान करहिं बर भामिनि ।
भै सुखमूल मनोहर जामिनि ॥
अँचइ पान सब काहूँ पाए ।
स्रग सुगंध भूषित छबि छाए ॥

२ रामहि देखि रजायसु पाई ।
निज निज भवन चले सिर नाई ॥
प्रेम प्रमोदु बिनोदु बड़ाई ।
समउ समाजु मनोहरताई ॥

३ कहि न सकहिं सत सारद सेसू ।
बेद बिरंचि महेस गनेसू ॥
सो मैं कहौं कवन बिधि बरनी ।
भूमिनागु सिर धरइ कि धरनी ॥

४ नृप सब भाँति सबहि सनमानी ।
कहि मृदु बचन बोलाईं रानी ॥
बधू लरिकनीं पर घर आईं ।
राखेहु नयन पलक की नाईं ॥

३५५ लरिका श्रमित उनीद बस सयन करावहु जाइ ।
अस कहि गे बिश्रामगृहँ राम चरन चितु लाइ ॥

Then, after bathing with his sons,   354
he summoned guru, priests, and kinsmen
and they feasted lavishly
until five periods of the night had passed.[86]

Lovely women sang songs of blessing   1
and the night became enchanting and joyful.
They all rinsed their mouths, partook of betel,
and were adorned with garlands and fine scent.
Gazing at Ram and receiving royal leave,   2
they bowed and went to their own abodes.
But the love and merriment, the splendor
and charm of that occasion and assembly
cannot be told by a hundred Sharadas and Sheshas,   3
Vedas, Brahmas, Shivas, and Ganeshas!
How, then, could I possibly narrate it—
can a worm take the earth on its head?
After honoring all his guests, the king   4
called for his queens and gently said,
"The brides are but girls, come to a strange house,
so protect them as the eyelids do the eyes.

The boys are weary and overcome with sleep.   355
See that they are put to bed."
Saying this, the king retired to his bedchamber,
fixing his mind on Ram's feet.

१ भूप बचन सुनि सहज सुहाए ।
जरित कनक मनि पलँग डसाए ॥
सुभग सुरभि पय फेन समाना ।
कोमल कलित सुपेतीं नाना ॥

२ उपबरहन बर बरनि न जाहीं ।
स्रग सुगंध मनिमंदिर माहीं ॥
रतनदीप सुठि चारु चँदोवा ।
कहत न बनइ जान जेहिं जोवा ॥

३ सेज रुचिर रचि रामु उठाए ।
प्रेम समेत पलँग पौढ़ाए ॥
अग्या पुनि पुनि भाइन्ह दीन्ही ।
निज निज सेज सयन तिन्ह कीन्ही ॥

४ देखि स्याम मृदु मंजुल गाता ।
कहहिं सप्रेम बचन सब माता ॥
मारग जात भयावनि भारी ।
केहि बिधि तात ताड़का मारी ॥

३५६ घोर निसाचर बिकट भट समर गनहिं नहिं काहु ।
मारे सहित सहाय किमि खल मारीच सुबाहु ॥

१ मुनि प्रसाद बलि तात तुम्हारी ।
ईस अनेक करवरें टारी ॥
मख रखवारी करि दुहुँ भाई ।
गुरु प्रसाद सब बिद्या पाई ॥

342

At his words, so naturally pleasing, the queens   1
made up golden beds inlaid with gems.
White as the froth of a fair cow's milk
were the many soft sheets they spread,
with fine pillows beyond description.   2
That jewel-room, fragrant with flowers,
lit by gem lamps, adorned with canopies,
was indescribable—only one who sees it can know.
Having arranged fine bedding, they brought Ram[87]   3
and lovingly made him lie on that bed.
Only after his repeated entreaties
did his brothers go to their own beds.
Beholding his dark and delicate body   4
the mothers all spoke affectionately.
"When you were wayfaring, dear son,
how did you slay the dreadful she-demon Taraka?

And those awful night-rangers—hardened warriors   356
fearing no one in battle,
Marich and Subahu—how could you kill them
along with their legions?

We swear on your head, son, it was by the sage's grace   1
that God averted so many calamities.
Guarding the sacrifice, you two brothers
acquired all knowledge by the guru's favor.

२ मुनि तिय तरी लगत पग धूरी ।
कीरति रही भुवन भरि पूरी ॥
कमठ पीठि पबि कूट कठोरा ।
नृप समाज महुँ सिव धनु तोरा ॥

३ बिस्व बिजय जसु जानकि पाई ।
आए भवन ब्याहि सब भाई ॥
सकल अमानुष करम तुम्हारे ।
केवल कौसिक कृपाँ सुधारे ॥

४ आजु सुफल जग जनमु हमारा ।
देखि तात बिधुबदन तुम्हारा ॥
जे दिन गए तुम्हहि बिनु देखें ।
ते ब्रिरंचि जनि पारहिं लेखें ॥

३५७ राम प्रतोषीं मातु सब कहि बिनीत बर बैन ।
सुमिरि संभु गुर बिप्र पद किए नीदबस नैन ॥

१ नीदउँ बदन सोह सुठि लोना ।
मनहुँ साँझ सरसीरुह सोना ॥
घर घर करहिं जागरन नारीं ।
देहिं परसपर मंगल गारीं ॥

२ पुरी बिराजति राजति रजनी ।
रानीं कहहिं बिलोकहु सजनी ॥
सुंदर बधुन्ह सासु लै सोई ।
फनिकन्ह जनु सिरमनि उर गोई ॥

A sage's wife was freed by touching the dust of your feet,   2
and your fame spread throughout the world.
Shiva's bow—tougher than a tortoise shell, diamond,
or mountain peak—you broke in the kings' assembly,
and winning world renown and Janaki, too,   3
you brought your brothers home wedded.
All these superhuman deeds of yours
were only managed by Kaushik's grace.
Today our birth in this world bears fruit   4
when we behold, child, the moon of your face,
and the days we spent without seeing you,
may God not reckon in our lives' account!"

Ram soothed all his mothers   357
with sweet and humble speech,
and meditating on the feet of Shiva, guru, and Brahmans,
let sleep overcome his eyes.

At rest, his face was perfectly charming,   1
like a red lotus contracted at twilight.
In every household, women stayed awake[88]
trading auspicious and ribald songs.
"Look, dears, how the city shines   2
on this splendid night!" said the queens
and went to sleep with the lovely brides,
like cobras hiding crest-jewels in their breasts.

३ प्रात पुनीत काल प्रभु जागे ।
अरुनचूड़ बर बोलन लागे ॥
बंदि मागधन्हि गुनगन गाए ।
पुरजन द्वार जोहारन आए ॥

४ बंदि बिप्र सुर गुर पितु माता ।
पाइ असीस मुदित सब भ्राता ॥
जननिन्ह सादर बदन निहारे ।
भूपति संग द्वार पगु धारे ॥

३५८ कीन्हि सौच सब सहज सुचि सरित पुनीत नहाइ ।
प्रातक्रिया करि तात पहिं आए चारिउ भाइ ॥

१ भूप बिलोकि लिए उर लाई ।
बैठे हरषि रजायसु पाई ॥
देखि रामु सब सभा जुड़ानी ।
लोचन लाभ अवधि अनुमानी ॥

२ पुनि बसिष्टु मुनि कौसिकु आए ।
सुभग आसनन्हि मुनि बैठाए ॥
सुतन्ह समेत पूजि पद लागे ।
निरखि रामु दोउ गुर अनुरागे ॥

३ कहहिं बसिष्टु धरम इतिहासा ।
सुनहिं महीसु सहित रनिवासा ॥
मुनि मन अगम गाधिसुत करनी ।
मुदित बसिष्ट बिपुल बिधि बरनी ॥

The Lord awoke at the sacred hour.[89] 3
Red-crested roosters began to crow,
bards and minstrels intoned his praise,
and townsfolk gathered reverently at the palace gate.
Saluting Brahmans, gods, guru, and parents, 4
the brothers happily received their blessings.
Their mothers lovingly beheld their faces
as they went with the king to the gateway.

Though innately pure, they all cleansed themselves[90] 358
and bathed in the holy river.
Completing the morning rituals,
the four brothers returned to their father.

As soon as he saw them, the king drew them to his heart, 1
and at his command they gladly took their seats.
The sight of Ram soothed the whole assembly
who reckoned it their eyes' supreme reward.
Then Vasishtha and Vishvamitra arrived 2
and were given splendid seats.
The king and his sons worshiped at their feet,
and seeing Ram, the two gurus felt intense love.
Vasishtha began recounting sacred lore 3
while the king and royal women listened.
The deeds of Gadhi's son,[91] which perplex even sages,
Vasishtha happily narrated in great detail.

४ बोले बामदेउ सब साँची।
कीरति कलित लोक तिहुँ माची॥
सुनि आनंदु भयउ सब काहू।
राम लखन उर अधिक उछाहू॥

३५९ मंगल मोद उछाह नित जाहिं दिवस एहि भाँति।
उमगी अवध अनंद भरि अधिक अधिक
अधिकाति॥

१ सुदिन सोधि कल कंकन छोरे।
मंगल मोद बिनोद न थोरे॥
नित नव सुखु सुर देखि सिहाहीं।
अवध जन्म जाचहिं बिधि पाहीं॥

२ बिस्वामित्रु चलन नित चहहीं।
राम सप्रेम बिनय बस रहहीं॥
दिन दिन सयगुन भूपति भाऊ।
देखि सराह महामुनिराऊ॥

३ मागत बिदा राउ अनुरागे।
सुतन्ह समेत ठाढ़ भे आगे॥
नाथ सकल संपदा तुम्हारी।
मैं सेवकु समेत सुत नारी॥

४ करब सदा लरिकन्ह पर छोहू।
दरसनु देत रहब मुनि मोहू॥

Sage Vamadeva affirmed, "All this is true!   4
Vishvamitra's fame fills the three worlds."
Everyone was delighted to hear this,
and Ram and Lakshman felt special exhilaration.

So the days passed, filled with constant blessing,   359
merriment, and celebration.
Avadh was awash with a bliss that swelled
and swelled beyond all bounds.

On a chosen day, the ritual threads were untied[92]   1
amid great joy and auspicious celebration.
Seeing these endless delights, the gods grew jealous
and begged Brahma for birth in Avadh.
Vishvamitra, though ever anxious to depart,   2
was held back by Ram's love and humility.
Daily witnessing the king's hundredfold affection,
that king of sages voiced lavish praise.
When he asked to leave, the king was overcome   3
and stood before him with his sons.
"Lord, all this bounty belongs to you,
and I am your servant, with my sons and wives.
Be always gracious toward these boys   4
and regularly bless me with your presence."

अस कहि राउ सहित सुत रानी ।
परेउ चरन मुख आव न बानी ॥

५ दीन्हि असीस बिप्र बहु भाँती ।
चले न प्रीति रीति कहि जाती ॥

रामु सप्रेम संग सब भाई ।
आयसु पाइ फिरे पहुँचाई ॥

३६० राम रूपु भूपति भगति ब्याहु उछाहु अनंदु ।
जात सराहत मनहिं मन मुदित गाधिकुलचंदु ॥

१ बामदेव रघुकुल गुर ग्यानी ।
बहुरि गाधिसुत कथा बखानी ॥

सुनि मुनि सुजसु मनहिं मन राऊ ।
बरनत आपन पुन्य प्रभाऊ ॥

२ बहुरे लोग रजायसु भयऊ ।
सुतन्ह समेत नृपति गृहँ गयऊ ॥

जहँ तहँ राम ब्याहु सबु गावा ।
सुजसु पुनीत लोक तिहुँ छावा ॥

३ आए ब्याहि रामु घर जब तें ।
बसइ अनंद अवध सब तब तें ॥

प्रभु बिबाहँ जस भयउ उछाहू ।
सकहिं न बरनि गिरा अहिनाहू ॥

४ कबिकुल जीवनु पावन जानी ।
राम सीय जसु मंगल खानी ॥

So saying, the king, with his sons and queens,
fell at the sage's feet, unable to speak.
Bestowing abundant blessings, the Brahman   5
left amid indescribable expressions of tenderness.
Ram and his brothers lovingly accompanied him,
till they received his order to turn back.

Ram's beauty, the king's devotion,   360
the rapture of the marriage festivities—
as he left, the moon of Gadhi's lineage
inwardly praised all these with delight.

Vamadeva and the preceptor of the Raghus*   1
once more narrated the tale of Gadhi's son.
Hearing of that sage's renown, the king mused
over the wondrous efficacy of his past deeds.
Obtaining his leave, the people departed   2
and the lord of men, too, went home with his sons.
People everywhere sang the saga of Ram's marriage,
and his pure fame permeated the three worlds.
From the day that Ram came home married,   3
all delights took up residence in Avadh.
The gaiety occasioned by the Lord's wedding
cannot be described even by Sharada and Shesh.
Knowing that the life of all poets is purified   4
by Ram and Sita's fame, treasury of blessing,

---

* Vasishtha.

तेहि ते मैं कछु कहा बखानी ।
करन पुनीत हेतु निज बानी ॥

५ निज गिरा पावनि करन कारन
राम जसु तुलसीं कह्यो ।
रघुबीर चरित अपार बारिधि
पारु कबि कौनें लह्यो ॥
उपबीत ब्याह उछाह मंगल
सुनि जे सादर गावहीं ।
बैदेहि राम प्रसाद ते जन
सर्बदा सुखु पावहीं ॥

३६१ सिय रघुबीर बिबाहु जे सप्रेम गावहिं सुनहिं ।
तिन्ह कहुँ सदा उछाहु मंगलायतन राम जसु ॥

I have recounted just a little of it
for the sake of sanctifying my speech.

To sanctify his own speech, Tulsi has told   5
of the renown of Ram.
But the Raghu hero's deeds are a boundless sea—
what poet has crossed it?
Those who reverently listen and then sing
of the joys of the sacred thread[93]
and nuptial rites will gain abiding joy
by the grace of Vaidehi and Ram.

Those who hear and sing with love   361
of the wedding of Sita and the Raghu hero
are forever inspired, for Ram's renown
is the abode of all auspiciousness.

[The end of the first stair of the *Rāmcaritmānas,*
which annihilates all impurities of the Kali Age.][94]

NOTES TO THE TEXT

१   रीति] MP; प्रीति GP

NOTES TO THE TRANSLATION

The Tyranny of Ravan

1   "Species," *jāti*; here Ravan specifically exempts these two life-forms from his boon of "limited immortality"—presumably because he considers them insignificant. For the same reason, in the Valmiki *Rāmāyaṇa*, he simply omits to mention them.

2   Maya (with short vowels) is one of the sons of Danu, hence a "demon," or more correctly, a kind of *asura*, the titanic and estranged cousins of the celestial *devas*. A master of fabrication and artifice (*māyā*), he is their architect and builder.

3   "Demigods," *jaccha;* a race of elemental beings who protect wild and beautiful places. Their king, Kuber, god of wealth, reigns over the mineral-rich Himalayas.

4   "Cloud-sound," *vāridanāda, meghanāda;* i.e., thunderclap. He will soon earn the epithet Indrajit, "victorious over Indra."

5   Durmukh (here, Kumukha): "dreadful-faced"; Akampan: "unshakable"; Vajradant (here, Kulisarada): "adamant-fanged"; Dhumketu: "smoke-banner"; Atikay: "huge-bodied."

6   All such rites "feed" the heavenly gods, and Brahmans are "gods on earth."

7   In the cosmic mandala, deities are stationed at the cardinal directions, generally Indra or Kuber (north), Surya (east), Yama (south), and Varuna (west); sometimes northeast, etc., are added, accounting for eight "directional guardians."

8   Most commentators gloss this as "Brahmans," though it can refer to any male member of the three upper social orders who is initiated in Vedic practice.

9   With this vocative and aside, Tulsi again signals that Shiva is narrating.

10 The stanza that follows, comprising Brahma's hymn, consists entirely of lyrical four-line *chand* verses, capped by the usual *dohā*.

11 "Giving up on our ingenuity," *chāri sayānī;* i.e., the gods recognize that they are unable to defeat Ravan on their own.

12 The cosmic mountain used by the gods and their demonic cousins to churn the ocean of infinity.

13 "Supreme energy," *parama sakti;* this refers to his feminine consort, Sita.

Ram's Birth and Youth

1 Literally, "the one holding the bow named *sāraṅga*"; an epithet of Vishnu.

2 According to tradition, Ram was born on the ninth of the bright fortnight of the month of Chaitra, under the asterism Abhijit (victorious), which Tulsi calls "dear to Hari."

3 The stanza that follows (up to *dohā* 192) comprises four lyrical *chand* verses. It is very popular and often recited in Ram temples, especially during his birth celebrations.

4 Most commentators interpret this as Vishnu/Ram recounting tales of his own and Kausalya's former lives; e.g., her request of him, as King Manu's wife Satarupa, to take birth as her son (see 1.149).

5 Tulsidas specifies, along with "birth rites," the Vedic ritual of *nāndīmukha śrāddha,* in which nine small balls of auspicious substances are offered to ancestors.

6 "Worshiping with lamps" refers to the *āratī* tray and ritual (see 1.96.1 and accompanying note). "Gestures of blessing" here approximates *nevachāvarī* (in modern Hindi, *nichāvar*), which refers to ritual hand gestures, often made by women, to remove inauspiciousness or the evil eye from a cherished person by taking it on themselves. It is sometimes translated "self-sacrifice."

7 Commentators disagree on whether the abundant gifts were being dispensed by the king or in a collective free-for-all; the latter sense seems more in keeping with the utopian spirit of the passage and the emphasis in Hindu tradition on the great virtue of giving gifts; note the second *ardhālī*'s observation that even the receivers did not hold on to their gifts.

8 Here, Shiva as narrator interjects a personal note, signaled by the address to Parvati in the second half of the line. The immortal crow Bhushundi will figure prominently in the final book of the *Mānas.*

9 Literally, "their mothers broke blades of grass," a gesture meant to protect an adorable child from the potentially malicious and covetous gaze of human beings and spirits.

10 Vishnu is said to bear these auspicious marks on the soles of his feet.

11 The angry Brahman Bhrigu once kicked Vishnu in the chest,

leaving a footprint-shaped scar that the Lord graciously accepted as a permanent adornment.

12 "Infant locks," *gabhuāre;* literally, "(hair) from the womb," a term referring to a child's hair prior to the first ritual tonsure.

13 The narrator here appears to be Shiva, signaled by the invocation of "Bhavani" in the next stanza, and by his earlier mention of having secretly gone to Avadh with Bhushundi to glimpse the infant Ram.

14 Literally, "sees in a dream/vision" (*sapanehũ*).

15 With this epithet, Tulsi foreshadows a later event in the story (3.18).

16 There is an apparent shift in this *caupāī* from past to present tense, suggesting a transition from straightforward narrative (the boys grow bigger and receive their first haircut) to Tulsidas's characteristic savoring of a devotional vision: toddler Ram's pranks at mealtime.

17 "Pure species," *pāvana mṛga;* although the second word is often translated "deer," it can refer to any wild animal deemed permissible for hunting. Ram's discriminate killing of these is also taken by some commentators to refer to his selection of souls who, by virtue of their deeds in prior lives, deserved liberation (as the next *caupāī* states).

18 Though it seems a non sequitur in translation, the second line of this *soraṭhā* begins with one of Tulsidas's commonest epithets for Ram (*kṛpāsindhu,* "ocean of compassion") and hails him (alone or as a dyad with Lakshman) as supreme God. The opening verses of the next stanza present a verbal icon that depicts Ram alone.

19 More literally, "Going along, the sage showed (them)"—but showed them what? Commentators mull over the extreme compression of this line, which seems to allude to Valmiki's passage in which Vishvamitra explains the devastation wrought on two once-flourishing lands by Taraka and her sons. Ram then twangs his bowstring, challenging her—a gesture that may be implied by the word "hearing," with which the second half of the line begins.

20 "His own state," *nija pada;* most commentators understand this as a boon of liberation, in which Taraka's soul experiences oneness with Ram or residence in his divine world. They reject interpreting the possessive pronoun as a reference to Taraka's being restored (as in some other Ram stories) to her former demidivine condition.

21 "Bow rite" or "bow sacrifice," *dhanuṣa jagya;* a reference to Sita's

svayaṃvara, or marriage tournament, in which a miraculous bow figures, and the conventional name for this episode in Hindi.

22 As at several other points, Tulsi omits a story recounted at length in the Valmiki version: here, that of the beautiful Ahalya's seduction by Indra, who assumed the form of her husband, the sage Gautam (*Rāmāyaṇa* 1.47–48). Discovering the couple, Gautam cursed them both. According to Valmiki, Ahalya was condemned to live invisibly in the deserted ashram, but most later Ram tales have her transformed into a boulder. In all versions, the curse is to end when Ram passes through the ashram and his feet touch the stone in which she is imprisoned.

23 The four numbered verses that follow, preceding *dohā* 211, are in lyrical *chand* meter.

24 To a modern reader this seems an anachronism, since Ram has not yet encountered Ravan. However, in Tulsi's world of recurring aeons and "many Ramayanas," it is reasonable to suppose that the saintly Ahalya divines the predestined story.

25 Although commentators generally gloss this as Tulsidas addressing the human mind/heart, the vocative here may equally be translated, "Oh foolish/wicked Tulsidas."

26 "On four sides," *cahū pāsa;* Tulsidas's idealized description of Sita's hometown has been used by some devotees as a guide to meditative visualization of a four-gated mandala, a practice the next *caupāī* seems to suggest.

27 This half line puns on Janak's epithet "Videha," which can mean "without a body." Tulsidas implies that the king lost bodily awareness on seeing Ram.

28 See "Prologue," n. 35. The unitary ultimate reality of "nondualist" tradition, referred to here as *brahma,* may be described only in negative terms. The Advaita resonance of the phrase appears to lend special flavor to the king's speculation, in the second half of the *caupāī,* that this transcendent and unitary reality might be present before him in "dual guise" (*ubhaya beṣa*).

29 "Watch of day," *jāma;* one of the eight three-hour periods into which the day was traditionally divided. Commentators point out that this time—late afternoon—is an ideal time for travelers to explore local sights, as the Raghu brothers will shortly do.

30 "Dharma's boundary wall," *dharama setu;* the word *setu* refers to a bridge, dam, or bund, and is frequently used to suggest the

restraining function of dharma, the religiously sanctioned moral code.

31 "Three fires," *tāpa traya;* literally, "triple heat." Most commentators understand this to refer to physical suffering (*daihika*), suffering caused by the gods or fate (*daivika*), and that caused by spirits or witchcraft (*bhautika*). The moon, as repository of the nectar of life (*soma*), is thought to be cooling.

32 "Forehead marks," *tilaka;* an adornment of the forehead, usually drawn with sandalwood paste, vermilion, or a pigment of fine clay. In popular art, Ram's forehead usually bears the U-shaped symbol (with a parallel median line) associated with followers of Vishnu and sometimes said to represent the footprint of the god. In parts of north India, it is also common to decorate the forehead with thin vertical lines of cooling sandalwood paste.

33 In describing Ram's beauty, Tulsi repeatedly uses stock phrases alluding to his having "defeated" or "triumphed over" tens of millions (*koṭi*) of Kamas, or to tens of millions of love gods ritually "sacrificing" themselves before him (as in the next *dohā*).

34 Literally, "young, royal *haṃsas.*"

35 The reference is to Janak's vow to marry his daughter only to the man who can lift and string the bow of Shiva.

36 The speaker anticipates what is to occur, even though the purported object of King Janak's tournament is only to lift and string the great bow, not to break it.

37 Tulsidas calls the site of this ritual—essentially a tournament to win Sita's hand—simply a "ground" (*bhūmi*), but commentators and visual artists picture it as an enclosed amphitheater (*raṅgbhūmi*), as succeeding verses confirm.

38 "Purification" (*sauca*) normally refers to defecation and ensuing cleansing.

39 "Mindful of the hour" is assumed to refer to the approaching morning worship, for which Vishvamitra will require various flowers and herbs. It is for the ostensible purpose of collecting these that the princes make their visit to the royal garden (*phulavārī*), occasioning the beloved episode that follows.

40 In this line, Tulsidas plays (in a manner that defies translation) on a series of words derived from the Sanskrit root *ram* (to please): *ramya* (pleasing), *ārām* (place of pleasure or rest, i.e., pleasure park), and, of course, the name *Rām,* which is commonly construed to mean "he who pleases."

41 Tulsi does not include the story of Sita's miraculous birth from a furrow, which identified her as the daughter of the earth goddess, and in the narrative he refers to King Janak and Queen Sunayana as her parents.

42 "Immemorial love" (*prīti purātana*) refers to the eternal, transcendent relationship of Ram and Sita as the divine dyad.

43 Although the divine sage Narad has made two earlier appearances in the *Mānas* (in the stories of the marriage of Shiva and Parvati, and of Vishnu's humbling of Narad's pride; see 1.66–70 and 1.124–138), the reference here is apparently to the *Adhyātmarāmāyaṇa,* in which the peripatetic sage visited Sita's family earlier in her life and predicted that she would meet her future bridegroom in a garden.

44 According to various *purāṇas,* King Nimi became disembodied through a curse and was later restored to life by the gods. However, he chose not to take another body but instead to reside unseen on the eyelids. It is said that, until then, created beings had possessed steady, unblinking eyes (like the gods), but Nimi's presence compelled them to periodically blink. Most commentators add, in explanation of Tulsi's use of the word *sakuci* (with embarrassment), the explanation that, since Nimi was an ancestor of Janak and hence a "father" to Sita, the sight of the first meeting of his daughter and future son-in-law caused him to discreetly absent himself—allowing Ram to gaze unblinking at his bride-to-be.

45 "Stale leavings," *juṭhārī;* a culturally charged word referring to food that has been defiled by being previously partaken of by another.

46 Throbbing or palpitation of the limbs on the right side of the body is considered auspicious for males; the left limbs convey the same message to females. The reverse (e.g., trembling in the left limbs of a male) is an inauspicious omen.

47 "Spoke casually," *batakahī*. Tulsi's use of this word in reference to Ram's preceding sermon is a delightfully humanizing touch: the infatuated Lord, intent on gazing at Sita (who has not yet seen him), "buys time" by delivering a series of platitudes, two of which ironically cite the impropriety of staring at a woman who is not of one's own clan—though it is understood by devotees that Sita is already, eternally, "his."

48 Literally, "the moon of *Sharad,*" the month (falling in autumn by the Gregorian calendar) that follows the end of the monsoon and is characterized by clear, dust-free skies.

49 By deliberately internalizing the vision of Ram's beauty and then closing her eyes (the poet likens Sita's lids to the characteristic Indian style of double door panels), Sita appears to go into a state of meditation. The ensuing description of the princes when they fully emerge from the bower (apparently "seen" only by her companions) thus unfolds inwardly for her, making Sita paradigmatic of the Ram devotee who meditates on the visualized Lord.

50 It appears that the next stanza is spoken by one of Sita's young friends (note the first-person pronoun in the third *caupāī*, and the vocative in the final one), who describes the brothers to her while Sita stands with closed eyes, visualizing them inwardly.

51 Large "lotus eyes" that are slightly bloodshot at the corners, a trait often poetically likened to the reddish veins at the inner edge of a lotus petal, are considered a mark of beauty, strength, and erotic charge in Indian art and are standard in the representation of deities and kings.

52 Literally: "(Like) Kama (in the form of a) young elephant's trunk," or "like the trunk of the child of Kama's elephant, (their) arms the limit of strength." I have chosen not to repeat the reference to Kama, and (in place of the commonplace "limit/epitome of strength") to add the adjective "supple," suggesting the dexterity of a young elephant's trunk, which seems to be implied.

53 "Ravishing," *lonā;* literally, "salty," i.e., "tasty."

54 "Enthralled," *parabasa;* literally, "under the control of another." Sita is visibly overwhelmed by Ram's charm, yet her forthcoming marriage depends on her father's vow; hence she is doubly, and worrisomely, "controlled" by others. The wily girlfriends become worried that they may have gone too far in thus "introducing" her to Ram.

55 "Icy one," *himakara;* literally, "maker of snow/ice," an epithet of the moon.

56 "Lovesick women," *virahinī;* a woman suffering in separation from her lover. Rahu is the demon who causes eclipses by devouring (temporarily, since he is only a bodiless head) the sun and moon.

57 The *Mānaspīyūṣ* takes these four categories (the third and fourth mean, literally, "low" and "lightweight") to correspond to the traditional fourfold order of Brahmanical social theory (3.407).

58 "Martial spirit," *bīra rasa;* the "flavor" or "mood" of heroism, especially as experienced through works of art.

59   Lines like this invite commentators to expand on Tulsidas's "outline." What story did King Janak tell Vishvamitra? According to some, he related the history of Shiva's bow and how it came into the possession of his family (as in the Valmiki version). Others cite a tale in which Sita, as a child, casually picks up the bow, and Shiva then commands her father, in a dream, to give her in marriage only to a youth capable of the same awesome feat.

60   In this celebrated passage, Tulsidas, having declared that Sita cannot be compared to worldly women, turns to otherworldly ones. Girā, "speech," an epithet of Sarasvati, is called (in effect) a "chatterbox" (*mukhara*); Shiva's wife, Parvati, is dismissed because she appears as his own left side (in the androgynous form known as *ardhanārīśvara*, the lord who is half woman); and Rati is found to be too morose because the body of her husband, Kama, was burned by Shiva's anger. Finally, in his most audacious move, the poet rejects Lakshmi, Vishnu's wife, whose "birth" (at the time of the churning of the cosmic ocean by the gods and their demon cousins, a myth that forms the basis for the next four verses) was accompanied by that of poison and liquor. This apparent poetic conceit may also be read as a theological assertion: a rejection of the common notion that Ram and Sita are earthly avatars of Vishnu and Lakshmi. For Tulsi, the hero and heroine of the *Mānas* are the ultimate divine dyad, of whom all other deities, including Vishnu and his consort, are but partial manifestations.

61   In some versions of the story, Ravan is present at Sita's *svayaṃvara*, in others, he has previously come (as is implied here) and tried unsuccessfully to lift the bow. Bana is the name of another powerful, demonic king.

62   "As though," *janu;* commentators observe that the feigned anger of Sita's father, though meant to put the arrogant kings in their place, is really intended to provoke Ram into lifting the bow.

63   "Micron," *tilu bhari;* literally, "the space of a sesame seed."

64   Agastya, who was miraculously conceived in a clay pot, once drank the entire ocean as a favor to the gods, to reveal the hiding places of demons in its depths.

65   Specifically, the poet invokes the *siras* tree, which is known for its delicate white blossoms.

66   Kama, god of love, wears fish-shaped earrings, and a pair of frolicking fish is a common symbol of eros. Although the basic

simile is clear—Sita's shyly glancing eyes are likened to fish and her face to the moon (understood to be a reservoir of watery coolness)—this difficult couplet has generated much commentary, with some preferring to take the word *ḍola* (a bucket or vessel used to draw water from a well) as *hiṇḍola* (swing, cradle), referring to the anxious upward and downward movement of Sita's eyes.

67 The figure is of a bee trapped in a lotus that has closed for the night.

68 Garuda, the divine eagle, feeds on snakes.

69 Lakshman calls on the mythical beings who support or uplift the earth and the directions of space.

70 Parashuram ("axe-wielding Ram," identified here by his clan name as "lord of Bhrigus") is a previous avatar of Vishnu still present in the world. A devotee of Shiva, he has a special attachment to the bow, as will soon become clear (see 1.268–285).

71 The shehnai is a double-reed instrument similar to an oboe; its auspicious sound often inaugurates festive events and is especially associated with weddings.

72 The *cātak* (fem. *cātakī*, used here) is a kind of cuckoo; reputedly it can drink only raindrops that fall during the astrological period known as *svāti*.

73 See the story of Ahalya, 1.210–211. Sita fears that the touch of Ram's feet might likewise liberate her from her body and thus separate her from him.

74 Parashuram (see n. 70) is the archenemy of Kshatriyas, whom he repeatedly massacred to avenge his father's murder. Like everyone else in the world, he has heard the sound of the great bow's breaking.

75 Sahasbahu ("thousand-arms") was a monstrous king, endowed as his name implies. Parashuram killed him after first hacking off his many limbs.

76 The magical bow, formed from the energy of all the gods, that Shiva used to destroy the three demonic citadels was the very one that Ram has just snapped.

77 The double meaning here is typical of this passage: on the one hand, Lakshman invokes a Brahman's vaunted ability to curse through powerful mantras; on the other, he taunts the sage to back up his sharp tongue with appropriate action.

78 Several earthy images enhance this couplet. In the first line, Parashuram is said to be "completely green" (i.e., unripe). The

second refers to a mass of raw sugar, formed of cane juice that has been boiled until it darkens and crystallizes. Vishvamitra likens it to Lakshman, but says that (in his case), the block (ingot) is actually cast from molten iron, hence it cannot be easily cut, nor will a piece of it simply melt in the mouth.

79　As a youth, Parashuram dutifully carried out his father's command to behead his mother because she had been guilty of an extramarital lustful thought; he then requested his father to restore her to life. Later, he slaughtered the warrior class to avenge his father's murder.

80　"Barely weaned," *dūdhamukha;* literally, "milk-faced."

81　"Venom," *kālakūṭa;* the world-destroying poison that emerged from the cosmic ocean when it was churned by gods and demons.

82　There is disagreement over the meaning of the word *bararai.* Although it can identify a kind of wasp, some commentators interpret it as referring to insane persons, and interpret the *caupāī* to mean: "Children and the mad are of one nature / and godly folk never fault them."

83　In this charming "aside," Ram contrasts his own "straightness" or "simplicity" with the "crooked" ways of the world. Some commentators interpret the line beginning "One known to be crooked" to also refer to the moon, which, when "curved" (that is, on the second of its waxing fortnight) is especially revered. Rahu, the eclipse demon, is only successful in "devouring" the moon when it is full.

84　Here Tulsidas puns on the word *guṇa,* which means both a "string" and "virtuous quality." Although the reference alludes to the nine strands of the sacred thread, commentators also explain the nine traits of a twice-born person as tranquility, self-restraint, austerity, purity, forgiveness, sincerity, knowledge, wisdom, and faith in the Vedic tradition.

85　Some commentators favor an alternate reading of this half line as: "that even a fearless one fears you." The word "such" (*asi*) in the preceding half line is understood by some to accompany Ram's gesturing toward his chest, to reveal the footprint-shaped scar from the kick given to Vishnu by Parashuram's choleric ancestor, Bhrigu. This revelation (suggested by the identification of Ram's speech as *gūṛha,* mysterious or enigmatic) precipitates the sage's recognition of Ram as avatar.

86　Parashuram possesses a bow of Vishnu's, comparable to Shiva's bow, which Ram has broken.

87　Literally, "forest of lotuses." Tulsidas plays on one of the epithets of "lotus" (*banaja*, "born in the forest"), pairing it with *bana* (forest), which (since lotuses do not literally form forests) here implies a profusion of the flowers, as on a lake.

The Marriage of Sita and Ram

1　An alternative reading is that Brahma became "confused," mistaking the amazing fabrications for real plants.

2　"Ceremonial vessel," *kalasa* (see "The Story of Shiva and Bhavani," n. 30); "fly whisks," *camara:* partly pragmatic and partly ornamental, fine fly whisks, usually of yak tail with silver handles, were used to fan both kings and deities.

3　Although this verse seems to imply that Sita is an earthly embodiment of Vishnu's consort, sectarian commentators argue that, since Sita-Ram are the ultimate divinity, "Lakshmi" here is invoked only in simile.

4　The verb *bācnā*, "to read," though rarely used in the poem, occurs three times in this passage, referring to the king's multiple "readings" of the letter. Many commentators assume the first to refer to a silent reading to himself, which causes him to manifest physical symptoms that might be caused by either happiness or grief. Naturally, his courtiers are alarmed, hence his second "reading" (presumably aloud) sets everyone at ease.

5　"Emotions," *rasa;* aesthetic "flavors" or moods.

6　As residents of Janakpur, the messengers consider Sita their own daughter and hence (following the customs of north Indian exogamy) will not accept gifts in her (future) in-laws' home.

7　That is, there is no need to wait for an auspicious astrological conjunction.

8　Peafowl are said to mate during the monsoon, and their mating calls often accompany the appearance of rain clouds.

9　"Elder women," *guru nārī;* literally, "guru women." This may mean both senior women of the family and the wives of Brahmans and teachers attached to the court.

10　In this half line, the Gita Press edition uses the phrase *prīti kai prīti* ("love's love," yielding a sense of "yet by the loving multiplication of love . . ."). However, the *Mānaspīyūṣ* favors the reading *prīti kai rīti* (customs of love) that is found in some old manuscripts, and I prefer this as well.

11 "Sacred squares," *caukē;* ritual squares, divided into four quadrants, which are filled with auspicious or costly substances such as pearls or gems.

12 "Gorgeously adorned," *saji navasapta;* literally, "adorned with the sixteen," a reference to the traditional types of adornment (from toe rings to tiara) that beautify a woman.

13 Bharat is assumed to be accompanied by his inseparable (but rarely singled-out) half-brother, Shatrughna.

14 Literally, "They rejoiced at continually hearing *panava* [a small double-headed drum] and *nisāna* [a large kettledrum]."

15 "Bearers," *kahāra,* refers to a caste traditionally charged with carrying water vessels and other loads, which were suspended from the two ends of poles borne on their shoulders.

16 King Dasarath's trusted minister, who will play an important role in sub-book 2, *Ayodhyākāṇḍ.*

17 This four-word half line contains archaic technical terms, and the *Mānaspīyūṣ* states that "no one has definitively identified (its) meaning" (3.755–757). Most traditional scholars believe that it refers to certain types of marching performers in royal processions who displayed martial arts by waving swords, staves, or heraldic banners, or by performing acrobatics, perhaps during periodic halts. I have tried for a simple composite rendering.

18 "Bluebird," *nīlakaṇṭha.* Though literally called "blue-throat" (also an epithet of Shiva), the bird, the Indian roller, actually has a blue crown and wing feathers. It is regarded as auspicious and figures in some royal rituals performed at the time of the autumn Dussehra (*daśaharā*) festival.

19 To the conventional adjective used to describe a breeze (*tribidha,* or "of three kinds," understood to mean cool, mild, and fragrant) is here added *sānukūla* ("of favorable direction").

20 Here the poet puns (untranslatably) on the name of the bird (*chemakarī,* a kind of hawk) and the word *chema* (protection, happiness, prosperity), which its call announced.

21 This *caupāī,* full of alliterative *s* sounds, puns on the Avadhi word *saguna* ("good omen," from the Sanskrit *śakuna*) and an identical one referring to God, and meaning "with attributes" (Sanskrit, *saguṇa*).

22   "Occult powers" (*siddhi*); supernatural abilities, usually eight in number, often associated with advanced yogic practice.

23   Although conceding the possibility of reading this half line as "like thirsty ones sighting a lake," the *Mānaspīyūṣ* concurs with most commentators in reversing the simile (3.777).

24   "Comforted," *juṛānī;* literally, it "made them cool," relieving the "heat" of their separation from Ram.

25   See "Prologue," n. 14.

26   In Hindu weddings, the bridegroom's procession usually arrives at the bride's family home just prior to the time set for the nuptial rites.

27   Literally, "that the two brothers become guests of our eyes."

28   A characteristic gesture of women in praying for good fortune.

29   Also known as Mārgśirṣ, this is the ninth month of the north Indian Hindu calendar and generally falls in November–December.

30   "Late afternoon," *dhenudhūri;* literally, the time of "cow dust," when cattle return from grazing outside the village, raising clouds of dust that catch the golden light.

31   This speech again points to Tulsi's conviction that Sita and Ram jointly comprise the ultimate divine dyad, Sita-Ram. Hence their "marriage" is an eternal reality that transcends the created universe, as Brahma discovers.

32   "Ultimate good," *apabaraga.* Commentators understand this to refer to the four types of liberation identified by Vaishnava teachers: *sālokya* (dwelling in the heavenly realm of the adored deity), *sāmīpya* (enjoying proximity to God), *sārūpya* (sharing the deity's form), and *sāyujya* (full absorption in God's being)— although some "dualists" regard even the last as merely a condition of extreme proximity ("in which one is absorbed into, e.g., one of the ornaments on the Lord's body," according to the *Mānaspīyūṣ,* 3:807).

33   Present- and past-tense forms are often not clearly distinguishable in Tulsi's poetic language and, according to commentators, alternate in many *Mānas* passages. Although I generally adopt past tense for telling the story, the description of Ram's beauty here suggests an inner visualization, and I follow commentators in adopting the present tense.

34   Shiva is often worshiped in the form of a *liṅgaṃ* with five faces. Since each bears a "third eye" in its forehead, the total is fifteen.

35   See n. 31; again Ram and Sita's separateness from and superiority to Vishnu and his consort are implied. In the second half of this line, Tulsi playfully suggests the oneness of multiple divine forms by using the epithets *Ramā* and *Ramāpati* for Lakshmi and Vishnu. The former means "the pleasing one" and the latter, "lord of the pleasing one," and both derive from the same verbal root as Ram's name.

36   Skanda, a son of Shiva and Parvati who leads the army of the celestials, has six heads, versus Brahma's four faces.

37   In many versions of the story of his seduction of the sage Gautam's wife, Ahalya, Indra is cursed by the angry husband to have his body covered with a thousand vaginas, which are later changed into eyes.

38   "Welcoming ceremony," *parichani;* a ceremony performed at weddings, in which a tray bearing an oil lamp and auspicious substances is rotated clockwise around the bridegroom's head in blessing and to dispel the evil eye. It is normally done by his future mother-in-law and her married friends who are *suhāgin,* unwidowed, as the women are here called.

39   Premodern Indian poetry idealized amply endowed women, whose languid, full-hipped gait was often likened to that of elephants. The common Sanskrit epithet *gajagāminī* (she who walks with the gait of an elephant), alluded to here, was used by Tulsi in the previous *dohā,* where I rendered it "shapely."

40   Indra's wife, Shachi, is accompanied by Brahma's wife, Sarasvati; Vishnu's wife, Lakshmi; and Shiva's wife, Parvati.

41   This passage is dense with cultural detail. "Fivefold instruments and chants" refers to the sounds of stringed instruments, clapped hands, finger cymbals, drums, and trumpets, as well as of Vedic chanting, bardic recitation, cries of "Victory!," the blowing of conchs, and women's ululation (or, according to some commentators, the sounding of kettledrums). "Sacred lamp" refers to the ceremony of welcome (and of worship of a deity) in which a tray bearing an oil lamp, flowers, incense, vermilion, unbroken rice grains, and other holy substances is circled clockwise around the head of the honored one. "Guest libation" refers to another of the "sixteen forms of service," done for both deities and guests, in which a vessel of pure water mixed with milk, curds, *kuśa* grass, mustard seeds, and rice is poured out in offering.

42   The four categories of lowly servitors—happy recipients of the ostentatious offerings heaped in front of Ram—include *bārī*

(rendered "artisans" here), which one dictionary defines as "a caste among Hindus who prepare and sell cups made of leaves."

43 This assertion is itself a figure in Indian poetics, known as *ananvyaya,* "the self-comparison."

44 The two are referred to as "fathers-in-law" (*samadhī*), suggesting a formality-ridden and potentially problematic social relationship that, here, is overcome by the prevailing mood of overwhelming love.

45 The name of another eminent sage in attendance.

46 Evidently other, lesser gods (and goddesses) do not. The tale of Sati has already illustrated this, and another example will come in sub-book 3, when Indra's son Jayant takes the form of a crow to attack Sita (3.1–2).

47 Another possible reading is, "Ram, seeing her, had his wishes fulfilled." However, most commentators reason that the half line invokes the Ayodhya party's longtime desire to find a bride suited to Ram's own perfection.

48 The text mentions one in particular, *madhuparka,* a mixture of three parts curd, one part honey, and one part ghee, that is especially pleasing to deities.

49 Both royal families belong to the solar line.

50 That is, women whose husbands are living; see n. 38.

51 The next four numbered verses, describing some of the climactic marital rites, are set in lyrical *chand* meter, and this pattern is repeated for four successive stanzas (to *dohā* 327).

52 An allusion to the river Ganga, which is said to flow from the toenails of Vishnu in heaven and to descend to earth by flowing through Shiva's matted hair. The *Mānaspīyūṣ* offers an alternate reading of the end of this line, preferring: "is the river of the gods, purity's apogee" (3.851).

53 Literally, "grasping of the hand," a key moment in the marriage ceremony, as it signals the first physical contact between groom and bride and forges a bond that is believed to outlast their physical lives.

54 Here, as in an earlier verse (1.215.4), Tulsi puns on the king's epithet *videha* (without a body), saying: "Videha could not utter the customary praise because the form of the dark youth rendered him bodiless [*videha*]," which commentators interpret to mean that he lost all self-awareness.

55 In one of the climactic events of the Hindu marriage ritual, the edges of the bride's and groom's upper clothes are tied together and, with him leading, they make seven slow circumambulations of the sacred fire.

56 In this line, Tulsidas twice identifies the gods as "wise" or "knowing" (*vibudha, sujāna*); the *Mānaspīyūṣ* suggests that this reflects their self-interested foresight, for they know that this marriage is a prerequisite to the eventual kidnapping of Sita and killing of their archenemy, Ravan (3.858).

57 Ram's dark arm is likened to a cobra and his cupped hand to a lotus. Sita's face is the moon, which is traditionally understood as a reservoir of the nectar of immortality.

58 Tulsidas has only hinted (in the townswomen's hopeful remarks at 1.311) at the plan to wed not only Ram but all four of Dasarath's sons to girls of Janak's clan. Mandvi and Shrutakirti are the daughters of Janak's younger brother, Kushadhvaj, and Urmila—the biological daughter of Janak and Sunayana—is Sita's younger half-sister.

59 *Śrutakīrti;* literally, "she whose fame is heard."

60 "Four states (of consciousness)," *cāriu avasthā;* according to commentators, this refers to waking, dreaming, deep sleep, and liberated, transcendent consciousness. Each of these (feminine) terms is then paired with a male consort, identified in *Mānas* commentaries as "creation," "luminosity," "wisdom," and "ultimate being."

61 Commentators observe that the traditional "four fruits" are all masculine words, and the words for the actions or deeds (*kriyā*) that produce them are feminine.

62 "Supplicant," *jācaka;* though often translated "beggar," the word here refers to anyone (especially a Brahman or mendicant) who looks to the king for maintenance.

63 The king says that deities and saintly people want or need *bhāva*— "emotion" or "feeling," but here implying sincere devotional love. Mere material gifts mean nothing to them (as, by implication, the vast dowry just presented means nothing to the Avadh ruler), just as the ocean does not need the libation of a palmful of water regularly offered by Hindu bathers.

64 "Inner nuptial chamber," *kohabara;* though defined in dictionaries as a room in which family deities are kept at the time of marriage, it is also, as an ensuing passage makes clear, one in which playful customary rites are enacted by the women of the family, teasingly

preparing newlyweds for conjugal pleasure. In the Mithila region of Bihar state (considered to be Sita's homeland), a room of this name is traditionally decorated with colorful murals painted by women, featuring pairs of birds, animals, and aquatic creatures; fish (see the next couplet), symbols of sexual love and fertility, are an especially common motif.

65   This refers to a male style of wearing a long, folded scarf (*dupaṭṭā*) by passing it under the right armpit and over the left shoulder.

66   This literal translation refers to a ritual female gesture to avert the evil eye from an especially beautiful male child or youth. As in comparable passages offering a visualization of Ram's beauty, commentators interpret the verb forms as present tense.

67   Here Tulsidas describes a women's custom in which the new bride and groom are each made to place a rich, juicy sweetmeat in the other's mouth. Shiva's wife directs Ram in doing this, as Brahma's consort does Sita.

68   The *Mānaspīyūṣ* mentions additional games that newlyweds are made to play, such as competing to snatch pieces of jewelry that have been dropped into a basin (3.886–887). Such pastimes may be relished in visualization (as the remainder of this line could imply) by devotees who inwardly assume the role of a *sakhī*, or intimate girlfriend, of Sita.

69   Literally, "five morsels"; five small balls of rice and dal set aside at the commencement of a meal as an offering to dogs, sinners, lepers, crows, and the infirm. Alternatively (or additionally), some understand it as five sips of water or morsels of food taken to the accompaniment of mantras saluting each of the vital breaths.

70   "Ribald songs," *gāri;* folksongs of teasing abuse, usually sung by women and often featuring sexual innuendo regarding extended-family relationships. This is further described later in this stanza. Though offered in fun, such songs may express resentment over the traditionally unequal relationship between bride's and groom's families. Tulsidas is careful to assure his audience that this is not the case here.

71   Here Tulsidas alludes to Sanskrit culinary treatises that identify four types of food preparations, respectively intended to be chewed, sucked, licked, and drunk.

72   "Rinsing water," *ācamana;* water with which to cleanse one's mouth and hands after a meal.

73 According to commentators, these gift cows were adorned with jewelry and rich fabrics.

74 "Inner apartments," *bhītara;* literally, "inside," i.e., the women's quarters.

75 Literally, "had stayed when coming" (and therefore would break the journey there again on their return).

76 "Leave-taking," *bidā* or *bidāī;* an emotional ceremony when a newly married girl formally departs from her maternal family.

77 Ganesh has two wives, Riddhi (prosperity) and Siddhi (success/attainment).

78 Literally, the verse says that Dasarath lovingly "nurtured" the supplicants and "made them stand erect." Some commentators interpret this to mean that he made them stop walking (so as to send them back to Videha), but I prefer the sense, favored by others, that he ensured that they were self-sufficient owing to their newly received riches.

79 The lake is identified as the Manas, or *Mānsarovar,* the sacred Himalayan pilgrimage place referenced in the poem's title.

80 Some manuscripts add another instrument here: the *bīna,* a type of lute.

81 "Perfumes," *aragajā;* this is said to be a yellow-tinted mixture of saffron, sandalwood, camphor, and other scents.

82 *Bakul, kadamba,* and *tamāl* are all considered auspicious evergreen trees and have uses in Ayurvedic medicine.

83 This catalogue of auspicious ingredients for the ceremonial greeting tray includes *dūb* grass, a hardy gray-green grass used in Vedic rituals, and *locan* (also called *gorocan*), a rare and fragrant yellow pigment excreted by certain kinds of cows.

84 "Folk customs," *loka rīti;* though Tulsi gives no detail of what these were, commentators propose that the mothers brought the couples into the nuptial shrine-room (see n. 64), tied their garments together, and made them play games, an ice-breaking invitation to intimacy. Doing such things in front of their elders naturally caused embarrassment to the young people, but the serene elder brother merely smiled inwardly.

85 Traditionally, the women in the groom's family did not travel with the wedding party or directly participate in the marriage rites at the bride's home.

86 How long did the meal last? Tulsidas specifies that it continued

through the fifth *ghaṛī* (a period of 24 minutes) of the night; i.e., two hours into the "watch" (a longer span of three hours) that begins after the conclusion of sunset rituals. Several commentators observe that even on such a festive occasion, the king was mindful of time and of the fact that the women would not eat until the men had finished their meal.

87   The poet uses a verb that may be translated "to lift" ("they lifted Ram"), suggesting childlike exhaustion. But it also means "to cause to rise," and the sense (as commentators note) seems rather to be that they made Ram arise from his seat and come to bed.

88   Literally, "awakeness" (*jāgarana*), an all-night ritual of devotional singing, often performed by women.

89   Literally, "sacred time of morning"; most commentators take this to refer to *Brahma-muhūrt* (the divine period), which begins well before dawn. The *Mānaspīyūṣ* notes that Ram's arising precedes (in the *caupāī*) the crowing of cocks, because "Lord Ram is knowledge itself; he is not informed of the sacred morning hour by the sound of any cocks" (3.997).

90   "Cleansed themselves," *kīnhi sauca;* this is generally understood to mean washing oneself after defecation. Even God (incarnate as Dasarath's four sons) has to do this, though Tulsi reminds us that the brothers are "inherently pure." The cleansing occurs outside Avadh's walls on the banks of the Sarayu.

91   Valmiki's version includes a long narrative merely alluded to here; since it concerns Vishvamitra's self-transformation from a Kshatriya king to a Brahman sage following bitter conflict with Vasishtha himself, it "perplexes even sages." In the Sanskrit epic, this tale is recounted by King Janak's family priest, Shatanand, soon after Vishvamitra, Ram, and Lakshman arrive in Videha (*Rāmāyaṇa* 1.50–64).

92   "Ritual threads were untied," *kaṅkana chore;* in this ritual, protective yellow amulet strings, tied on the wrists of the bride and groom before marriage, are removed. According to C. N. Singh, this signals the end of a period of celibacy vows and the beginning of conjugal life (personal communication, March 2011). The *Mānaspīyūṣ* notes that it is accompanied by raucous rites in which the women pour water on the men (3.1004).

93   Commentators have mused over the fact that Ram's sacred-thread ceremony, merely alluded to in a half *caupāī* (1.204.3), is apparently

cited here as something to be "sung." One explanation is that the two obligatory life-cycle rituals that occur in this book become a symbolic summation of its content. Another is that the "thread" referred to here is the wristlet tied on at the start of the marriage ceremonies (*Mānaspīyūṣ* 3.1011–1012).

94 This Sanskrit colophon, reminding readers of the allegory of Lake Manas with its ghats and stairways, is found in some manuscripts and has become standard in printed editions.

GLOSSARY

AVADH (*avadha;* unconquerable) the kingdom and city of Ayodhya

BHAVANI (*bhavānī,* feminine form of *bhava*) Parvati, the great goddess, Shiva's consort

BHRIGU LORD (*bhṛgupati*) Parashuram

cakor the chukar partridge which, according to legend, forever craves sight of the moon and feeds on its beams (and occasionally on fire); a poetic trope for fervent lovers and devotees

GAURI (*gaurī;* fair, light-complexioned) Parvati

GIRIJA (*girijā;* "mountain-born girl") Parvati

haṃsa mythical bird that lives in the Himalayas, feeds on pearls, and has the ability to separate milk from water; a literary trope for the enlightened soul, it is often depicted by Tulsidas as flying above or floating on Lake Manas; sometimes identified with the bar-headed goose that breeds in Central Asia and winters in India, crossing the Himalayas in its annual migrations

HARA (*hara*) Shiva

HARI (*hari;* lion- or tawny-colored) Vishnu/Ram

JANAKI (*jānakī;* "daughter of Janak") Sita

KAMA (*kāma;* love, desire, eros) the god of love, who is also called "bodiless" because, having been burned to ashes by Shiva, he lives invisibly in all created beings

KAUSHIK (*kauśika;* "descendant of Kusha") epithet of sage Vishvamitra

KHARA (rough, harsh) name of a demon general in Ravan's service, who will be slain by Ram in *Aranyakāṇḍ* (3.18–20)

kinnara a semidivine being with the head of a horse

KOSALA (*kosala*) realm of which Avadh is the capital

KUMBHAKARAN (*kumbhakarṇa;* "pot-ears") Ravan's gigantic elder brother, who sleeps for six months at a time

MAHESH (*maheśa;* "the great lord") Shiva

MAINA (*mainā*) the wife of King Himalaya and mother of Parvati

MAYA (*māyā;* fabrication, semblance) the illusory power of the gods, often personified as a goddess

NIGHT-STALKERS (*niśācara*) earthly demons, or *rākṣasas,* who are most powerful and hunt their prey by night

377

RATI (*rati;* "passion") the wife of
Kama, god of love

RAVAN (*rāvaṇa;* "he who causes
lamentation") the gods' nemesis
and the antagonist of the
Ramayana

SHAMBHU (*śambhu;* pleaser) Shiva

SHANKAR (*śaṅkara;* auspicious,
benevolent) Shiva

SHARADA (*śāradā;* autumnal)
epithet of Sarasvati, goddess of
speech, art, and learning and the
wife of the creator-god Brahma

SHESH (*śeṣa;* "the remainder") the
thousand-headed divine serpent;
with his thousand tongues, also a
literary trope for eloquence

SHRI (*śrī;* auspicious) epithet of
goddess Lakshmi; sometimes
used for Sita

UMA (*umā;* mother) Parvati

VAIDEHI (*vaidehī;* "Videha's
daughter") Sita

VAIKUNTH (*vaikuṇṭha;* relating to
Vikuntha, i.e., Vishnu) Vishnu's
heavenly world

VASUDEV (*vāsudeva;* descendant
of Vasudeva, a deity) epithet of
Vishnu

VIBHISHAN (*vibhīṣaṇa;* terrifying)
Ravan's pious junior brother,
who is a devotee of Vishnu/Ram

378

BIBLIOGRAPHY

Editions and Translations

Kalyāṇ Mānasāṅk. 1938. Edited by Hanuman Prasad Poddar. Comment-
ary by Chimanlal Goswami and Nanddulare Vajpeyi. Gorakhpur: Gita
Press.

Mānaspīyūṣ. 1950. Edited by Anjaninandansharan. Commentary by
Ram Kumar Varma, Ram Vallabh, and Rambalakdasji. 7 vols. Gora-
khpur: Gita Press.

Rāmcaritmānas. 1962. Edited by Vishvanath Prasad Mishra. Ramnagar,
Varanasi: All-India Kashiraj Trust.

Tulsī granthāvalī, pratham khaṇḍ, vol. 1: *Rāmcaritmānas.* 1973. Edited
by Ramchandra Shukla et al. Varanasi: Nāgarīpracāriṇī Sabhā.

Atkins, A. G., trans. 1954. *The Ramayana of Tulsidas.* 2 vols. New Delhi:
Birla Academy of Art and Culture.

Bahadur, Satya Prakash, trans. 1978. *Rāmcaritmānas.* Varanasi: Pracya
Prakashan.

Dev, Satya, trans. 2010. *Tulsi Ramayan in English Verse.* New Delhi:
Vitasta Publishing.

Dhody, Chandan Lal, trans. 1987. *The Gospel of Love: An English Render-
ing of Tulasi's Shri Rama Charita Manasa.* New Delhi: Siddharth
Publications.

Goswami, Chimanlal, trans. 1949. *Śrīrāmacaritamānasa.* Gorakhpur:
Gita Press.

Growse, Frederic Salmon, trans. 1978. *The Rāmāyaṇa of Tulasīdāsa.*
New Delhi: Motilal Banarsidass. Reprint, Kanpur: E. Samuel, 1891.

Hill, W. Douglas P., trans. 1952. *The Holy Lake of the Acts of Rāma.*
London: Oxford University Press.

Nagar, Shanti Lal, trans. 2014. *Shri Ramcharitmanas.* 3 vols. Delhi:
Parimal Publications.

Prasad, R. C., trans. 1988. *Tulasidasa's Shriramacharitamanasa* (The
Holy Lake of the Acts of Rama). Delhi: Motilal Banarsidass.

Other Sources

Lutgendorf, Philip. 1991. *The Life of a Text: Performing the* Rāmcarit-
mānas *of Tulsidas.* Berkeley: University of California Press.

————, trans. 1994. "Sundarkand." *Journal of Vaisnava Studies* 2: 4, 91–127.

————, trans. 1995. "*Ramcaritmanas:* From Book Five, The Beautiful Book." In *The Norton Anthology of World Masterpieces,* expanded edition, ed. Maynard Mack. New York: W. W. Norton, 1: 2316–2332.

————, trans. 2001. "From the Ramcaritmanas of Tulsidas, Book Five: Sundar Kand." *Indian Literature* 45, 3 (203): 143–181.

McGregor, Stuart. 2003. "The Progress of Hindi, Part 1." In *Literary Cultures in History: Reconstructions from South Asia,* ed. Sheldon Pollock. Berkeley: University of California Press, pp. 912–957.

Stasik, Danuta. 2009. "Perso-Arabic Lexis in the *Rāmcaritmānas* of Tulsīdās." *Cracow Indological Studies* 11: 67–86.

INDEX

ABOUT THE BOOK

Murty Classical Library of India volumes are designed by Rathna Ramanathan and Guglielmo Rossi. Informed by the history of the Indic book and drawing inspiration from polyphonic classical music, the series design is based on the idea of "unity in diversity," celebrating the individuality of each language while bringing them together within a cohesive visual identity.

The Hindi text of this book is set in the Murty Hindi typeface, commissioned by Harvard University Press and designed by John Hudson and Fiona Ross. The proportions and styling of the characters are in keeping with the typographic tradition established by the renowned Nirnaya Sagar Press, with a deliberate reduction of the typically high degree of stroke modulation. The result is a robust, modern design.

The English text is set in Antwerp, designed by Henrik Kubel from A2-TYPE and chosen for its versatility and balance with the Indic typography. The design is a free-spirited amalgamation and interpretation of the archives of type at the Museum Plantin-Moretus in Antwerp.

All the fonts commissioned for the Murty Classical Library of India will be made available, free of charge, for non-commercial use. For more information about the typography and design of the series, please visit *http://www.hup.harvard.edu/mcli*.

Printed on acid-free paper by Maple Press, York, Pennsylvania.